The
Dark Side of the Screen

The
Dark Side of the Screen:
Film Noir

Foster Hirsch

A DA CAPO PAPERBACK

Library of Congress Cataloging in Publication Data

Hirsch, Foster.
   The dark side of the screen.

   (A Da Capo paperback)
   Reprint. Originally published: San Diego: A. S. Barnes, 1981.
   Bibliography: p.
   Includes index.
   1. Gangster films — History and criticism. 2. Moving-pictures — United States —
History. I. Title.
[PN1995.9.G3H5 1983]   791.43′09′09355   83-7559
ISBN 0-306-80203-1 (pbk.)

This Da Capo Press paperback edition of *The Dark Side of the Screen: Film Noir* is an unabridged republication of the first edition published in California and London in 1981. It is reprinted by arrangement with Oak Tree Publications.

Published by Da Capo Press, Inc.
A Subsidiary of Plenum Publishing Corporation
233 Spring Street, New York, N.Y. 10013

Contents

Also by Foster Hirsch

Love, Sex, Death, and the Meaning of Life: Woody Allen's Comedy
Laurence Olivier
A Portrait of the Artist: The Plays of Tennessee Williams
Joseph Losey
Who's Afraid of Edward Albee?
Elizabeth Taylor
The Hollywood Epic
Edward G. Robinson
George Kelly
A Method to Their Madness: The History of the
    Actors Studio
Harold Prince and the American Musical Theatre
Acting Hollywood Style
The Boys from Syracuse: A Biography of the Shuberts
Neo-Noir (*in preparation*)

Acknowledgments

The Motion Picture Section of the Library of Congress, Washington, D.C.; the Library of Performing Arts, New York Public Library at Lincoln Center; the Library of the Motion Picture Academy of Arts and Sciences, Beverly Hills; the Beverly Hills Public Library; the Brooklyn College Library; Scribner's, for permission to use quoted material from *The Killers*; Vintage, for permission to use quoted material from *The Maltese Falcon, The Big Sleep*, and *The Rebel*; the Thalia Theater, New York City, for their two seasons of *films noirs*; the Los Angeles Public Library, Downtown Branch, for their rare copies of the original editions of the novels and stories of Cornell Woolrich; the Whitney Museum of American Art; Ted Sennett; Peter Cowie; Allen Eyles; Murder Ink., New York.

**Visual material edited and designed by
Bill O'Connell**

1
The City at Night

A car weaves crazily through the dark deserted streets of downtown Los Angeles. As it lurches to a halt, a man crawls out, stumbles into an office building, falls at his desk as he begins to talk into a tape recorder, narrating in a clipped tone a story of a doomed love affair. The speaker, Walter Neff, is an insurance salesman who, on a routine house call, became enamored of a bored and sexy housewife. The two of them, in record time, began an affair and concocted an elaborate plan to do away with the woman's husband—after he had been insured for double indemnity. But their ingenious scheme to defraud Walter's insurance company backfired, and the conspirators were undermined by their own mounting distrust of each other, as well as by a shrewd and suspicious claims investigator. The estranged lovers' final meeting takes place in the woman's house, at night, in dark shadows, in pointed contrast to their first encounter in the house on a sunny mid-afternoon. They shoot each other. The woman dies; the man is able to stagger back to his office where he unburdens himself on tape to the zealous claims man who is also his friend. Having revealed the truth, Walter dies in the friend's arms.

The policeman and the city: Barry Fitzgerald, in *The Naked City*, looks out over his turf.

After a dinner in his honor, marking twenty-five years of faithful service, a mild-mannered bank clerk named Christopher Cross decides to celebrate by walking home instead of taking the bus, as he usually does. He gets lost in the winding streets of Greenwich Village. Turning a corner, he stumbles upon a scene of violence—a man attacking a woman—and he runs to call the police as the woman (Kitty Marsh) and her boyfriend (Johnny), who were having a typical argument, confer quickly before Johnny steals away. Kitty and her "rescuer" strike up a conversation. She is clearly a dame on the make, though the shy clerk is so delighted to be talking to a pretty woman that he doesn't see her for what she is. The poor guy is hooked, a goner; and before he has a chance to get his bearings, he is stealing money from his bank in order to support Kitty in a smart Village apartment. She and Johnny see the older man as easy prey, as someone who can be easily swindled, but they are both too dumb to realize that Chris has no money—they are as blind to who he really is as he is to the truth about them. They manage, though, to take him for all he is worth and then some, living high on the money he has stolen; and they contrive as well to steal his identity. The clerk is a Sunday painter, and through a chain of coincidences, the two-timing woman begins to sell his canvases as her own work. When Chris discovers the full extent of her duplicity, when she reveals her true face to him and taunts him for his ugliness, his blindness and gullibility, he kills her. But it is Johnny, always slinking around corners and hiding behind doors, who gets caught (and executed) for the murder while Chris goes free, becoming a Bowery bum unable to come forward as the painter of his own now highly-priced work.

These are the stories of two of the most famous *films noirs, Double Indemnity* (1944) and *Scarlet Street* (1945). In theme, characterization, world view, settings, direction, performance, and writing, the two dramas are focal points for *noir* style, as representative of the genre as *Stagecoach* is of westerns or *Singing in the Rain* of musicals. *Double Indemnity* and *Scarlet Street* are about doomed characters who become obsessed with bewitching women. The insurance man and the bank clerk live regular, self-contained lives, yet a chance encounter releases wellsprings of suppressed passion and forces a radical transformation of character. Both men end up killing the women who have tempted them away from their humdrum lives. Victims of fate, both Walter and Chris fall into traps from which there is no escape; Walter is hopelessly caught when he first meets his client's sultry wife, the clerk is doomed when he rounds a corner and finds what he thinks is a damsel in distress. Both films suggest that the obsessiveness, the irrationality, the violence, the wrenching psychological shifts triggered by their infatuation with luscious, deceitful women were lying in wait beneath the characters' bland masks. Sexual release plunges both men into irreversible calamity.

Freed from their former, middle-class selves, both Walter and Chris prove resourceful. Realizing at last a long-held fantasy of duping his company, Walter plots an ingenious swindle. He and his paramour can claim double indemnity if her husband dies—or seems to die—on a train. (Deaths by accidents on trains yield high premiums because of their rarity.) Walter applies himself with evident relish to formulating a perfect crime, exulting in the cleverness of his plan to stage the husband's fatal fall from the rear platform of a train; Walter himself "plays" the husband, whom he has already killed. Chris Cross, though an utter fool in his relations with Kitty, turns out to be a smart embezzler and, when he has the chance to get rid of his nagging wife, rises triumphantly to the occasion. Her former husband, a sea captain she has presumed dead, returns, promising Chris that, for a price, he will disappear once again. But Chris tricks him, and the Captain to his utter surprise is reunited with his wife while Chris walks away a free man. That Chris is not all meekness and pliancy is announced also in a droll scene when, dressed in an apron, he chops meat as his wife scolds him. The emasculating apron notwithstanding, Chris wields the chopping knife heartily, a sly look in his eye: this soft-spoken clerk is obviously seething with murderous rage.

Both Walter and Chris are at first sexually stalled. Walter is unmarried, and his closest attachment is to his colleague, the claims investigator, a father figure whom he tries, perhaps unconsciously, to outwit and to outrage in his clandestine affair with a married woman. The investigator is a figure of authority but also and more crucially of propriety as well; he is a strait-laced bachelor whose life is his job and who is as obsessive in his pursuit of false claims as Walter is in his scheme to defraud the company. The claims man believes Walter's nice-guy image, responding to him as the perfectly behaved son, and never for a moment suspecting him as Phyllis Dietrichson's partner in crime. He dislikes Phyllis the moment he sees her, perceiving her as in some way a threat to his own relationship with Walter. He is offended by Phyllis' obvious sexuality. Clearly there is a strong connection between the two men; Walter, half dead, races back to the office to confess to his friend and then dies, purged, in the older man's arms. The comradely devotion and loyalty that bind them are an antidote to the poisonous sexuality that links Walter to Phyllis. Is *Double Indemnity* covertly anti-woman and pro-homosexual? The film's tangled, ambiguous, loaded sexual currents, at any rate, are typical of *noir* thrillers.

The triangular relationship in *Scarlet Street*, involving Chris, Kitty, and Johnny, is also kinky. The woman likes the man who regularly beats her up; Johnny is a sadist, and the more brutal his behavior, the more devoted and clinging Kitty becomes, whereas she scoffs at the man who treats her like a princess. Are there in this story, as in *Double Indemnity*, some disguised parent-child hostilities? Chris is old enough to be Kitty's father, and his posture toward her is paternal and kindly. He sometimes drops by unannounced when Kitty is entertaining Johnny on the sly. Before admitting Chris, she kicks Johnny's hat and shoes under the bed and hides him in the bathroom: is daughter sneaking in an affair behind Daddy's back? Does the child have guilty secrets from her parent?

The doomed, unheroic protagonists of both films are triply victimized—by women, by their own psychological imbalances, and by fate.

Before the fall: Christopher Cross (Edward G. Robinson), the fated anti-hero of Fritz Lang's archetypal *Scarlet Street*, preparing to walk home after the dinner in his honor. Little does he suspect that his casual nighttime stroll through the winding streets of Greenwich Village will plunge him into a *noir* nightmare.

Seemingly average men who go haywire, whose lives fall apart because they took an initial wrong turn, Walter Neff and Chris Cross are archetypal *noir* losers.

The female characters in *Double Indemnity* and *Scarlet Street* are equally representative figures. For both Phyllis and Kitty, sex is only a means to an end. The end is money. Greedy and selfish, knowingly using their bodies as destructive weapons, the women face their doom with less conscience than their male partners. Walter and Chris are allowed a token repentance: the insurance man unburdens himself in a therapeutic confession, the clerk turned murderer wanders the city in a state of terminal alienation. Dazed and radically split from his former self, he squanders his days in a limbo of self-punishment. The women present false faces to the world, but beneath their masks beat hearts of steel.

Though their effect on men is the same, the two women are not exactly alike. The cunning housewife has no feelings for anyone, while dumb, careless Kitty is genuinely attached to her callow boyfriend. Phyllis is a figure of Machiavellian evil, chilling and reptilian, while Kitty is presented on a distinctly less sophisticated level, as a dimwitted whore with just enough savvy to know how to look out for herself. Phyllis makes a career of murdering people who get in her way. She killed her husband's first wife; once she meets Walter, she wants to kill her husband; and when Walter becomes a possible threat to her, she tries to kill him too. She has pretended to a sexual interest in him that she does not feel; while courting him, she has been carrying on with her stepdaughter's boyfriend. The character is a misogynist's vision of woman as a male-attracting embodiment of evil. Phyllis is a castrating Eve in a nightmare inversion of the Garden of Eden myth. As written by Billy Wilder and Raymond Chandler, working from James M. Cain's original novel, and as played by Barbara Stanwyck, Phyllis is the ultimate *femme fatale* of the 1940s thriller, a contemporary Circe luring unsuspecting men with her siren's song.

In the harsh world of both *Double Indemnity* and *Scarlet Street*, survival means doing unto others before they do unto you. Wives murder husbands, murderers are wolves in sheep's clothing, stepmothers steal boyfriends from their stepdaughters, loyal employees turn with a vengeance against their employers. The mildest-seeming people are capable of fierce crimes of passion: appearances are more than deceiving in this Hobbesian universe, they are positively fatal to the unwary. Life is built on quicksand, as a nighttime stroll that takes the clerk a few blocks out of his way leads directly into a labyrinth without exit, as a routine visit to a client's house on a sunny afternoon precipitates the hapless salesman into the darkest possibilities of the self, a waking nightmare triggered by lust and concluding in a bloodbath. The characters have no place of refuge in this cruel naturalistic world, this life-as-a-jungle setting. Alone and unpro-

tected, they are truly strangers, to themselves as well as to others. The world is littered with pitfalls against which the individual has, at the most, meager defenses. Like Walter and Chris, most of the protagonists of *film noir* are the playthings of designing women, of their own dark, subterranean inclinations, and of a malevolent fate.

Double Indemnity and *Scarlet Street* are enacted in settings that strongly reinforce the films' cheerless vision. *Double Indemnity* takes place in Los Angeles, *Scarlet Street* in New York, but the two cities are shown in a narrow and subtly stylized way—in Robert Warshow's resonant phrase, they are "cities of the imagination." The New York of *Scarlet Street* is entirely studio-created, airless and claustrophobic, with no sense of a world going on outside the frame. The Greenwich Village in which the story begins, and in which most of the action occurs, is a clear-cut fabrication, bearing only the remotest connection to reality. Village streets, like those in the film, are in fact winding and irregular. But there is no sense in the film of a real community. The film's streets are eerily deserted, layered with shadows: a symbolic terrain. When Chris Cross starts his walk into the zigzagging, darkened streets, he is clearly doomed.

Like many of the dark films, *Scarlet Street* takes place primarily at night and in a limited number of settings. There are only three important interiors: Chris's office, his cluttered apartment, and the mirrored, white apartment he rents for Kitty. Hunched over his desk in his cramped, barred office, Chris looks like an imprisoned animal. A large portrait of his wife's first husband, a lusty sea captain, dominates the living room of his overstuffed apartment, displacing him in his own home. The apartment is dim, the furniture dusty and squat. These rooms without light or air are indications of the people who inhabit them, the pinched, crabby wife and the meek clerk with the busy inner life. The apartment Kitty lives in, with its sleek and empty whiteness, is equally expressive of character. Chris stabs Kitty to death as she lounges in her white bed framed by mirrors, her image split and multiplied in a strong visual echo of her duplicity.

Double Indemnity is played out against a

The conspirators perpetrating the perfect crime, in *Double Indemnity*. Night, railroad tracks, high-contrast lighting, a corpse, the glum, masked faces of Barbara

Stanwyck and Fred MacMurray: this shot contains several key *noir* ingredients.

larger canvas. There are vestiges throughout of the real Los Angeles, of actual streets and houses rather than studio-created replicas. The film is designed as a series of visual contrasts between night and day, shadow and light. The opening scene, Walter's car racing unsteadily through the nighttime city, is followed by a flashback set on a sunny afternoon in a Spanish-style house in Pasadena. Day is contrasted to night in this back-to-back sequence, as the past intersects the present. Both scenes maintain a mood of impending doom. Walter's first meeting with Phyllis is played out against a bright, waning Southern California afternoon, as the slanting sun streams through the windows, baking the adobe walls and tiled floors of the comfortable suburban living room. But the venetian blinds break up the flow of the streaming sunlight, casting ominous barred shadows onto the walls. The two conspirators-to-be look trapped in the hot, bright room. The air is thick with sex, and

with catastrophe. Intent on killing each other, the former lovers meet for the last time in the same room, now totally darkened. The pitch-black house encloses their final descent. Between the light and shadow opening and the circumambient darkness of the finale are many scenes set in deceptively normal daytime surroundings. The two murderers meet on neutral ground in Jerry's Market, conferring in whispered tones in the baby food section, their desperate plotting ironically played off against the flat lighting of an ordinary, featureless surburban grocery.

These deeply unromantic films, shot through with visual and verbal ironies, take a sneaking delight in their displays of passion gone wrong and of murderous calculation confounded. The films keep their distance from their twisted characters—a mordant humor seeps through even the darkest moments of the action. *Double Indemnity* was directed by Billy

Wilder, *Scarlet Street* by Fritz Lang, men of Germanic origin not noted for their warmth or emotional generosity. Like the fate that hovers over their luckless characters, their direction is utterly controlling. They create closed worlds from which a sense of the flow of life has been rigorously excluded. There seems to be no world outside the frame, and there are almost no other people on view besides the principals. These stories of obsession and self-destruction are enacted in a deliberately created vacuum, then—a sealed-off environment of airless rooms, and of threatening, lonely streets. The camera keeps its distance, offering only occasional comment through a recurrent high angle or a disorienting low one. The high angle, which peers down on the characters (catching Chris in his cashier's cage, for instance), is a visual intimation of doom. It seems to trap the characters and emphasizes their helplessness against both the external and internal forces that bedevil them. The low angle (Phyllis in a bath towel at the top of the stairs, seen from Walter's point of view) provides occasional disquieting images of one character's power over another. For the most part, though, both Wilder and Lang use the camera as a neutral observer of the characters' breakdowns. Relying on dramatic lighting and on settings that reflect the characters' states of mind, their methods are muted adaptations of Expressionism. At the end of *Scarlet Street*, to signal Chris Cross' delirium, Lang uses an all-out Expressionist technique that departs from his prevailing understatement: the neon lights flashing madly outside Chris' flophouse room, and the voices rooting around in his head, colliding in demented echo and repetition, are subjective renderings of the character's collapse, and provide a bombastic epilogue to Lang's remarkably cool film.

Wilder's seamless direction maintains its taut surface throughout, never becoming overtly theatrical, like the ending to *Scarlet Street*, where Lang emphasizes the character's de-

Characterization through costume and setting (in *Scarlet Street*): Christopher Cross, dressed in an apron, is doing housewifely chores in the kitchen, and a portrait of his wife's first husband, which dominates the livingroom, seems to displace him in his own home. Yet the shot is filled with Langian ironies, because meek, emasculated Chris will outwit his wife and her former husband, and will murder the woman (Kitty Collins) who makes a fool of him. In *noir*, visual information is often misleading, double-edged.

rangement to show beyond any doubt, and therefore to satisfy the censors, that Chris is indeed punished for his crime. Like Wilder's, Barbara Stanwyck's performance is quintessentially *noir*. Stanwyck, who plays Phyllis Dietrichson with the steeliness for which she is famous, is the undisputed queen bee of *noir*—hard, mannish, her face a taut mask, her eyes beady and suspicious, her voice honed to a cutting edge. Her acting is unrelieved by a moment's softness or shading. Yet this is not an operatic version of a fatal temptress: Stanwyck's method is one of subtraction rather than theatrical embellishment as she reduces expression and gesture to a minimum. She plays in a narrow, tight emotional range, creating a recognizable American housewife of a certain type and class—except that *something* is missing, some crucial human element omitted. Her face frozen, her voice and body forbiddingly rigid, she seems like a somnambulist, a walking zombie in a waking nightmare. Stanwyck's skillful work is like a painting of a recognizably real scene in which nature, on closer inspection, looks too neat and still and poised. Her character, as a result, is more a mask, a symbolic idea, of a monstrous woman than a fully flesh-and-blood representation of her; and in this sense she is playing the character as James M. Cain originally conceived her in his novel: predatory and not fully human, the essence of aggressive, unlovely female sexuality. Cain's almost cartoon-like villain is a caricature of the wicked stepmother of folk lore and fairy tales, and the film has the integrity not to blunt the characterization by adding humanizing touches.

Stanwyck's acting is thus an imitation of reality in only the narrowest possible sense. Her deliberately monochromatic delivery is the signature of the hard-boiled manner prevalent in thrillers of the period. It is one of the conventions of *noir* that, like Stanwyck, tough dames and guys hardly move their facial muscles or their lips, their darting, narrowed eyes the only movement in their masks. Stanwyck's performance created a sensation; never before in American films had a female character been presented as so devoid of softening, feminine touches, and never before had death and sex been linked so explicitly and powerfully. Stanwyck plays the character with startling suggestions of perversity.

Double Indemnity is also seminal because it represents a one-time-only collaboration between James M. Cain and Raymond Chandler, two of the leading writers of the hard-boiled school. Chandler didn't care for Cain. He thought Cain's work had too many sensational elements, and he was offended by the feverish, erotic quality of Cain's writing, its hothouse sultriness. With his English school training and his upbringing by a genteel mother, Chandler was put off by what he considered Cain's lack of polish. Reluctantly, he accepted the assignment of adapting Cain's novel into a screenplay, and he was desperately unhappy working with Billy Wilder because he felt Wilder did not allow him sufficient creative freedom. But working together, uneasy as the collaboration may have been, Wilder and Chandler preserved the texture of Cain's novel—a trim novel in the hard-boiled manner becomes a trim, hard-boiled movie—and made a few changes that actually strengthened the material, as Cain later admitted. They decided to give the story a flashback framework, beginning at the end as Walter is dying. Avoiding a straightforward treatment of time immediately introduces the requisite hopeless tone: the story, in a sense, is over before it begins, with the hero's grim fate then hovering over the entire film. The adapters retain Cain's first-person narration, keeping it to a minimum, while choosing passages that express the narrator's cynical, world-weary, yet peculiarly matter-of-fact manner. The narration has added dramatic impact because in the film it is a confession to Walter's friend and colleague, whereas in the novel it was a mere literary convention, a report addressed to no one in particular.

A neurotic *noir* triangle (in *Double Indemnity*): accurately enough, the shot suggests a closer connection between Walter Neff and his colleague (Edward G. Robinson) than between Walter and Phyllis, who is separated from the two men as she hides behind the door to Walter's apartment.

In character types, mood, themes, and visual composition, *Double Indemnity* and *Scarlet Street* offer a lexicon of *noir* stylistics. Set in cities at night, the two films dramatize the fateful consequences of an obsession. The two anti-heroes are driven wild by desire for provocative, unavailable women. The men's passion destroys the ordered, mundane surface of their former lives, and hurls them into a maze of crime and punishment. Both films depict private worlds turned upside down in a manner that is rigorously controlled. With their use of shadows, their muted patterns of chiaroscuro, and their settings that comment on the characters, the films contain visual echoes of German Expressionism. Made by two masters of the claustrophobic style, *Double Indemnity* and *Scarlet Street* are impressive examples of the topography of *noir*, and as such a helpful starting point for a study of one of the richest and most critically neglected of American film genres.

At the time, Wilder and Lang did not know that they were making *films noirs*. They would probably have called their stories thrillers or crime dramas and let it go at that. *Film noir* as a descriptive term was coined by French critics in the postwar period, as a response to what seemed to them a distinctly darkened tone to the American cinema. During the war, American movies were not shown in France, and when a few were finally released in 1946 French critics (who had long watched the American studio film with particular interest) noticed decided tonal shifts. The thrillers seemed to the French *cinéastes* more sombre in style and more pessimistic in tone than the usual American movie of the thirties. Marked by a startling cynicism and ending often in defeat, the "new wave" of crime dramas contradicted the customary optimism of popular American pictures. These downbeat stories of murder and passion, of ordinary lives gone hopelessly astray, of evil women casting their net and fatally contaminating the American male, seemed to the French to represent a shift in the national psyche. They saw a loss of energy and confidence, and a growing disillusionment with traditional American ideals. In these dark films, money and love, as well as individual enterprise, lead not to fulfillment and the happy ending, but to crime and death—to defeats of nightmarish proportion. Appropriately enough, the French called these stories of tabloid sex and murder "*film noir*"—"black film." The first sustained discussion of the films appeared in 1955, in *Panorama du film noir américain*, by Raymond Borde and Etienne Chaumeton.

Film noir, then, was "discovered" by the French during a remarkably fertile period in French film criticism, when the close study of American genre films led to the formulation of the *auteur* theory. French critics saw the formularized studio films as opportunities for idiosyncratic directors with subversive tendencies to rework standard stories, to undermine generic conventions. The discovery and naming of *film noir* occurred at a time when French critics, under the influence of André Bazin and writing for *Cahiers du cinéma*, were excavating American entertainment movies with an ingenuity that has had a lasting impact. The French "taught" Americans how to read aspects of their own popular culture. Regarding the popular studio offerings as potential works of art some two decades before most Americans were ready to do so, the French were especially attracted to the B movie, as opposed to the A productions with a more obvious cultural pedigree. Low budget *films noirs*, made quickly and not always with A casts or directors, and frequently appearing at the bottom of the ubiquitous double feature, provided particularly rich grist for the *auteur* critics' mill. These thrillers with mostly unpretentious packaging contained a wealth of material waiting to be "retrieved" and explicated by clever critics; here, in these modest crime stories with their loaded sexuality and their pathologi-

The role of the *femme fatale—noir's* Circe, the wicked woman who destroys every man she meets—is emphasized in this poster for *Scarlet Street*.

cal characters, was an intriguing image of the American Dream gone bad.

Film noir became an accepted critical term in America only in the late sixties, at a time when Americans themselves began to take American films more seriously. Contemporary reviews of *film noir* were not, on the whole, either favorable or enlightened. Only Manny Farber, ever on the alert for disrespectful stories about the underside of American life, fully appreciated the *noir* flavor. Lacking Farber's irreverence, most of the forties reviewers disapproved of the cold tone of the films, of the fact that the dramas offered few characters the audience could care about. Though the writers at the time were alert to the Freudian motifs that filtered into the crime thriller (they cited an epidemic of Oedipal complexes), they were impatient with the quantity of unbalanced characters. Further, the reviewers sniffed at the pulp origins of the films, disdaining Raymond Chandler, for instance, several decades before he was to become a cult figure.

Night and the City: the archetypal *noir* title.

On the whole, the reviewers preferred *noir* when it was set in the real world rather than when it took place in the studio; thrillers such as *The Naked City* and *Boomerang* that had a documentary look got the best notices, just as *The Lost Weekend* or *Body and Soul*, stories that seemed to have a social conscience, received the stamp of approval. The particularly high-strung *noir* thrillers, relying primarily on murky photography and a studio-created atmosphere, were regarded with suspicion. Individual films were critically successful, but for the most part *noir* in the forties was unappreciated; the crime film trend of the period had to wait some three decades before its full richness began to be savored.

Film noir erupted in full creative force during a comparatively concentrated period. In an early and influential article, "Notes on *Film Noir*" (1972), Paul Schrader places its outer limits from *The Maltese Falcon* in 1941 to *Touch of Evil* in 1958. In a more strict dating, Amir Karimi, in *Toward a Definition of the American Film Noir*, limits the period from 1941 to 1949. Later critics suggest that the true heyday of *noir* lasted only a few years, from Wilder's *Double Indemnity* in 1944 to the same director's *Sunset Boulevard* in 1950. But the long-range view, with *noir* extending from the early forties to the late fifties, is the most sensible, for the crime films of this period are noticeably different in

theme and style and mood from those made before or after.

Films noirs share a vision and sensibility, indicated by their echoing titles: *No Way Out, Detour, Street with No Name, Scarlet Street, Panic in the Streets, The Naked City, Cry of the City, The Dark Past, The Dark Corner, The Dark Mirror, Night and the City, Phenix City Story, They Live By Night, The Black Angel, The Window, Rear Window, The Woman in the Window, D.O.A., Kiss of Death, Killer's Kiss, The Killing, The Big Sleep, Murder My Sweet, Caught, The Narrow Margin, Edge of Doom, Ruthless, Possessed, Jeopardy*. These wonderfully evocative titles conjure up a dark, urban world of neurotic entrapment leading to delirium. The repetition of key words (street, city, dark, death, murder) and things (windows and mirrors) points up the thematic and tonal similarities among the films.

Just as *noir* is a subdivision within the American crime film, so there are several offshoots within what Raymond Durgnat has called "the family tree of *film noir*." In a delirious article (written in 1970), Durgnat kneads and twists *noir* like a sculptor playing with putty. His fancy critical juggling yields eleven sub-categories within *noir*. Durgnat's eleven story types can be conflated to three basic patterns: stories about cool private eyes; flailing victims; and hard-core criminals. Certainly all three basic character types can and do appear within a single film, but one of these characters dominates the action and in turn influences the style of the film. The dramas with private eyes as their heroes are cooler than the ones that focus on characters whose lives are coming apart. In its brief history, *noir* changes its focus, mood, and visual style, as its point of view shifts from objective to subjective and its decor slides from studio stylization to location realism.

Looking at *The Maltese Falcon* and *Touch of Evil*, the two films frequently cited as forming the outer limits of the cycle, suggests some general tendencies about its thematic and stylistic evolution. *The Maltese Falcon* is directed by John Huston in a sedate manner, with only occasional low angles and theatrical lighting to call attention to the oddness of the characters. The focus of the action is on a private eye, the now-legendary Sam Spade (Humphrey Bogart), as he investigates the murder of his partner Miles Archer and searches for the mysterious, priceless, and finally ineffable falcon. Spade is a cool character, and the film for the most part maintains his wary, questioning point of view. Spade regards the crooks (played by Sydney Greenstreet and Peter Lorre, those droll masters of menace) with scornful disbelief, and he keeps his distance from the lady in the case (Mary Astor) as well. He never entirely capitulates to the allure of Brigid O'Shaughnessy, the first of a long line of calculating beauties in movie mysteries, a skillful and dangerous liar. His basic integrity remaining intact, Spade then keeps at arm's length from crime and from designing women; and Huston's sly, understated direction provides the appropriate field within which Spade can conduct his inquiries.

Orson Welles' *Touch of Evil,* about a psychotic law enforcement officer in a Mexican border town, is pitched in an altogether different key, the quiet chiaroscuro and occasional oblique angles of *The Maltese Falcon* inflected to baroque proportions. Welles offers an overheated summary of what were by 1958 the conventions of the *noir* style. A looming, restless, hyperactive camera, a barrage of tilted, disfiguring angles, complex and self-infatuated patterns of shadows, exotic settings—the film explodes

as a series of visual fireworks, the syntax of *noir* slashed and then reconstructed as if for the last time. Unlike Huston, Welles never leaves well enough alone, is never content merely to serve the needs of his story. If Welles exploded Shakespeare in his wild and woolly film versions of *Othello* and *Macbeth*, he was certainly not about to stand quietly to the side in his direction of a pulp crime novel.

The difference between the two films is emblematic of general shifts in the treatment of crime subjects. Coming at the beginning of a cycle, and presenting character types (the private eye, the crafty heroine, the comic opera villains) which were fresh if not exactly original, *The Maltese Falcon* did not have to rely on visual pyrotechnics in order to sustain audience interest. If the film represents an early, relatively straightforward depiction of characters and a

Richard Widmark, in *Night and the City*: a beleaguered *noir* anti-hero, on the cover of Borde and Chaumeton's pioneer 1955 study of *film noir*.

The city at night, with its darkened skyscrapers and a row of blinking neon lights at the bottom of architectural canyons, provided a recurrent backdrop for *noir* title sequences. (The credits here are for *Cry of the City*.)

story pattern that were to become *noir* conventions, then *Touch of Evil* can be seen as the last, brilliant flourishes of *noir's* decadence. Welles' baroque and masterly orchestration of effects stands in sharp counterpoint to Huston's measured rhythm. In a general way, the two films indicate an overall development within the *noir* canon from objective to subjective accounts of crime, as Sam Spade's cool outsider's view of the criminal scene is replaced by the agitated viewpoint of the crackpot sheriff who dominates the later film.

As *noir* shifts its focus from the investigator who makes skeptical forays into criminal settings to the feverish criminals hopelessly entangled in webs of crime, its tone grows noticeably darker, more menacing and unsettled. The change of emphasis from the investigator to the criminal cannot be traced in a neat chronological curve, but in general *noir* heats up, gets crazier, toward the latter part of the 1940s. The films present the world as an increasingly unsafe place. In the postwar period many thrillers were about neurotic characters lured into a world of crime; victims and good men gone wrong, they are not hardened criminals who willfully set themselves up in opposition to society. Rather, they are often middle-class family men; steady, likable fellows who happen to be in the wrong place at the wrong time, tricked by a twist of fate, seduced by the promise of sex or the chance to make quick illegal money. Standing between

John Huston's *The Maltese Falcon* (1941), often cited as the first *film noir*, takes place in neat studio interiors, with the action photographed primarily from neutral medium shots, as in this representative still. In contrast, Orson Welles' *Touch of Evil* (1958), frequently called *film noir's* epitaph, has exotic settings (like the gaudy strip joint in these two shots), packed frames, and disorienting camera angles.

the cynical investigator and the committed criminal, the *noir* victim is the most interesting and most original of the genre's anti-heroes, the ideal patsy for the world view that is at the core of *noir*. Like the protagonists of *Double Indemnity* and *Scarlet Street*, this luckless recurrent character type walks a tightrope across a landscape strewn with traps ready to spring at the slightest misstep, the smallest detour. 'The world is a dangerous place' is one of the axioms of *noir*— and it is especially so for the man who has lived according to the rules. The solid bourgeois is a prime target, his straight and narrow virtue an invitation to downfall, a thin shield against churning inner dissatisfactions. No one is immune from the temptations of sex and money, *noir* says—and the seemingly mundane characters, the ones living small, repressed, outwardly conventional lives, like the ripe victims of *Double Indemnity* and *Scarlet Street*, are the most susceptible of all.

The three major *noir* character types—the sleuth, the criminal, the middle-class victim and scapegoat—all inhabit a treacherous urban terrain filled with deceiving women and the promise of money easily and ill-gotten. The city,

minatory and bewitching, is a powerful and inescapable presence in *noir*; but, like the characters who walk through its mean streets, it too comes in various styles. Again, neat dating is impossible as *noir's* phases overlap, but there are some general patterns: the earliest period (for which Lang's *Scarlet Street* and *The Woman in the Window* are pre-eminent examples) presented cities that were primarily studio-created, deliberately lacking the fullness and density of a real city. Shown, most typically, at night, the studio city of darkened rainy streets was eerily deserted, its pools of shadows pregnant with menace. The simplified and semi-abstract cityscapes of the studio-made thrillers provided the appropriate backdrop for stories of entrapment. Films set in this environment were claustrophobic psychological studies, stories of obsession and

The textures of a studio city and of a real city are contrasted in these scenes from Lang's *Woman in the Window* and Dassin's *Naked City*. Typically, the shot from the studio-made film looks posed, neatly balanced; the eerily deserted, rain-slicked street emphasizes the isolation of the character (Edward G. Robinson, as a meek professor turned murderer). The busy shot from *The Naked City*, with Don Taylor as a plain-clothesman moving against the flow of traffic, has qualities of spontaneity and immediacy that Lang deliberately avoided.

confinement in which the world begins small and then progressively closes in on the fated protagonists. In these dramas of wriggling, harried, increasingly desperate characters, the outside world is filtered through only in limited doses, as, in a sense, an "accessory to the crime."

After the war, the thriller took to the streets of real cities (while studio dramas continued to be made as well), and the new location look encouraged the development of different kinds of crime stories. The location films opened up the crime picture, giving it a semblance of documentary authenticity that the studio-based films, with their heavily controlled lighting and creation of atmosphere, deliberately avoided. The location thrillers had a wider and more open frame, a greater number of settings, and a visual style that was not as stiff and manipulated as in the studio-created "cities of the imagination." The greater amount of camera movement in the location films, as well as the dominant use of the camera as an objective recording instrument, gave the action the look of an on-the-spot journalistic report. Passing by, at the rear and the edges of the frame, were glimpses of a random

Films noir shot on location often chose unusual backgrounds or, through compositional means, transformed reality to match the mood of the story. Here, Robert Siodmak sets up a shot for *Criss Cross*, while Burt Lancaster waits on the porch of a house in the old Bunker Hill section of Los Angeles, a popular location for forties thrillers because of its bizarre Los Angeles-Victorian architecture.

reality, a flow of life, that could not be absorbed by crime dramas confined to the studio. Such films as *Call Northside 777, Boomerang* and *The House on 92nd Street* dramatized true-life stories as a salute to policemen or the FBI or crusading journalists who cracked tough cases. The semi-documentary thriller thus had a different tone than the more stylized and claustrophobic *films noirs*. The realistic stories of detection were essentially conservative in their outlook, whereas the studio films tended to be subversive, slyly undermining the middle-class status quo with their depiction of middle America gone haywire. The location stories of police procedures had clear-cut separations between the good guys (the men who represented and staunchly upheld the law) and the bad (the criminals who hid from the light of day in the bowels of the urban underworld), whereas in the stylized *noirs* innocence and guilt, virtue and vice, were presented in much more complex ways.

Yet the straightforward semi-documentary thrillers were not the only kind of crime film to take advantage of the real city. Again dates overlap, and the hard-hitting exposé dramas with a Neo-Realist technique appeared at much the same time or anticipated by only a year or two the location film with a more neurotic component, such as *The Naked City* (1947), *Kiss of Death* (1948), *Criss Cross* (1948), *Side Street* (1949), and *Night and the City* (1950), in which the real city became more than a merely neutral and uninflected backdrop. In these manneristic pieces, reality is transformed. In the brilliant *Night and the City*, for instance, a real London, oozing with slime and enshrouded with fog, becomes a maze of crooked alleyways, narrow cobbled streets and waterfront dens: a place of pestilential enclosure. In *The Window* (1949), New York in midsummer is rendered as a wasteland of abandoned buildings, empty lots ringed by fences, and sweltering tenements—an infested environment that seems to be a breeding ground for crime.

The difference between the airless studio city and the real city of later films suggests the range of themes within which *noir* operates. The fabricated city, or the fragments of it that represent the whole, forms the appropriate setting for stories of psychological focus, while the real city backgrounds indicate a shift to a broader social canvas. The fake and the real cities point up the distinction between *noir's* "private" and "public" modes, between closed-form stories of festering neurosis on the one hand and the more open-form stories that connect in some way to contemporary social realities on the other.

Though sometimes it did go "public," *noir* worked best when it bypassed specific contemporary problems to concentrate instead on private obsession and trauma. The genre's full flavor was curtailed when a film was designed to make a social point, when a story had an anti-communist bias, or exploited nuclear anxiety, or crusaded against criminal syndicates, or networks of German spies. *Noir*, adapted to the demands of exposé or patriotism or moral statement, proved less vigorous and original than when it dealt with small-scale, intimate portraits of criminals by design (*Double Indemnity*) or default (*Scarlet Street*), its focus specifically psychological rather than social.

The crime films of the thirties reflected their times in a direct way, whereas *noir's* connection to the forties is less precise, less a matter of portraying specific social issues than of reflecting, generally and metaphorically, the mood of the country during and after the war. French *cinéastes* felt, after all, that the very qualities which gave the style its name reflected the impact of the war on American society. In *Panorama du film noir américain*, Borde and Chaumeton make the point that few *films noirs* were made from 1941, when *The Maltese Falcon* appeared, to 1945, when the war ended. They write that *noir's* full flowering had to wait until 1945–46, as if the studios had agreed to withhold the negative imagery of *noir* in order to concentrate on patriotic war stories (the industry doing its part in the nation's war effort) or purely escapist entertainment, like musicals and light comedies, which supplied a diversion during a period of anxiety. The two French critics cite the number of full-fledged *noir* dramas in the immediate postwar period as a sign of contemporary disillusionment and malaise, while Raymond Durgnat suggests, plausibly though not persuasively, that "late forties Hollywood is blacker than thirties precisely because its audience, being more secure, no longer needed cheering up."

To read *noir*, however, as a series of social notations either in sympathetic response to or in reaction against a national frame of mind is tricky because it is not primarily a social form, in the way that the stories of gangsters in the thirties were. The gangster's rise and fall took place in a public arena, and the films (partly to placate the censors) assumed a propagandistic cast, claiming to be social documents aimed at eliminating public enemies. The reformist strain of the gangster saga may have been spurious or half-hearted, but the films captured the social

In these two scenes from *The Naked City*, New York becomes a place of entrapment, a blank, menacing background for climactic *noir* chases.

flavor of their period. The public focus of the gangster's career—his activities made headlines—does not continue into *film noir*, where the emphasis is distinctly private, underground. The typical *noir* anti-hero is in hiding, from himself as well as from society; and his criminal activity, unlike the gangster's, is not the stuff of folk legends.

Yet in a number of ways, *noir* offers a symbolic social and psychological profile of its era. The genre's heyday covers a particularly disruptive time in American history; the forties began with the specter of war and concluded with the Congressional witch-hunt for communists, as well as with the prospect of a war in Korea. Even though the theater of action was on foreign soil, American lives were profoundly changed by the war. American cities may not have been directly under fire, but still the daily rhythm of life shifted; if there were no bread lines, there were at least war rations. The war stimulated the domestic economy, but the work force was significantly different from what it had been in the years of pre-war isolationism. Because men were needed in the armed services, women for the first time entered the job market in large numbers, and the place of women, both at home and on the job, changed radically. It is, in fact, in the way that it reflects the new status of women in American society that *film noir* is most closely connected to its period. Like everything else that *noir* touched, it transformed the new role of

In *Night and the City*, Dassin presents London as an imprisoning environment of barred windows and foul narrow alleyways, as in this shot (with Googie Withers, in flight from her husband).

women into a negative image. Passed through the *noir* filter, the "new woman," forced by social circumstance and economic necessity to assert herself in ways that her culture had not previously encouraged, emerged on screen as a wicked, scheming creature, sexually potent and deadly to the male. The dark thrillers record an abiding fear of strong women, women who steer men off their course, beckoning them to a life of crime, or else so disrupting their emotional poise that they are unable to function.

Noir's treatment of women is thus symptomatic of the way in which the genre transforms reality: women who in real life were strengthened by their wartime experience, while their husbands were away, appear in films as malevolent temptresses, their power confined almost entirely to a sexual realm, their strength achieved only at the expense of men. *Noir's* parade of weak, uncertain, woefully neurotic men

and fire-breathing dragon ladies is thus a nightmarish distortion of contemporary realities. It is one of the ongoing complaints of feminists that American films, made mostly by men (and by men who are economically and socially dominant), have seldom been able to portray women as intelligent, independent, and strong-willed without either turning them into monsters, as in *noir*, or else marrying them off in the last reel (the inevitable fate of the career gals played by Rosalind Russell, for instance), thereby "proving" that a woman is calmed down, and removed from the world of masculine striving, once she gets a man. Female ambition is seen then as merely a channeling of sexual frustration.

The anti-woman bias that runs through American films reaches an apotheosis in *noir*, where beautiful spider women proliferate. There are other kinds of women in the films—meek wives infected with a fuddy-duddy morality, strong women like Lauren Bacall who achieve something of a parity with the men they fall for. But the dominant image is the one incarnated by Barbara Stanwyck in *Double Indemnity*: woman as man-hating fatal temptress. The force and persistence of this image of women as amoral destroyers of male strength can be traced, in part, to the wartime reassignment of roles, both at home and at work.

The only character type in *noir* connected directly to the period, without any symbolic exaggeration, is the veteran, returning home after the war in a disoriented state. He is shell-shocked and violent (William Bendix in *The Blue Dahlia*, Robert Ryan in *Crossfire*), re-entering a world whose laws he doesn't understand (Burt Lancaster in *Criss Cross*, Alan Ladd in *The Blue Dahlia*). When he surfaces in *noir*, the returning soldier has the disconnectedness of an ex-con; he seems both amnesiac and somnambulist. The crime dramas absorb the soldiers into the *noir* world rather than focusing directly on such problems of the immediate postwar situation as demobilization, the severely shaken economy, the loss of Roosevelt and readjustment to a new President. Specific social traumas and upheavals remain outside the frame.

Noir never insisted on its "extracurricular" meanings or its social relevance. But beneath its repeated stories of double and triple crosses, its private passions erupting into heinous crimes, the sleazy, compromised morality of many of its characters, can be glimpsed the political paranoia and brutality of the period. In its pervasive aura of defeat and despair, its images of entrapment, the escalating derangement of its leading characters, *noir* registers, in a general way, the country's sour postwar mood. This darkest, most downbeat of American film genres traces a series of metaphors for a decade of anxiety, a contemporary apocalypse bounded on the one hand by Nazi brutality and on the other by the awful knowledge of nuclear power.

Film noir is a descriptive term for the American crime film as it flourished, roughly, from the early forties to the late fifties. It embraces a variety of crime dramas ranging from claustrophobic studies of murder and psychological entrapment to more general treatments of criminal organizations. From stylized versions of the city at night to documentary-like reports of the city at midday, from the investigations of the wry, cynical sleuth to the "innocent" man momentarily and fatally tempted by luxury, to the desperate flailings of the confirmed and inveterate criminal, the genre covers a heterogeneous terrain. In range of theme and in visual style, it is both varied and complex, and in level of achievement it is consistently high. *Film noir* is one of the most challenging cycles in the history of American films.

2
The Literary Background:
The Boys in the Back Room

Noir did not spring full-blown in the early forties. It has a complex ancestry, drawing on literary, artistic, and cinematic precursors to arrive at its own unique blend of American and European styles. The hard-boiled school of crime writing which flourished in the pages of pulp magazines in the twenties and thirties had a great impact on the *noir* tone. *Noir* also shows temperamental and philosophical affinities with the brand of naturalism practiced early in the century by such novelists as Theodore Dreiser and Frank Norris. In visual design, *noir* recalls the stark night world transformations of German Expressionism. The genre's most significant directors—Fritz Lang, Billy Wilder and Robert Siodmak—brought to their assignments on American thrillers the kind of visual styling they had developed in Germany in the twenties during the Golden Age at UFA. As a final major influence, *noir* absorbed some of its iconography from the American gangster film popular in the thirties.

In 1940, in an unappreciative review of the hard-boiled writers, Edmund Wilson called them "the boys in the back room," "the poets of the tabloid murder." Wilson's skepticism was in

Dashiell Hammett and Raymond Chandler began their careers in the rough-cut yellow pages of *Black Mask*, the best-written and best-edited of all the pulp magazines.

fact a minority opinion, since the tough guy writers were generally well received by the literary establishment (though not by movie reviewers of the period); the best of them—Dashiell Hammett, Raymond Chandler, James M. Cain, and Horace McCoy—had enjoyed a steadily growing reputation. For both the writers and their protagonists, "hard-boiled" was first and foremost a matter of style. It was a stance, a way of observing and behaving that demanded the suppression of any openly expressed feeling. Hard-boiled toughness was indicated by appearance, by occupation, by personal habits, and by manner of speech. Dressed typically in trench coat and fedora, a constant smoker and a heavy drinker, the hard-boiled hero was a man of the city, usually though not always engaged in criminal detection, a cop or a gumshoe. Moving through the criminal underworld with a shield of ironic and wary detachment, this self-conscious he-man figure used violence to contain violence; he twisted or circumvented the law in order to uphold the law. His morality was flexible and utilitarian. Though he might resort to devious means to get the job done, he was not for sale: he had a fundamental integrity. (The paradoxical morality of the hard-boiled hero is suggested by the title of a recent study of private eye fiction: *Saint with a Gun*.)

This urban searcher spoke a particular lingo: terse, laconic, and earthy; the stories in which he starred were written in a style that imitated his own toughness. Often presided over by first-person narrators, the hard-boiled stories had a salty, clipped, no-nonsense tone. The first significant hero in the hard-boiled vein was the Continental Op, conceived by the first important hard-boiled writer, Dashiell Hammett. "Hammett took murder out of the Venetian vase and dropped it into the alley," wrote Raymond Chandler in his well-known defense of the realistic mystery story, "The Simple Art of Murder." "[Hammett] wrote at first (and almost to the end) for people with a sharp, aggressive attitude to life. They were not afraid of the seamy side of things; they lived there. Violence did not dismay them; it was right down their street . . . He was spare, frugal, hard-boiled, but he did over and over again what only the best

writers can ever do at all. He wrote scenes that seemed never to have been written before." Chandler saluted Hammett for taking crime back to the streets, to a "not very fragrant world" where people "commit[murder] for reasons, not just to provide a corpse," and away from the aristocratic country house settings of the so-called classical detective story that had dominated the field until the twenties. Hammett's mysteries were revolutionary in both style and substance, and must be seen in context as a reaction to the prevailing conventions of the form at the time he began writing.

Before Hammett, the major names in the mystery field are Edgar Allan Poe, Arthur Conan Doyle, and Agatha Christie, whose work represents three phases of the literature of crime and detection. Histories of the genre, from Howard Haycraft's pioneering survey, *Murder for Pleasure* (1941), to Julian Symon's *Mortal Consequences* (1972), invariably cite Poe as the father of the detective story. Poe's pre-eminent place rests on only three short stories, "Murders in the Rue Morgue," "The Mystery of Marie Roget," and "The Purloined Letter." But in them Poe introduced elements that have been staples of the literature of crime ever since. In "Murders in the Rue Morgue" (1841), Poe introduces the prototype for the character of the eccentric detective. Independently wealthy, Poe's C. Auguste Dupin lives in seclusion in a baroque ancestral mansion, accompanied only by a friend who is the Boswell to his great skills, the modest court reporter who narrates the story. (Poe's characters anticipate Conan Doyle's Watson and Sherlock Holmes by forty-five years.) Dupin and his companion love the dark. During the day, Dracula-like, they remain secluded behind shuttered windows, while at night they wander at random through Paris, seeking not so much adventure as suitable subjects for contemplation. As his admiring friend tells us, Dupin is a wizard of ratiocination, able to pierce any mystery with his uncanny powers of deduction. The murders that occur in the Rue Morgue, which completely baffle the police, offer a signal challenge to Dupin's reasoning skills. The deaths of an obscure laundress and her daughter—the first instance of what was to become a classic mystery motif, that of the locked room puzzle—seem to defy any rational explanation; the conflicting reports of several witnesses who overheard a babble of strange accents before the murders cause further confusion. But Dupin cracks the case with a virtuoso display of his reasoning faculties—concluding, after an argument of serpentine complexity, that the murders were perpetrated not by any human agency but by a gorilla escaped from a traveling circus that entered the top-floor apartment through a window after climbing up a drainpipe!

"Murders in the Rue Morgue" introduces many motifs that were to become conventions of the detective story and of *film noir*: the peculiar and incisive investigator, a lordly, detached figure; the locked-room puzzle; the city as a dark and dangerous setting; the clash between the detective, in business for himself, and the dim-witted police; the last-minute explanation of the crime after a series of hypotheses has been tested and proven false; the withholding of the truth until just before the "final curtain"; the hero's pleasure in the intricate processes of deduction and ratiocination; the labyrinthine route to the solution of the crime. This story and its two successors were enormously popular, which makes the long interval between their publication in the early 1840's and the emergence of Sherlock Holmes in 1886 something of a mystery in itself. Since the first appearance of Conan Doyle's sleuth, however, the genre has sustained its popularity through a number of changes in structure and style.

Like Poe, Conan Doyle created his detective as a respite from other kinds of writing which he took more seriously and for which he wanted to be remembered. The enduring appeal of the Holmes stories, like that of Poe's mysteries, is in the oddities and compulsions of their protagonist, and in the evocation of mood and setting, rather than in plotting. Conan Doyle's narrative construction is often haphazard, and sometimes delirious—habitués are more likely to return to the stories again and again for the sake of Holmes himself, and the London atmosphere, and not for their elements of mystery.

But it is the element of detection that dominated crime literature until the emergence of the hard-boiled school in the twenties. In these pre-hard-boiled stories, whodunit is paramount, and ingenuity of plotting takes precedence over style or character drawing. This kind of puzzle story, of which Agatha Christie's are among the most popular, sets up a mock-battle with the reader, teasing him into a series of wrong guesses. But the writer had to play fair; he could be tricky, but he couldn't cheat; above all, the guilty party had to be on the premises from the beginning. Stories in the Christie mold were set in confined locations: a train, a ship, most often a country house. A murder is committed; the cast of characters, distinctly limited in number, contains many suspects. The detective questions the house guests or passengers, as the case may be, his suspicions pointing now one way, now another, while the reader engages in his own simultaneous process of inquiry and deduction, toying with hunches that may or may not tally with those of the detective. The revelation of the murderer, at any rate, is meant to be a jolt: by convention, the least likely character is usually the guilty one.

It was exactly this type of story—the tale of classical detection—that the hard-boiled school intentionally superseded. The mysteries built on the house-party plan took place in a remote environment—in a sylvan country setting, most typically—and were enacted by caricatures of English nobility and the servant class. In locale, as well as in social notation, the classical detective stories existed in a never-never land utterly alien to the urban American crime milieu. American crime stories and films put crime back where it belonged—in the mean streets of the real world. Stories featuring Nick Carter, the earliest hard-boiled hero, appeared in pulp magazines in the latter part of the last century, but the pulps did not achieve widespread recognition, nor did they become a literate and significant aspect of American popular culture, until the twenties. And the pulp that loomed over the field was *Black Mask*, founded in 1920 by H.L. Mencken and George Jean Nathan. The two men were more interested in their *Smart Set* magazine and, within a year, sold *Black Mask*. In 1926, the editorship was assumed by Captain Joseph T. Shaw, who took the magazine serious-

Humphrey Bogart, as Sam Spade in *The Maltese Falcon*.
Hollywood's first hard-boiled hero, a brooding,
tight-lipped loner who keeps his feelings to himself.

ly, never referring to it as a "pulp" but as "the book" or the "rough paper" magazine. Shaw set high standards for his writers, holding out for a taut style and for characterization. He published the first efforts of both Hammett and Chandler, and used their stories as models for his other writers. The Captain was known in the trade for his ready blue pencil—he tolerated no padding or fat, and he personally edited every story that appeared during his long tenure. Though quality varied, "the book" achieved a level of performance that is now legendary.

Colloquial, racy, vivid, *Black Mask* style (like that later to dominate *film noir*) imitated the lingo of the real criminal world. Style and form are so well matched that it is surprising that crime stories had not always been written in this way, in the accent of street-wise hoodlums and burly cops and gumshoes; but the fact is that *Black Mask*'s gritty realism was something new

in the field—a conscious rebellion against the sissified English murder mysteries.

The use of language in these crime stories was part of a larger revolution in written language, with its roots in the nineteenth century, in the work particularly of Mark Twain, Henry James, and Walt Whitman, who in their different ways sought to introduce the sounds and rhythms of vernacular American speech into literature. Prose in nineteenth century America was formal and ornate. Poe begins "Murders in the Rue Morgue" with a discourse on the deductive faculty: "The mental features discoursed of as the analytical, are, in themselves, but little susceptible of analysis. We appreciate them only in their efforts. We know of them, among other things, that they are always to their possessor, when inordinately possessed, a source of the liveliest enjoyment." The dry, abstract language is likely to alienate the contemporary mystery reader. Here, for striking contrast, representing the *Black Mask* tone at its strongest and purest, is the opening of *The Maltese Falcon* (1929):

> *Samuel Spade's jaw was long and bony, his chin a jutting v under the more flexible v of his mouth. His nostrils curved back to make another, smaller, v. His yellow-grey eyes were horizontal. The v motif was picked up again by thickish brows rising outward from twin creases above a hooked nose, and his pale brown hair grew down—from high flat temples—in a point on his forehead. He looked rather pleasantly like a blond Satan. He said to Effie Perrine: "Yes, sweetheart?"*

Poe is oratorical; Hammett is swift, concrete, simple. Between the two writers lay generations of experiments in tone and style intended to bring prose closer to spoken language. The process, overall, was one of a general chastening and simplification. In this assimilation of the American tone into literature, the crucial book is *Huckleberry Finn* (1884), in which Twain's use of his hero as narrator enabled him to write in a distinctly colloquial manner. Huck speaks directly to the reader in the voice of rural America, with Twain hovering above the page as a sly master of ceremonies. Twain uses the first person technique to introduce greater realism and immediacy into the texture of his writing, and the "I" through whom we receive impressions in many of the hard-boiled stories and *films noirs* performs the same function.

The major link between the kind of experiments with language that Twain was making and the vernacular tang of the hard-boiled style is Ernest Hemingway, who is generally acknowledged as the true father of the tough crime writers of the twenties and thirties, their stylistic and philosophical headmaster. Hemingway did

Ole Andresen (Burt Lancaster) awaits his executioners, in the film adaptation of Hemingway's authentically hard-boiled short story, "The Killers."

more than any other single writer to legitimize the colloquial mode in American prose; he perfected a clean, idiomatic style. He and the hacks cranking out a penny a word for the flourishing pulp jungle had much in common: a concern for the true sounds and rhythms of American speech and a posture of American toughness and durability. The typical Hemingway hero held on to his stance of self-reliant masculinity in a way that paralleled the hard-boiled stars—the Sam Spades and Philip Marlowes—of the *Black Mask* brigade. Hemingway's men keep a tight rein on their emotions, guardedly resisting feelings, their fiercely willed stoicism a shield against chaos. The struggle for control and the denial of feelings are reflected in Hemingway's spare, taut, compulsively worked-over language, where everything is concrete and immediate, where descriptions (whether of climate or landscape or food or people) are confined to a tight neutral tone, like a journalist reporting the externals of a scene as they seemed to him to be at the time.

Chaste and withheld, with a simplicity arrived at through rigorous self-discipline, the Hemingway style quickly became the dominant mode of American realism. Yet beneath the compact tough guy stance is a creeping sense of hysteria, an ongoing hint that the hard-boiled pose can crack at any moment. It is in exactly this tension between surface and subtext, between the seeming poise of the characters and the language and the underlying unrest, that Hemingway transcends the *Black Mask* school. For the most part, the image that the hard-boiled heroes present to the world is accurate, whereas Hemingway's stoics—the wounded Jake Barnes in *The Sun Also Rises*, or Frederick Henry, fleeing from war in *A Farewell to Arms*—often construct a facade which is almost the opposite of what they really are "deep down." The split in Hemingway's characters between their public and private selves is often decisive, while in much crime writing the characters have no private selves at all.

Hemingway honed the hard-boiled style, but only one of his novels (*To Have and Have Not*) and only a few of his short stories ("The Killers" pre-eminently) qualify as specifically hard-boiled. Harry Morgan, the hero of *To Have and Have Not*, is a full-fledged tough guy who tries to make ends meet running a fishing boat from Havana harbor. Betrayed by a rich client, who steals off without paying the money he owes, Harry slips into criminal activity, illegally transporting a group of Chinese and Cuban revolutionaries. A determined man, capable of violence, he dislikes trafficking with criminals, but he compromises because he sees no other way to support himself. A heavy drinker who spends his time in bars, he is also a terrific lover. Killed in a shootout aboard his boat, Harry Morgan, like the old fisherman in *The Old Man and the Sea*, makes a superhuman effort to survive against enormous odds. His defeat is rendered in heroic terms, as the action of a special man. Harry is a more exalted figure than the tight-lipped private eye, but the world he moves in, the challenges he faces, and the posture he assumes, are all much the same as those of the lesser Spades and Marlowes of the pulps and of *noir*.

"The Killers" is Hemingway's one perfectly realized piece in the hard-boiled vein. Two hired gunmen enter a diner to wait for the nightly appearance of "the Swede," whom they have been paid to kill. When the Swede doesn't show, the zombie-like killers go to his rented room, to find him lying on his bed in the dark, waiting to give himself up to their dark mission. The killers shoot him and then leave town, as quickly and as quietly as they arrived.

Hemingway tells us nothing about the Swede's background, or about his feelings. We see him only from the outside, as a startlingly passive victim. And yet the story reverberates with a sense of powerful, unexpressed feelings. Hemingway's clenched, metallic dialogue—which is to become the standard "voice" of *noir*—and his terse scene-setting contain a palpitating subtext. The Swede's existential resignation, the character's despair and world-weariness, are ingrained in the willed, deadly flatness of the language.

*Nick opened the door and went into the room.
Ole Andreson was lying on the bed with all his
clothes on. He had been a heavyweight
prizefighter and he was too long for the bed. He
lay with his head on two pillows. He did not
look at Nick.*

"What was it?" he asked.

*"I was up at Henry's," Nick said, "and
two fellows came in and tied up me and the cook,
and they said they were going to kill you."*

*It sounded silly when he said it. Ole
Andreson said nothing.*

"Thanks for coming to tell me about it."

"That's all right."

*Nick looked at the big man lying on
the bed.*

*"Don't you want me to go and see the
police?"*

*"No," Ole Andreson said. "That
wouldn't do any good."*

"Isn't there something I could do?"

"No. There ain't anything to do."

"Maybe it was just a bluff."

"No. It ain't just a bluff."

Ole Andreson rolled over toward the wall.

The short, simple sentences, the repetitions, are thick with menace and implication. Hemingway uses the colloquial style more knowingly and for deeper purposes than the "poets of the tabloid murder," but the high and low versions of the hard-boiled manner share a world view as well as use of language.

Though Hemingway's influence was pervasive, he was never considered *merely* hard-boiled. The first writer who was legitimately and literately hard-boiled without being anything else was Dashiell Hammett, whose tough-sounding mysteries were intended as a challenge to the genteel, formula-ridden puzzle stories of the British crime school. Hammett wrote for mood and character rather than for story—the solution was often less important than atmosphere, local color, dialogue, tone. It was clear to almost everyone who read him that Hammett was a born writer who just happened to work in a particular genre. Hammett had only ten fruitful years as a writer, from the mid-twenties to the mid-thirties; but in that time, in his stories for *Black Mask* starring The Continental Op, and in his famous novels, he built a solid reputation as the Hemingway of the pulps.

Fat and oily, the antithesis of the romantic hero, The Op seems to have no life at all apart from his determined pursuit of criminals. We never catch a glimpse of him in a private moment. He is always on stage, radiating toughness. He never changes, he never removes his mask, he has an emotional range approaching zero. Only his ready use of violence is capable of surprising us. Yet he is a real presence, a character of some stature, a primitive version of the hard-boiled anti-hero central to the private eye tradition in crime literature of the twenties and thirties and to *film noir* in the forties.

Hammett's writing stood above the hack work that inundated the crime field because of his taut, slangy style, filled with precise descriptions of characters and settings, his character drawing, and his themes. Like Chandler after him, Hammett chafed at the supposed limits of crime fiction, and he introduced motifs not previously associated with the genre. The feeling that something new and interesting is happening in Hammett's work is deepened in his novels. *Red Harvest*, *The Maltese Falcon*, *The Dain Curse*, and *The Glass Key* (but not *The Thin Man*, which was never intended to be more than an agreeable entertainment, brisk and witty) all deal with serious themes that enlarge the limits of category fiction. The four novels open the enclosed mystery frame to larger issues: *Red Harvest* and *The Glass Key* touch on political corruption, exposing shady collaborations between bosses of politics and crime. *The Dain Curse* flirts with ideas of false religion and of the power of cults—long before cults were a widespread part of American life. *The Maltese Falcon* is less programmatic than these other socially-oriented crime pieces, but it contains the most pungent of all the hard-boiled characters—Sam Spade—and through him becomes a kind of informal essay on the code of the tough guy. Two famous

speeches in the novel reveal the essence of that code. Early in the story, Sam Spade, in what is for him an expansive mood, recites an anecdote to Brigid O'Shaughnessy about a man named Flitcraft. One day, while walking to work, Flitcraft is nearly hit by a falling beam. The near-accident gives him a sense of the randomness and absurdity of life; he decides to walk away from the safe, contained life of work, family, and responsibilities he has created for himself. He disappears, re-settles in some other city, and, after a period of time, rebuilds his life in the same mold as before the incident with the falling beam.

Fully aware that this is a world in which falling beams can cause an absurd end for an innocent bypasser, Flitcraft proceeds imperturbably. The knowledge of the absurd doesn't destroy his life; he carries on much as before, business as usual: but the event gives him rare clear-sightedness. Beneath the seemingly unruffled surface of his life, Flitcraft sees into the abyss. Hammett summarizes:

> *Flitcraft had been a good citizen and a good husband and father, not by any outer compulsion, but simply because he was a man who was most comfortable in step with his surroundings . . . Now a falling beam had shown him that life was fundamentally none of these things. He, the good citizen-husband-father, could be wiped out between office and restaurant by the accident of a falling beam. He knew then that men died at haphazard like that, and lived only while blind chance spared them. It was not, primarily, the injustice of it that disturbed him: he accepted that after the first shock. What disturbed him was the discovery that in sensibly ordering his affairs he had got out of step, and not into step, with life.*

Flitcraft's strange story epitomizes the hard-boiled world view. Like Flitcraft, Spade is clear-sighted—pitilessly so, in fact—proceeding as if the world makes sense and adds up to something when he knows it really doesn't. Like Flitcraft, Spade leads an ordered life, maintaining a sense of purpose in the face of disorder and irrationality.

The Flitcraft episode is extraordinary for a number of reasons. This richly suggestive allegory, which seems oddly placed in a crime story, is indicative of Hammett's unconventional methods. Supplying mood and philosophical context, and conveying a sense of Spade's measured, wary character, the story does not advance the narrative in any direct way—Hammett's inclusion of it moves *The Maltese Falcon* toward literature and away from pulp fiction.

Spade's speech to Brigid at the end is equally trenchant in its revelation of character. Spade tells Brigid that he has been wise to her from the beginning. The jig is up, he announces, as she attempts to work her female magic on him. Though Sam is attracted to her, charmed by the skill of her performance, he is not going to protect her. He is not going to violate his code for her. "When a man's partner is killed," he says, in a speech that typifies the clipped, terse tone he always adopts, "he's supposed to do something about it. It doesn't make any difference what you thought of him. He was your partner and you're supposed to do something about it . . ."

These two beautifully written passages, the Flitcraft story and the explanation to Brigid, summarize the moral foundation of the hard-boiled code. In the face of uncertainty and duplicity, Sam Spade retains his honor. He is not lily-white by any means—he had an affair with his partner's wife, he is not above using deception and violence to gain his ends. He is cynical and hard to reach emotionally. But, like Flitcraft, he endures, held together by an inner toughness. He commands respect. He is, in short, an ideal character for Humphrey Bogart, the quintessential *noir* actor.

Like the typical Hemingway hero, Spade attends to the task at hand, concentrating on the physical details of the moment. Hammett's

"RAYMOND CHANDLER IS A STAR OF THE FIRST MAGNITUDE"
—Erle Stanley Gardner

THE BIG SLEEP

by RAYMOND CHANDLER

Published in 1939, *The Big Sleep* was Chandler's first novel, the first of ten that starred Philip Marlowe.

forefinger and thumb pinching their end while right forefinger and thumb smoothed the damp seam, right forefinger and thumb twisting their end and lifting the other to Spade's mouth.

Hammett wrote about a world he knew (among his various jobs, he had been a Pinkerton man) in a tight, lean, vernacular style that seemed to him the appropriate medium for his characters and settings. As he was drawn more and more in the thirties and forties to radical political causes, his crime fiction began to appear irrelevant to him, though his short career was also attributable to his spectacular ill-health, his fight against both tuberculosis and alcoholism. Hammett's body of work is slim. When he could no longer write the way he wanted to, he simply stopped. Hammett's reputation as the progenitor of a new kind of crime novel, as a symptomatic political figure, as the inspiration to his long-time companion Lillian Hellman, and as an innovator of the clenched tough guy style, has continued to rise; if anything, he is in danger of being over-rated. Of its kind, *The Maltese Falcon* is supreme—it maintains a perfect pitch throughout—but nothing else in the canon comes anywhere near the same level of performance. Hammett knew his own limits, as well as those of the genre in which he worked, and he surely would have scoffed at high-toned re-appraisals that make him a writer of the first rank, co-equal with Hemingway, or that attempt deep readings of material never intended to be more than intelligent, finely crafted entertainment.

Raymond Chandler was more defensive about his writing than Hammett, and he worked as both practitioner and critic to lift crime fiction to full-fledged literary status. In contrast to Hammett's proletarian roots, Chandler's background was blue-blood. He was raised in England, where he attended Dulwich College and received a fine classical education. Returning to his native America as an adult, Chandler saw it with the eyes of a foreigner, and with a clarity perhaps possible only to an outsider. Chandler did not begin writing until he was middle-aged, and he developed his mature style quickly. His

description of how Spade makes a cigarette is similar to Hemingway's accounts of how his characters fish, or steer a boat, or fight a bull, with superb control and a mastery that comes from absolute concentration:

Spade's thick fingers made a cigarette with deliberate care, sifting a measured quantity of tan flakes down into curved paper, spreading the flakes so that they lay equal at the ends with a slight depression in the middle, thumbs rolling the paper's inner edge down and up under the outer edge as forefingers pressed it over, thumbs and fingers sliding to the paper cylinder's ends to hold it even while tongue licked the flap, left first story, *Blackmailers Don't Shoot*, was published in *Black Mask* in 1933. His first novel, *The Big Sleep*, appeared, to popular and critical success, in 1939. There followed nine other novels between 1940 and 1959. As with Hammett, the list is slight, as crime fiction goes (compare Hammett's and Chandler's lean output to the vast numbers of books by Agatha Christie or Ellery Queen or John Dickson Carr).

A studied craftsman who insisted that good writing was good writing regardless of genre, Chandler worked, like Hammett, for tone and characterization rather than narrative drive. He was, in fact, a poor storyteller, and his novels are often confusing conflations of motifs derived from several different short stories. (Chandler referred to the process of turning short pieces into novels as "cannibalization.") His work is distinguished not by its tension, though the reader has a lingering curiosity as to how the story ends, but by its evocation of setting (Chandler is the poet laureate of Southern California) and by its wry tone—in short, by its fine writing. And in Philip Marlowe, Chandler created a private eye, a proper *noir* hero, worthy of following Sam Spade. Chandler had a more romantic temperament than Hammett, and his private eye was a more exalted figure than any of Hammett's characters. In *The Simple Art of Murder*, Chandler defined his concept of the ideal detective:

. . . *down these mean streets a man must go who is not himself mean, who is neither tarnished nor afraid. The detective in this kind of story must be such a man. He is the hero, he is everything. He must be a complete man and a common man and yet an unusual man. He must be, to use a rather weathered phrase, a man of honor, by instinct, by inevitability, without thought of it, and certainly without saying it. He must be the best man in his world and a good enough man for any world. I do not care much about his private life; he is neither a eunuch nor a satyr; I think he might seduce a duchess and I am quite sure he would not spoil a virgin; if he is a man of honor in one thing, he is that in all things. He is a relatively poor man, or he would not be a detective at all. He is a common man, or he could not go among common people. He has a sense of*

character, or he would not know his job. He will take no man's money dishonestly and no man's insolence without a due and dispassionate revenge. He is a lonely man and his pride is that you will treat him as a proud man or be very sorry you ever saw him. He talks as the man of his age talks, that is, with rude wit, a lively sense of the grotesque, a disgust for sham, and a contempt for pettiness. The story is his adventure in search of a hidden truth, and it would be no adventure if it did not happen to a man fit for adventure. He has a range of awareness that startles you, but it belongs to him by right, because it belongs to the world he lives in. If there were enough like him, I think the world would be a very safe place to live in, and yet not too dull to be worth living in.

Chandler's work doesn't quite match this beautifully written description, but it does reveal his sense of the story of detection as a kind of modern urban romance, a quest for truth, with the private eye hero the self-appointed preserver of decency and order in a tarnished world.

Guided by his own code, morally flexible but not corruptible, maintaining his integrity while resorting, if necessary, to violence and double-dealing, Chandler's hero has much the same tough guy posture as The Op and Sam Spade. And like Spade and the others, he too is sexually ambiguous; beautiful women find him appealing, but he remains sexually aloof, almost monkish. Essentially wary of women, he is more at ease in the world of male friendships. The most impassioned relationship in any of the Marlowe books is the one between the detective and his male friend Terry Lennox, in *The Long Goodbye*. The decided misogyny that runs through Chandler's stories is to become a dominant motif in *noir*.

Concealing a festering evil beneath seductive masks, women are typically the villains in Chandler's work, their beckoning sexuality a trap for the tempted male. Like most hard-boiled heroes, Marlowe responds to women as objects to appraise; he inspects and judges them. "I sat down on the edge of a deep soft chair and looked at Mrs. Regan," Marlowe says in *The Big Sleep*.

Chandler's men and women communicate in a language of inuendo and wisecrack which is a cover-up for their true feelings. In the film of *The Big Sleep*, Humphrey Bogart and Lauren Bacall capture exactly the kind of low-keyed mutual baiting that is a metaphor for sexual attraction in Chandler's writing.

She was worth a stare. She was trouble. She was stretched out on a modernistic chaise-lounge with her slippers off, so I stared at her legs in the sheerest silk stockings. They seemed to be arranged to stare at. They were visible to the knee and one of them well beyond. The knees were dimpled, not bony and sharp. The calves were beautiful, the ankles long and slim and with enough melodic line for a tone poem. She was tall and rangy and strong-looking. Her head was against an ivory satin cushion. Her hair was black and wiry and parted in the middle and she had the hot black eyes of a portrait in the hall. She had a good mouth and a good chin. There was a sulky droop to her lips and the lower lip was full.

Marlowe keeps his distance from Mrs. Regan, not venturing beyond verbal flirtation; but toward her sister Carmen, he reacts with revulsion. "She stood there for a moment and hissed at me, her face still like scraped bone, her eyes still empty and yet full of some jungle emotion." After he throws her out of his apartment, he goes to his bed, where she had been lying in wait for him. "The imprint of her head was still in the pillow, of her small corrupt body still on the sheets. I put my empty glass down and tore the bed to pieces savagely." Carmen's blatant sexuality offends Marlowe's asceticism. To him, she is a foul creature, a warped jungle animal, and he regards her with open distaste.

In *Farewell, My Lovely*, Velma Grayle (the name has echoes of the Arthurian motifs present throughout the canon) is another dangerous woman, pretending, like most of Chandler's female characters, to be something she is not. A former dancer in a downtown strip joint, Velma has transformed herself into the wife of a millionaire. In order to protect her new identity, she kills a few men, a slippery gigolo and the big dumb ex-con Moose Malloy, who has hired Marlowe to track her down. Velma's sexual come-on is a little subtler than Carmen's— money and social status are really more important to her than sex—but she is equally poisonous.

In *The Long Goodbye*, Eileen Wade pollutes Marlowe's friendship with Terry Lennox. Eileen killed Lennox's wife, a crime for which Lennox (who has fled to Mexico) is accused and of which Marlowe believes him innocent. The fidelity to his friend costs him dear; he is jailed, beaten, mistreated by the police to a degree unprecedented in the private eye canon. Yet he is true to a masculine code of honor which the mad female is determined to corrupt. Embarked on a killing spree that includes her lover and her neurotic novelist husband, whose tough pose she chips away at and ultimately destroys, Eileen is the most fiendish of Chandler's villains. The

character is excessive, almost as if in creating and then in destroying her, Chandler is settling a personal score against the female sex.

Chandler's conniving women are threats to the poise and attempted self-sufficiency of his male characters, and only when the women are killed is the moral and sexual order of Marlowe's world restored. Sexual tensions in Chandler— the war between the hard men and the even harder women—are powerful and elemental; the only heterosexual mingling that Chandler seems to accept is the one in which the partners are buddies, sparking each other's wit and irony, and maintaining their distance with clever give-and-take. The sly sexual baiting in Chandler is captured beautifully in the exchanges between Humphrey Bogart and Lauren Bacall in *The Big Sleep*, where the two express their feelings in a volley of barbed witticisms. As in Restoration comedy, their mutual verbal slicing is an index of sexual attraction.

Bacall and Bogart, in *The Big Sleep*.

Often in trouble, Chandler's private eye nevertheless maintained a stoical mask. In these two shots from *Murder, My Sweet* (the film version of *Farewell, My Lovely*), Dick Powell as Philip Marlowe undergoes a grueling interrogation by his arch-opponents the police, and is thrown into jail when he is accused of a crime that, of course, he did not commit.

Chandler's characters address each other indirectly, in a diction coated with innuendo and duplicity. Often the people Marlowe interviews aren't being straight with him, and their clever evasions are communicated in a wry tone; the characters are often putting each other on, playing a cagey game of sexual baiting and oneupmanship:

> *"Tall, aren't you?" she said.*
> *"I didn't mean to be."*
> *"Handsome, too," she said. "And I bet you know it."*
> *I grunted.*
> *"What's your name?"*
> *"Reilly," I said. "Doghouse Reilly."*
> *"Are you a prizefighter?" she asked . . .*
> *"Not exactly. I'm a sleuth."*
> *"You're cute," she giggled. "I'm cute too."*

Chandler's dialogue is consistently terse, salty, with an effective rhythm. Listen to the beat as Marlowe talks fresh to Mrs. Regan:

> *"I'm not crazy about your manners," I said. "I didn't ask to see you. You sent for me. I don't mind your ritzing me or drinking your lunch out of a Scotch bottle. I don't mind your showing me your legs. They're very swell legs and it's a pleasure to make their acquaintance. I don't mind if you don't like my manners. They're pretty bad. I grieve over them during the long winter evenings. But don't waste your time trying to cross-examine me."*

Almost all of Chandler's people are smart-alecks, and his novels considerably enrich the distinctly American tradition of the wisecrack.

Chandler is more manneristic than Hammett, allowing his fondness for similes occasionally to run wild: "He looked about as inconspicuous as a tarantula on a slice of angel food cake." These verbal fillips which spice nearly every page of the Marlowe books are a measure of Chandler's concern with style. *How* the story is told is often more important to him than *what* the story is about; many passages, glittering set-pieces, can be enjoyed quite apart from their connection to the narrative, such as this gorgeous paragraph of scene-setting in *Farewell, My Lovely*:

> *We curved through the bright mile or two of the Strip, past the antique shops with famous screen names on them, past the windows full of point lace and ancient pewter, past the gleaming new nightclubs with famous chefs and equally famous gambling rooms, run by polished graduates of the Purple Gang, past the Georgian-Colonial vogue, now old hat, past the handsome modernistic buildings in which the Hollywood flesh-peddlers never stop talking money, past a drive-in lunch which somehow didn't belong, even though the girls wore white silk blouses and drum majorettes' shakos and nothing below the hips but glazed kid Hessian boots. Past all this and down a wide smooth curve to the bridle path of Beverly Hills and lights to the south, all colors of the spectrum and crystal clear in an evening without fog, past the shadowed mansions up on the hills to the north, past Beverly Hills altogether and up into the twisting foothill boulevard and the sudden cool dusk and the drift of wind from the sea.*

As a skillful literary stylist working within the conventions of the mystery story, Chandler remains unsurpassed.

The private eye genre returned, ignominiously, to its pulp origins in the work of Mickey Spillane, whose character of Mike Hammer has none of the finesse or integrity that distinguishes Marlowe or Spade. "A good name for a duke," Mrs. Llewellyn Lockridge Grayle tells Marlowe at the end of *Farewell, My Lovely*. Nobody could say that to Mike Hammer, the antithesis of royalty in both name and manner. If Marlowe represents for Chandler, as many of his critics claim, an ideal fantasy version of himself, then Hammer is a fantasy self-image for Spillane. The distance between the two characters charts the difference between Chandler's refinement on the one hand and Spillane's hopeless crudeness on the other. Spillane makes no pretense of being an artist—he is merely in the business of marketing garish right-wing fantasies of the threat to the national fibre of communists and homosexuals. To preserve the macho patriotic ideal, Hammer resorts to vigilante justice, his violence excused as a necessary way of maintaining law and order against contaminating foreign elements. The Hammer books represent a lunatic right-wing fringe, enlisting sex and violence in the cause of Americanism. Raw to an absurd degree, naked testaments to Spillane's utterly meretricious sensibility, the books would not deserve notice except for the disturbing fact of their unprecedented popularity. A culture does not buy fantasies that have no connection to it, and the record sales of Spillane books indicate the degree to which he has plumbed the lowest common denominator.

Spillane's work is the nadir of the hard-boiled school. His fiction confirms the worst elements that critics of the crime novel have customarily charged against it: its exploitation of sex and violence and sensational crime, its sleazy atmosphere, its misogyny, its lack of aesthetic standards.

The detective is the most famous, but certainly not the only, incarnation of the hard-boiled style. Although crime is usually present, either centrally or peripherally, in the hard-boiled novel, the element of detection is not. James M. Cain and Horace McCoy, along with Hammett and Chandler the leading writers of the hard-boiled school and major influences on *noir* style, do not write stories about private eyes or about searches for missing persons. Their focus is on the criminal rather than the investigator, and the shift in vantage point involves adjustments of tone and characterization as well. In Cain's most famous stories, the criminals serve as narrators, so the novels are not mysteries in the usual sense: in Cain, we know whodunit, and why, right from the start. The suspense comes not from locating the guilty person but from examining him, from penetrating his consciousness as he tells us his story.

Cain felt that he belonged to no particular school or tradition; he especially disliked the hard-boiled label attached to his work. But hard-boiled it definitely is. His writing is more feverish than the work of Hammett or Chandler, but like them Cain writes about crime in a stylistically self-conscious way, creating

Recently reissued in paperback, James M. Cain's novels, like those of Hammett and Chandler, are attracting a growing number of admirers.

restrained investigator, but seen up close, in sustained intimate focus, through their own words. The absence of an intervening consciousness between the sexually voracious criminals and the reader gives Cain's stories a sensational aura. "Nothing Cain has ever written has been entirely out of the trash category," writes W. M. Frohock, in *The Novel of Violence in America*. "He has schooled himself grimly to produce the kind of effect he wants, with every sentence supercharged and a new jolt for the reader on every page . . . Cain works on the assumption . . . that he can do with the reader just about what he likes. The reader is a sort of victim, whose weaknesses are there to be exploited."

Cain's two best-known protagonists, Frank in *The Postman Always Rings Twice*, and Walter Neff in *Double Indemnity*, are led to crime through animalistic passion. By chance, both characters meet sexually enticing and available women. Frank is something of a hobo, a knockabout wanderer, who drifts by a country luncheonette-gas station. When he sets eyes on the proprietor's wife, he decides to stay on as handyman and station attendant. Walter Neff meets Phyllis on a routine call in the course of selling insurance. The sight of these two women unbalances both men. The women are embodiments of male sexual fantasies, and the heroes' luck in encountering them, and then in beginning affairs with them, constitutes what Cain has called "the wish come true." But in Cain, hot sex is a trap, the beginning of the end. Sex leads quickly to crime as the new lovers plan to murder the woman's unloved husband. Once the lovers commit murder, their passion becomes stained and corrupted beyond repair. The conspirators begin to distrust each other, in little ways at first, and end up locked in a fierce battle of wills, their passion turned to hatred.

Double Indemnity served as the basis for one of the most trenchant *films noirs*. *The Postman Always Rings Twice* was emasculated in its screen adaptation, made by the wrong studio (tinselly MGM), and miscast in two of its roles (Lana Turner too poised and glamorous for Cora, Cecil Kellaway far too refined for Cora's dimwitted and gross husband). Elements of Cain's

through a vigorous vernacular mode a hard-edged picture of hard-edged characters. His major pieces—*The Postman Always Rings Twice* (1934), *Double Indemnity* (1936), *Serenade* (1939), and *Mildred Pierce* (1940)—anticipate aspects of *noir* sensibility as much as the work of Hammett and Chandler.

Chandler, the chief critic of the hard-boiled literary tradition, disliked Cain's writing. It is not difficult to see why. Cain's sexually explosive novels violate Chandler's sense of decorum; in Cain's work, twisted characters are not, as in Hammett or Chandler, observed from the disapproving gaze of a moralistic and sexually

Cecil Kellaway, John Garfield, and Lana Turner in the
1946 MGM film of *The Postman Always Rings Twice*,
which undercut the novel's hothouse atmosphere. The
film's well-scrubbed surface (indicated in this shot)
missed the sour, mordant quality of Cain's writing.

work filtered into most of the crime films of the
forties: the link between sex, greed, and crime;
the deadly irony (Frank escapes punishment,
through legal technicalities, for a crime he did
commit, and is then condemned to death for a
crime of which he is innocent); the tough, dispassionate, slangy first-person narration.
Frank's story, we learn at the end, is told from
his cell on Death Row. Walter's story is told just
before he and Phyllis decide to commit suicide
by jumping off the ship that is carrying them to
a life of exile. Although we don't know, until
the end, where the stories are told, or at precisely what point in time, an aura of doom
nonetheless hovers over both narrations.

The fact that the narrators are recalling
events that have already taken place gives these
stories of sex and murder a reflective overlay;
the cool, matter-of-fact quality of the narration,
as in many of the voice-over commentaries in
noir, creates a striking contrast to the powerful
feelings that put the hapless protagonists where
they are now. The narrators look back on their
hot-bloodedness with a mixture of rue and
irony, recollecting their wrong-headed lust with
distance if not exactly tranquility. Here is the
voice of Walter Neff, as he begins his story of
passion gone wrong:

James M. Cain's *Serenade* is a delirious sexual escapade, all but unrecognizable in the laundered Hollywood adaptation, starring Mario Lanza, a most unlikely *noir* hero.

I drove out to Glendale to put three new truck drivers on a brewery company bond, and then I remembered this renewal over in Hollywoodland. I decided to run over there. That was how I came to this House of Death, that you've been reading about in the papers. It didn't look like a House of Death when I saw it. It was just a Spanish house, like all the rest of them in California, with white walls, red tile roof, and a patio out to one side. It was built cock-eyed.

The clash between the narrator's dry, mordant tone and the sensational substance of his story is one of the hallmarks of the hard-boiled tradition, providing the kind of ironic distancing that lifts *Double Indemnity*, like other novels of its type, above tabloid intrigue to the level of consciously crafted literature.

In addition to *Double Indemnity* and *The Postman Always Rings Twice*, Cain has written two other deeply *noir* novels, *Serenade* (an extraordinary story utterly disembowelled in a foolish, laundered film version starring Mario Lanza, a most unlikely *noir* hero) and *Mildred Pierce* (splendidly adapted into Joan Crawford's most successful star vehicle). Both stories again concern obsession leading to murder, though the actual crime in each case is much less central than in the earlier books.

Serenade was too sensational to be translated intact to films—and it would still be unfilmable today, though for different reasons than in the forties. Set in a variety of locations, from rural Mexico to Hollywood to New York, *Serenade* is narrated by an opera singer—an unusual *noir* occupation—whose voice changes radically in quality (and here is the story's wild, dotty premise) according to his current sexual orientation. He lost his voice when he discovered that he was attracted to men, and then allowed himself to be seduced by a wealthy, decadent patron. In a smoky den he meets a ravishing senorita whom he wins in a card game. His desire for her, which is consummated in a church (in the novel's most delirious and virtuoso set-piece), revives his voice. His manhood and his art restored, he goes to Hollywood where his star rises and falls in record time. Lured back to New York by his former male lover, he re-enters the world of opera as the effete man and the passionate senorita wage battle over his body and soul. In a climactic scene, the senorita thrusts a sword through the hovering homosexual—a phallic thrust to save her man's phallus for herself. She and the singer once again become fugitives. She returns to Mexico as he follows in hot pursuit, and the story comes full circle, ending where it began, with the hero in much the same ravaged emotional and sexual condition as at the opening. *Serenade* is awash in gross sexual stereotyping: nowhere else in the hard-boiled canon is homosexuality presented with the naked disapproval and contempt evident here. Homosexuality in the novel is a threat not only to the character's self-image but also to his art.

Sex with a Mexican spitfire is thus both cleansing and restorative, while sex with his male patron is utterly degrading.

For all its exotic settings and references, *Serenade* is quintessentially *noir* in its depiction of sex, with homosexuality replacing the traditional *femme fatale* as the hero's nemesis. Whatever the orientation, sex in Cain (as in *noir*) is a supremely destructive force; it has the power to transform personality, and to give in to it is a certain invitation to disaster. Although the Mexican prostitute is a vital figure, restoring the hero to his best self, she is ultimately menacing since her passion leads to murder. Cain cannot imagine sex as both dynamic and safe.

"In the spring of 1931, on a lawn in Glendale, California, a man was bracing trees." So begins *Mildred Pierce*, in a voice of rational and objective observation that offers a strong contrast to the intense first-person narrator of *Serenade*. The cool narration is misleading, since the novel turns out to be as full of sexual obsession as Cain's other work—it begins as a seemingly conventional domestic melodrama and then descends by degrees into a dark pit of *noir* pathology. Mildred Pierce, in fact, is more monomaniacal than any of Cain's other characters, her every action guided by her twisted love for her spoiled-rotten daughter. Mildred is a typical American mother who wants her children to enjoy all the "finer things," which to her means the things only money can buy. In some respects Mildred is normal and admirable: she is a good hard worker, she is resilient, ambitious, clever, as she set herself up in the restaurant business, graduating in record time from waitress to baker to entrepreneur. But all her good points are disfigured by her intense and single-minded desire to win the approval of her disdainful daughter. She soils herself to maintain Veda's "love," marrying a man she does not really care for, a ne'er-do-well with money, just so Veda can have entrée to the world of high society.

There are moments of startling perversity in the novel, as when Mildred admits that she is glad it was her other daughter who died of pneumonia and not Veda, and when she sleeps with Veda, to soothe and protect her. Mildred's sick attachment to her daughter contaminates and finally overwhelms her, just as the singer's homosexuality in *Serenade* and Frank's lust for Cora in *The Postman Always Rings Twice* fatally discolor them. For Mildred, men are merely convenient stepping stones toward her fantasy goal of an indissoluble union with her daughter. Going after money and social status for an unusually twisted reason, Mildred Pierce represents a deformed version of the Horatio Alger myth.

The misogynistic streak in Cain's work is carried to grotesque proportions in the character of Veda, who is intolerably precocious intellectually and sexually—she is a nymphet version of the castrating *femme fatale* who was to become a *noir* fixture. Like Cain's other vixens, Veda is indeed deadlier than the male, ravenous, libidinous—and only sixteen when she sleeps with and then, when he spurns her, shoots her no-account stepfather.

Cain is a forceful, knotty, occasionally maddening writer. As he dramatizes the destruction of his sexually overloaded characters, as he attacks American Momism and the American bitch, his voice is harsh and authentic. Fiercely misanthropic, Cain's writing exudes a low-consciousness tabloid mentality that has kept some readers at a distance. But his work reflects a true aspect of the hard-boiled tradition. Cain is a shrewd American original whose four major novels are striking premonitions of the sensibility that underlies *film noir*.

Like many of the tough guy writers, Cain has always been popular abroad, especially in France and Italy, if not consistently on native grounds. He has, however, enjoyed a recent resurgence in America, while Horace McCoy, traditionally listed along with Cain, Hammett, and Chandler as a tough-guy writer who could really write, has yet to be fully appreciated at home. McCoy's novels are all out of print, and yet his work is flavorful, well-crafted, authentically hard-boiled. His limited fame rests on one novel, *They Shoot Horses, Don't They?*, a slashing social satire much admired by French writers and critics: Camus hailed it as an American masterpiece. A successful film adaptation in 1969, with Jane Fonda and Gig Young, failed to

The dance marathon as social metaphor. Bonnie Bedelia, Bruce Dern, Jane Fonda, and Red Buttons as contestants, in the film adaptation of Horace McCoy's hard-boiled novel, *They Shoot Horses, Don't They?* The success of the 1969 film did not spur a revival of interest in McCoy, who remains the most neglected of the major tough guy writers.

push McCoy out of the literary limbo he has occupied since the thirties.

They Shoot Horses, Don't They? introduces a number of changes into the tough guy novel. Instead of a wisecracking, tight-lipped hero, its protagonist is a woman (who is among the most embittered of hard-boiled characters) and the story, unlike most in its vein, has an explicit social context. It is a Depression novel, set at a dance marathon in an arena on a crumbling Santa Monica pier. The characters enter the contest to earn money. The two leading characters are aging kids who have traveled to California to be movie stars; the boy retains a naive optimism about his possibilities, the girl is ravaged by her experiences in Hollywood. She has come to the marathon as a last resort. Tart, morbid, poised

to expect the worst, Gloria, unlike many of the fated *noir* protagonists whom she resembles, actively seeks her own death. At the end of her rope, her life nothing but the ashes and rubble of the American Dream, trapped in an absurd contest on a rotting pier at the edge of the American continent, she is "saved" by her partner, who at her insistence becomes her executioner.

Prefiguring a *noir* pattern, Gloria's story begins at the end, with her death, so that a sense of her own utter despair hangs over the novel. We know from the start that Gloria is a marked character. The story is told in retrospective fragments as the boy stands trial for her murder.

Gloria's biting manner, her mask of toughness, is not simply a given, as it is in many hard-boiled novels, but a response to a specific social condition, to a Depression America that offers no support to the have-nots. *They Shoot Horses, Don't They?* is probably the most socially pointed novel in the tough guy canon; in its splintered narrative construction, and its use of the claustrophobic dance-hall setting as a metaphor for the times, it is more self-consciously literary than most of the mystery stories to which it is related in tone, while McCoy's staccato dialogue rings with the echo of Hammett and Hemingway at their most caustic.

Hammett, Chandler, Cain, and McCoy wrote novels and stories that inspired some of the most highly acclaimed *films noirs*. But the writer whose sensibility is most deeply *noir*—Cornell Woolrich—does not have the literary prestige of the hard-boiled quartet. The pulp base of Woolrich's style is less disguised than in the writing of the others, but Woolrich is a better storyteller than Hammett or Chandler and a master in building and sustaining tension.

Like other writers in the mystery-thriller field, Woolrich works within formulaic patterns. A Woolrich story begins typically in an ordinary and undramatic environment: a cafeteria, an office, a tenement, a city street at noon. Woolrich stresses the ordinariness of his urban settings and of his characters, his blue-collar workers, secretaries, housewives, clerks. He begins in a tone of exaggerated casualness, paying attention to seemingly small matters—to scraps of conversation, details of dress and behavior, to time—that are to figure importantly in the ensuing mystery. A dry, reportorial manner, in Woolrich's stories, is invariably a prelude to nightmare, as the seemingly everyday setting and the bland characters come quickly under attack.

A man has an argument with his wife and stalks out of the house for a night on the town. In a bar, he strikes up a conversation with a woman in an exaggerated hat who agrees to go with him to dinner and to the theatre, and then says good-bye without ever telling him her name. The man returns home to find his wife has been murdered. His one alibi—the one person standing between him and the gas chamber—is the phantom lady with the hat.

A little boy who tells tall stories happens, by chance (it is a stiflingly hot New York summer night and for relief he is on a fire escape), to see his upstairs neighbors commit a murder. When he tells his parents, they threaten to pun-

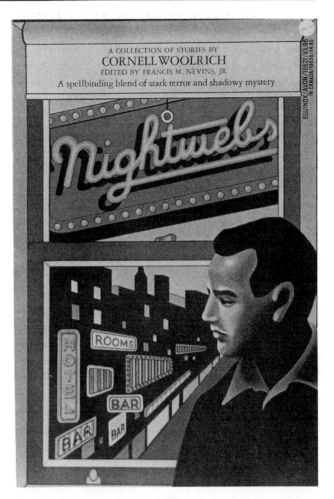

A COLLECTION OF STORIES BY
CORNELL WOOLRICH
EDITED BY FRANCIS M. NEVINS, JR
A spellbinding blend of stark terror and shadowy mystery

Nightwebs

The *noir*-inspired cover for a recently published collection of stories by Cornell Woolrich, the most *noir* of all mystery writers.

ish him for his lies. When he goes to the police, he is sent home. The neighbors find out about his "story," and when the boy is locked in his room by his irate father (his mother has been called to visit an ailing sister), the murderers close in on him.

A man confined to a wheelchair has little to do but peer across a courtyard into the windows of the facing buildings. What begins as a casual inspection of the comings and goings of his unsuspecting neighbors escalates to obsessive interest when the observer discovers a murder—a man across the way has done in his invalid wife, though how can this be proven? No one believes him, including his detective friend. He begins to deal directly with the murderer, who then tracks him down, an invalid alone in his apartment: the perfect victim.

A spoiled young man, despite his sister's pleas, is determined to run off with a floozy. When he calls at his fiancée's apartment, she is dead. Caught red-handed, the boy is sentenced to the chair. His sister, who is convinced of his innocence, sets out on a search for the murderer that takes her into a tough urban nightworld. When she discovers a link between the murdered girl and a nightclub, she applies for a job as a dancer. The gross entrepreneur goes wild over her, but when he finds out that she is a double-dealer, he orders his henchmen to finish her off.

These four archetypal Woolrich tales— ''Phantom Lady,'' ''The Boy Cried Wolf,'' ''Rear Window,'' and ''Angel Face'' are expert variations on a formula. Innocent characters are accused of or in some way involved in a murder, and saved at the last minute after a series of escalating catastrophes. The Woolrich world is a maze of wrong impressions as the author sets traps for his luckless protagonists and then watches as they fall into them. Filled with pitfalls and sudden violence, the landscape in Woolrich is the kind of place where a single wrong turn, a mere chance encounter, triggers a chain reaction in which one calamity follows another. Standing in the wings manipulating the movements of his players as though they were figures on a chessboard, Woolrich is a master contriver. His characters, more thinly conceived than those of his more illustrious hard-boiled predecessors, have no inner life, no history at all in fact apart from their immediate use to the author as pawns in his clever games.

Often Woolrich presents a story from the point of view of a criminal or an amateur avenging sleuth. The first person mode, with its necessarily limited perspective, increases the aura of claustrophobia and entrapment which hovers over all of Woolrich's work—Woolrich's characters seldom see the light, and are rarely prepared for what happens to them. As he operates above his near-sighted characters, watching them pinned and wriggling against their ghastly fates, Woolrich's humor is pitch black. An alcoholic and a recluse, Woolrich had a grim comic sense, a piercing irony, and a firm belief that the world was at best indifferent to its inhabitants, at worst an active conspirator against our well-being.

"Black," "night," and "death" appear with obsessive recurrence in Woolrich's titles: *The Bride Wore Black, The Black Curtain, Black Alibi, Rendezvous in Black, The Black Angel, Night Has a Thousand Eyes, Dead Man Blues, I Married a Dead Man.* Two recent collections of Woolrich stories are called *Nightwebs* and *Angels of Darkness.* Night, darkness, the menacing streets of the city at night, the city as a landscape of doom: these supply the inevitable *mise en scène* for Woolrich's taut stories of black deeds, sudden eruptions of foulness, grisly twists of fate. One of Woolrich's unfortunate protagonists suffers from amnesia; many of his characters are plagued by self-division, by conflicts between their rational daytime selves and their night-time alter egos, just as the typical Woolrich fable customarily begins in the ordered, daytime world before it plummets into darkness. The Woolrich canon is rife with visual and psychological dou-

Two Woolrich avenging angels — (left) a ravaged, maddened Jeanne Moreau, in François Truffaut's *The Bride Wore Black*, and (right) a triumphant, sane one portrayed by Susan Hayward, in *Deadline at Dawn*.

bleness, as day is contrasted with night and sanity teeters on the edge of darkness.

Woolrich's writing lacks Chandler's metaphoric frills and his characters are not as complex as Cain's, but he is a superb craftsman. The Woolrich style is colloquial and easy; it imitates the tone of his primarily working class characters. The opening of "Angel Face" conveys the author's rough-hewn, idiomatic quality:

I had on my best hat and my warpaint when I dug into her bell. You've heard make-up called that a thousand times, but this is one time it rated it; it was just that—warpaint.

I caught Ruby Rose reading at breakfast time—hers, not mine. Quarter to three in the afternoon. Breakfast was a pink soda-fountain mess, a tomato-and-lettuce, both untouched, and an empty glass of Bromo Seltzer, which had evidently had first claim on her. There were a pair of swell ski slides under her eyes; she was reading Gladys Glad's beauty column to try to figure out how to get rid of them before she went out that night and got a couple more. A Negro maid had opened the door, and given me a yellowed optic.

"Yes ma'am, who do you wish to see?"

"I see her already," I said, "so skip the Morse code." I went in up to Ruby Rose's ten-yard line. "Wheeler's the name," I said. "Does it mean anything to you?"

"Should it?" She was dark and Salome-ish. She was mean. She was bad medicine.

The opening of "Rear Window" has the dry, matter-of-fact quality with which Woolrich typically begins his stories of crime and terror: "I didn't know their last names. I'd never heard their voices. I didn't even know them by sight, strictly speaking, for their faces were too small to fill in with identifiable features at that distance. Yet I could have constructed a timetable of their comings and goings, their daily habits and activities. They were the rear-window dwellers around me." Woolrich's scene-setting is precise and richly evocative of mood and atmosphere, as in this description of a bar in *The Black Angel*:

The Oregon Bar . . . on Third above Forty-ninth, in the first half-hour after twelve that same night. It was deep and narrow, like an alcove piercing the building it was situated in. It was dark with a sort of colored darkness that was

the tint of it. Although there were lights, and they were dusky orange, copper-rose, and other similar feverish tones, it was the darkness you were conscious of more than them; its overall cast was dimness, a confetti-like twilight.

Woolrich's stories often take place in a sickly, yellowish half-light. Inhabiting cramped, foul-smelling rooms in rundown hotels and tenements; hanging out in bars, all-night cafeterias and movie houses, many of his characters never seem to see the light of day.

Woolrich's manipulations of his puppet-like characters, his ironic detachment, his evident enjoyment in subjecting his characters as well as his readers to situations of ulcer-inducing tension, his deliberately narrow emotional range, his clipped vernacular dialogue, his dark city settings, link his methods to those of *film noir.* Woolrich was enormously popular in the forties, and though he continues to have a loyal following, he has not received his full recognition as a skillful popular artist (the best in his field, in fact), a writer with a distinct moral vision, dark and unsettling, and streaked with flashes of mordant comedy.

Woolrich is located at the least literary end of the hard-boiled spectrum, where pulp formulae and a genuine if unexalted literary sensibility intersect. The tough guy heritage trickles down from Woolrich to the tabloid sensationalism of dime novels and stories and novelettes of the pure pulp variety. But the hard-boiled tradition can be traced "upward" as well, to serious, non-formulaic literature, to art. Hemingway's famed style and that of the *Black Mask* genre writers: both techniques share a concern for realistic description, and an interest in crackling dialogue that depends on echo and repetition. In addition to Hemingway, other serious writers—Graham Greene, Nelson Algren, John O'Hara, and Albert Camus among them—write in a style and deal with themes and settings that overlap with those of the tough guy tradition. Algren's novels and short stories, set characteristically in the Chicago underworld; Greene's spy novels; O'Hara's *Appointment in Samarra*; and Camus' *The Stranger* are all manifestly hard-boiled and *noir*-like.

Although it is not usually regarded as such, Camus' *The Stranger* is one of the greatest of all hard-boiled novels. In depth and impact, it eclipses its literary forebears, but it owes a debt to them, one that Camus himself has acknowledged. Like many French writers and critics, Camus admired the American tough guys for their style and control, and in *The Rebel*, he provides a trenchant analysis of their hard-boiled "realism": The American tough novel of the thirties and forties, he notes,

claims to find its unity in reducing man either to elementals or to his external reactions and to his behavior. It does not choose feelings or passions to give a detailed description of, such as we find in classic French novels. It rejects analysis and the search for a fundamental psychological motive that could explain and recapitulate the behavior of a character . . . Its technique consists in describing men by their outside appearances, in their most casual actions, of reproducing, without comment, everything they say down to their repetitions, and finally by acting as if men were entirely defined by their daily automatisms. On this mechanical level, men, in fact, seem exactly alike, which explains this peculiar universe in which all the characters appear interchangeable, even down to their physical peculiarities. This technique is called realistic only owing to a misapprehension . . . it is perfectly obvious that this fictitious world is not attempting a reproduction, pure and simple, of reality, but the most arbitrary form of stylization.

In *The Stranger*, Camus writes in a style based on the work of the American genre specialists he admires. The persona that he creates for Meursault, his doomed narrator, deliberately echoes the tough guy stance of the heroes of American detective fiction. Like them, Meursault is impassive and deeply private. "Mother died today. Or, maybe, yesterday; I can't be sure," the novel

---

Opposite: Woolrich voyeurs tracked by the killers whose crimes they have overseen: James Stewart and Raymond Burr, in *Rear Window*; Paul Stewart stalks Bobby Driscoll, in *The Window.*

Graham Greene's mysteries are filled with *noir* motifs in theme, characterization, setting, and mood, as suggested in this climactic scene from Greene's *The Third Man*.

opens, unforgettably, establishing at once Meursault's mechanical response to people and events. Meursault lives in a rented room, in physical surroundings that recall those of the American detectives. He has no close personal ties. He has a routine job. He drifts into a casual friendship with a neighbor, and into an affair. Like the American sleuths, he is more observer than participant. Every Sunday, he ritualistically watches the parade of pedestrians that passes in the street below his room. He seems to have no feelings. He reacts only to external stimuli, such as the oppressive heat, the touch of his girlfriend's hands on his body, the soothing coolness of the ocean.

Willfully, he lives on the surface. Meursault is the prototype of the uncommitted existentialist, experiencing life as it happens, yet separated from it as well by his sense of its absurdity.

The central act, as in crime novels and *film noir*, is a murder. Meursault kills an Arab because it was hot, because the Arab had earlier terrorized him and his friend Raymond when they were walking along the beach, and because he felt like it. Like many *noir* heroes, Meursault is caught in a web of circumstance and coincidence, yet unlike the typical *noir* protagonist, who struggles against the tightening net, Meursault is casual and ironic in the face of catastrophe. For Meursault, casually killing another person is no more important, and no less important, than anything else in his life. It is just something that happened. Even though Meursault is the narrator, he remains an enigmatic figure, a stranger, to himself, to others, to the universe. Camus' landmark novel is the ultimate *film noir* story, carrying the recurrent *noir* motifs of a malevolent, jesting fate and of alienated, puzzled, set-upon characters to their blackest depth.

Noir also drew at least marginally on another literary tradition, that of naturalism as it was practiced early in the century by writers like Dreiser and Norris. Adapting to American settings and character types the philosophical premises developed in the late nineteenth century by Zola in France, the naturalist writers took a hard view of the consequences of the capitalist system. Their setting is the American city (Chicago in *Sister Carrie*, San Francisco in *McTeague*), their aim to chronicle in unsparing and minutely realistic detail the effect of the city's economic structure on its victims. Although the naturalists professed absolute detachment, their writing became feverish as it recorded their characters' inevitable corruption and decline. *Greed*, Erich von Stroheim's masterful adaptation of *McTeague*, contains both the sober, uninflected realism and the occasional Expressionistic heightening that mark many of the naturalist novels.

Quite unlike that of the hard-boiled writers, the naturalists' vision tended to be epic and grandiose. Their stories typically take place over a long period of time, to underline the portrait of economic and psychological collapse which is their recurrent subject. The naturalists regarded their characters as representative American types whose histories pointed moral lessons with national overtones; thus, Dreiser's saga of an ambitious young man who kills a poor girl so that he can enter the world of the very rich is called *An American Tragedy*. In striking contrast to the trim stories and novelettes of the tough guy school, the naturalist novels are big, fat books and are customarily written in a laborious and flat-footed manner.

But the naturalists and the hard-boiled crime writers overlap in some respects. Both introduced to American writing what was at the time a new kind of realism; both presented the big city as a ferocious, suffocating place; and both worked for an objective mode in which to present their versions of harsh urban realities, though both ended up embellishing their observations with strokes of literary flourish.

Fate in the naturalist novel is as dark and as relentless as in the grimmest crime novel or *film noir*. In the naturalists' view, as in that of *noir*, the world is a harsh place in which the lone person hasn't a chance. The naturalists thought

everyone was a victim of heredity and environment, and unable, no matter how hard the struggle, to withstand the combined impact of these two forces; the inevitable downfall of their characters is thus a collusion between personal failings—greed, lust, pride, all the deadly sins writ large—and those of capitalist society. The trapped protagonists in the naturalist novel surface in *noir* on a smaller, less bombastic scale.

Combining the objectivity and harshness of naturalism with the tough, stylized realism of the hard-boiled crime school, *film noir* draws on a rich literary tradition. The echo of the themes and style of serious writing that permeates *noir* adds immensely to its palette, making it one of the most accomplished and most intelligent of the Hollywood genres.

The hard-boiled anti-hero as existential saint: Marcello Mastroianni as Meursault, in Luchino Visconti's film of *The Stranger*.

3

The Cinematic Background:

From Expressionism to Neo-Realism

The cinematic origins of *film noir* can be traced to the German Expressionist films of the late 1910s and twenties, to the American crime film of the thirties, and to one contemporary and less central source as, following the war, *noir* absorbed some of the concerns of Italian Neo-Realism. Expressionism and Neo-Realism are, of course, strikingly dissimilar, the German style edging toward nightmare, the Italian straining for documentary veracity. Sometimes the two modes collide within the same film; more often the divergent styles result in two distinct sub-categories within the *noir* keyboard.

As an artistic vision, whether in painting or film, Expressionism reveals a distinctly Germanic rather than American temperament. It may indeed be that its Expressionist aura accounted for the relative unpopularity of *noir* in America: in visual style and moral sensibility, the films may simply have been too downbeat for general American taste. Expressionist artists pledged themselves to creating works that reveal personal, inner truths rather than to recording a merely objective and external reality. Strongly influenced by the work of such Post-Impressionists as Van Gogh, Cézanne, and Gauguin, Ex-

The *trompe l'oeil* city, in Lang's Expressionist drama, *Metropolis*—a visual foreshadowing of the menacing, indifferent *noir* city.

pressionism flourished in Germany from approximately 1910 to the mid-twenties. Such artists as Kirchner, Kokoschka, Jawlensky, Pechstein, Kandinsky, Nolde, Schmidt-Rotluff, and Beckmann cultivated an angular, hallucinatory, violently emotional style, one that sought images of chaos and despair, and that seemed to celebrate the artists' own instability. The Expressionist artist embraced his madness, converting inner demons into images of tumult and breakdown which radiated a terminal bleakness. Painting as he felt, faithful only to his own inner vision, he created phantasmagoric transformations of reality. Night, death, psychic disorder, social upheaval are the recurrent themes of the Expressionists' apocalyptic sensibility. The typical Expressionist work conveys a powerful sense of chaos, both personal and cosmic. In *The Scream*, Munch's influential proto-Expressionist lithograph (1893), the inner turmoil of the screamer is answered by the uneasily undulating lines with which the scene is rendered, as if the world both reflects and participates in the central figure's evident breakdown. To depict their gloom-ridden images, Expressionists used funereal colors—muddy, heavy purples, blacks and browns—painting in obvious defiance of nature and also of the Impressionists, who had been concerned with the effects of light on natural scenes, and who celebrated the natural world and man's comfortable place within it. The Expressionist "cry" signaled a release of inner turbulence, though in portraying powerful feelings of doom and disorder, the artists certainly did not banish them. Expressionist transformation heightens chaos, it does not dispel it.

The gloomy, fatalistic vision, the intoxication with breakdown, of the Expressionist artists, was translated into German films during their so-called Golden Age, which began in the late teens and extended to the end of the silent period. Countering the mimetic tradition that dominated American silents, the German Expressionist dramas were set in claustrophobic studio-created environments where physical reality was distorted. Stories about the loss or the impossibility of individual freedom dominated the "haunted screen" (as Lotte Eisner calls it in her brilliant study of the Expressionist film).

Images of death, of a relentless fate, and of the divided soul appeared with insistent repetition. To convey their dark themes, the films developed a distinct visual vocabulary consisting primarily of chiaroscuro and distortions of time and space. Mood (*stimmung*) was all-important, as the films' shadow-filled, artificial settings and theatrical high-contrast lighting, which dramatically divided the image into criss-crossing shafts of light and dark, gave intense visual expression to the negative stories. Space in the high German Expressionist film is fractured into an assortment of unstable, zigzagging, splintery lines, of spinning circles and twisted angles. The conflicting shapes and patterns of movement convey restlessness, chaos, as if the physical world has assumed the dementia of the bewitched characters.

The most famous film in the full Expressionist style is *The Cabinet of Dr. Caligari* (1919), which is set in a hallucinatory landscape, a crazy quilt of anti-naturalistic shapes and angles. Vertical lines form visual prisons, slanting in ways that entrap the characters; horizontal lines swerve in haphazard directions in a mad mockery of the laws of gravity. This lopsided world is revealed at the end to be an imaginary one—the ravings of a madman—but the film-makers slipped (intentionally perhaps) because the sets remain Expressionist even after the narrator has been discredited as a lunatic. The film thus offers no normal world to oppose to that of the insane asylum in which the inmate relates his story to a friend, as both the inner story and its frame share the same disfigured and nightmarish setting.

The inner story, about how Dr. Caligari trains a somnambulist to commit a series of murders, is one of personality takeover. In his provocative reading of German films, *From Caligari to Hitler*, Siegfried Kracauer suggests that the Caligari figure is symptomatic of a thrust in German society toward the need for a

---

Dr. Caligari feeds Cesare, his somnambulist; Cesare in a trance, in *The Cabinet of Dr. Caligari*, the grimly prophetic Expressionist thriller, a madman's nightmare enacted in distorted, symbolic settings.

The child-murderer (Peter Lorre) trapped in a warehouse, in Lang's *M*. As indicated in this shot, Lang's decor has overtones of Expressionist distortion and paranoia.

tyrant. Kracauer makes a remarkably convincing case for Caligari and his somnambulist as premonitions of Hitler's relation to the German people: in Kracauer's interpretation, Caligari is a madman-tyrant whose ability to control the minds and actions of others leads to massive moral as well as social perversion. For Kracauer, the authority-crazed Caligari, and the weak-willed, puppet-like somnambulist, committing crimes in his sleep, prefigure aspects of the Nazi mentality that was to infect Germany.

Later Expressionist films, for the most part, do not distort the real world to the degree that *The Cabinet of Dr. Caligari* does. Many of the dramas are set in an approximation of reality that is then invaded by Expressionist elements. In such representative films as Murnau's *The Last Laugh* (1924) and Fritz Lang's *M* (1931), Expressionist subjectivity is reserved for climactic passages where the protagonists recoil in humiliation and defeat. In both films, the central characters are marginal, collapsing figures. The "hero" of *The Last Laugh* is a hotel porter, proud of his rank, who is demoted, because of his advanced age, from doorman to lowly lavatory attendant. As he descends to his new position, the film takes on darker tones; as the character sinks in self-esteem, the city seems to tower above him, its thrusting spires mocking his fall. The court where he lives, and where he had enjoyed a privileged place, becomes a sea of cruel laughing faces, cackling like a set of macabre masks in an Ensor carnival. Shapes, objects, perspective, begin to shift and dissolve in a taunting dance. In the man's visions, the revolving door of the hotel that had been the center of his life now appears as a gigantic totem, whirling in mockery of his downfall.

The protagonist of *M* is a murderer of children in flight from groups of criminals and police who are determined to capture him. As his pursuers track him down, the city streets become increasingly shadowed and solitary. As in Murnau's film, the Expressionist tendencies of Lang's *mise en scène* are emblematic of an internal reality; the dark streets, the abandoned storage area where the haunted man takes refuge, the frames within the frame that seem to box the character into corners, all reflect the child murderer's mounting agitation.

These early Expressionist films, with their tormented protagonists in flight from an alien society, and their stylized urban settings, exerted a deep influence on the subject matter as well as the visual temper of the American *film noir*. Expressionist motifs filtered into *film noir*, in diluted but nonetheless significant ways, because the German style offered an appropriate iconography for the dark vision of the forties thriller and also because a number of German directors fled to Hollywood from a nightmare society, bringing with them the special sensibility that permeated their early work. Adjusted to the taste of American producers and their audiences, Expressionist elements in *noir* are more muted than those in the German films. The world of *noir* is not distorted to the degree that it is in *The Cabinet of Dr. Caligari*. A recognizable physical reality dominates the *noir* thriller, as it does throughout the American cinema, but the films contain an undercurrent of Expressionist motifs that functions as a kind of visual italics, supplying mood and texture and removing the stories from a merely bland, everyday context.

In moments of tension, *noir* dramas crawl with shadows. The image darkens to indicate sudden fear, to suggest that the characters are about to be attacked or to crack up. A consistent vestige of Expressionism throughout *noir* is the nightmare sequence, where for a few moments, under the protection of a dream interlude, the film becomes overtly subjective, entering into the hero's consciousness to portray its disordered fragments. One of the earliest and best of these Expressionist nightmares occurs in *Murder, My Sweet* (1944), where a short sequence dramatizes Marlowe's drug-induced delirium.

"Starring *You* and Robert Montgomery": Hollywood's half-hearted Expressionism. The ad for *Lady in the Lake* calls attention to the film's visual gimmick of using the camera as Philip Marlowe's eye, a diminished version of Expressionist subjectivity.

The sequence is composed of objects, characters, and places that have appeared as part of the realistic "furniture" of the story, and which in the hero's nightmare spin crazily and haphazardly in space. The fragmented, free-floating images of the dream symbolize Marlowe's drug-induced mania, and their disorder, their violation of reality, can therefore be explained as his temporary hallucination. An American thriller can accommodate Expressionist distortion at this pitch in short spurts only.

The Expressionist emphasis on subjective experience is likewise of only limited use in an American film. The *noir* thrillers often carry a first-person narration, a device retained from the crime novels of the tough guy school. But the point of view of the *images* is seldom first-person, and certainly not in the same way as in the deeply Expressionist paintings and films, where the "I" that views the scene is manifestly neurotic, unstable, approaching if not actively embracing a kind of demented ecstasy. The hard-boiled narrator strives to be objective, to divest himself of exactly the kind of private and visionary slant sought by the Expressionists. In films, at any rate, a first-person point of view is bound to look like a gimmick, a self-conscious departure from the camera's observing, recording function, its predisposition to witness the scene rather than to create it. Films, and certainly major studio American films, gravitate toward a neutral rendering of a recognizable physical reality rather than toward the delirious inner landscapes, the overwrought transmutations, of full-fledged Expressionism. Subjective experience in *noir* is for the most part limited to the interpolated dream sequence or to the visual trick of using the camera as the eye of a central character, as in Robert Montgomery's awkward *Lady in the Lake*, the opening section of *Dark Passage*, and in isolated climactic moments in many thrillers, where the image blurs or dissolves into wavy patterns to suggest a character's loss of consciousness or his derangement or sudden terror. In *Lady in the Lake*, the camera "stands in" for Philip Marlowe, while the other characters look directly into the lens, on the pretext that they are talking to him. The device is strained, and not at all a rendering of the kind of subjective experience the Expressionists had in mind.

In *The Night of the Hunter*, Charles Laughton used Expressionist design in a more forthright way than was usual for most American films. In selected passages, Laughton employs non-realistic space and a heightened chiaroscuro that are overtly Germanic. This story of a preacher crazed by greed who terrorizes a widow and her children is shot through with daring stylistic changes. At key moments, as the preacher pursues the children through rural landscapes, the film becomes as stylized as a German Expressionist drama of fate. Retreating from the real world in which most of the action is set, these scenes seem to be taking place on a vast sound stage, where real time and space have been suspended. Laughton favors dramatic silhouettes, with the preacher outlined in black against a blank horizon. The disorienting close-ups in these passages, the prominence of objects, the extreme chiaroscuro, the angularity, the clean, sharp compositions, enclose the action in a timeless and dream like ambience. A scene in which the children float on a raft is surely the most lyrical use of Expressionism in the American cinema. The modulations from realism to theatricality lend the film a strange and ethereal quality, one that seemed at the time (1955)—and would seem so now—to cut across the grain of American film-making. Laughton's great work may well be the most visually experimental, and certainly the most intensely Expressionist, of all American *films noirs*; but *The Night of the Hunter* was so decisive a financial failure that Laughton never got another chance to direct. Though this particular film contains a greater amount of Germanic stylization than most American thrillers, the level of visual inflection that prevailed in *noir* was in fact unusually high: the films have a special mood and aura, a tenebrous, minatory atmosphere, that perhaps lend them a touch of "something foreign" and that certainly sets them apart from standard major studio realism.

As influential as German Expressionism in forging the *noir* style was the homegrown gangster story that had flourished, in various permutations, throughout the previous decade. Like the later *noir* thriller, the gangster saga took place in an urban setting, involved criminal activity, and ended in the defeat of the anti-social protagonist. But the gangster story, reflecting different social conditions, had a different tone than the forties' *film noir*. During the Depression, the gangster emerged as both a living presence—his activities chronicled in the news—and as a folk hero. As a fictional character, the gangster was strikingly different from the typical *film noir* anti-hero. The gangster may ultimately have been defeated by the system (the censors saw to it that his story was, in the final

Full-blown Hollywood Expressionism: Robert Mitchum, as the preacher in Charles Laughton's *Night of the Hunter*, which is closer in spirit and visual design to the German Expressionist films than any other *noir* thriller.

reel at least, a reminder that crime does not pay, no matter how attractive its temporary rewards); but the gangster, especially as embodied by such charismatic actors as James Cagney and Edward G. Robinson, was a figure of vitality and enterprise, a man who carved for himself a life of glamor and power that offered vicarious satisfaction to thwarted Depression audiences. The *noir* protagonist is etched in a different mold—resolutely small-scale, unheroic, defeatist. He is, typically, a knotted, introspective character, cowering in the corner in flight from his crime, or else hopelessly entangled in the aftermath of his ill-considered actions. The fates may also be against the gangster, but he reacts heroically rather than with the fear and trembling that is characteristic of the *noir* criminal.

The gangster's essential energy was engrained in the staccato rhythm in which his story was told. The thirties gangster film moved at a clipped pace, its colloquial dialogue snapped out in a rat-tat-tat beat. Little Caesar and Scarface had brute force as they hacked their way up the ranks of the underworld. They were dumb but nervy and stubborn, and their drive was rewarded with all the trappings of bourgeois success. In their hunger for money and power, they are less alienated from the American mainstream than the introverted characters of *noir*, who usually want to escape from themselves and from a past which continues to haunt them. The gangster, on the other hand, is a public figure who craves fame and recognition.

The prevailing tone of the gangster story, then, is more upbeat than that of *noir*. In its unique way, the typical gangster saga is something of a celebration of self-assertiveness, whereas *noir* focuses on stories of doom and withdrawal. Cagney and Robinson challenge the world; the *noir* hero wants mostly to be left alone. The neon sign that blinks on and off outside the window of Scarface's apartment, proclaiming that "The World Is Yours," is an ironic counterpoint to the action, especially at the end as the bullet-ridden thug lies sprawled in the gutter. But the sign is also something that Scarface truly believed in, the creed that sustained him. As a motto for a character in *noir*,

"The World Is Yours" would only be seen as a mockery; no character in *noir* who knows the score would believe it for a minute.

The three archetypal gangsters—Little Caesar, Tom Powers (*The Public Enemy*), and Scarface—were all in some way sexually wounded or incomplete. Little Caesar (Edward G. Robinson) had no time for women and seemed capable of an emotional commitment only to his hometown friend and partner, Joe. Tom Powers (James Cagney), in his most characteristic gesture, smashes a grapefruit in Mae Clarke's face. Tom can relate to women only as mother figures or as whores. Scarface (Paul Muni) has an incestuous attachment to his sister. In each case, acting in a kind of blind obedience to powerful inner forces, the characters never confront their problems. The films all suggest, though, that there is something fearfully—fatally—wrong with the gang lords, and that in some way their climb to power is generated by displaced sexual energy.

But the classic gangster stories are not psychological case studies in the way that many *noir* films attempt to be. With their craggy looks and their harsh voices, Cagney and Robinson certainly suggested that Little Caesar and Tom Powers were not average or normal; both actors perform with an intensity that at least hints at the characters' psychopathic maladjustments. But the films are concerned primarily with the gangsters' public functions, their notoriety as public figures, rather than with their twisted psychology. In most of the films, the gangsters are figures *in* society, rather than isolated outside it.

The gangster story is a social drama, set in a specific place and time: the American big city, typically either New York or Chicago, during the Prohibition-Depression era. Representing an aggressive native response to adversity, making capitalistic profit out of national misfortune, the gangster grew out of the social conditions of his

Shadows, bannisters, prison-like bars, chiaroscuro: Expressionist motifs in thirties crime dramas. Edward G. Robinson, in *Little Caesar*; George Raft, in the 1935 version of Dashiell Hammett's *The Glass Key*.

time. When Prohibition was repealed, the gangster lost his chief means of livelihood, and both as a movie icon and a folkloric hero, he began to fade.

The city in the thirties gangster story is not quite the same city that appears in *film noir*. With its documentary shots of city streets, and its sense of the pulse and flow of city life, the prologue to *The Public Enemy* is unusual, for most gangster films are confined to interiors—studio sets built to imitate reality. In *Little Caesar* and *Scarface*, the city is glimpsed mostly through windows. The gangster drama is enacted against immutable settings: the tenement kitchen and bedroom; the backroom meeting place with its pool table and naked overhanging light, and the inevitable blinking neon sign outside that gives evidence of an ongoing life beyond the circumference of the story; the ritzy apartment, done up in white, that indicates the gangster has arrived; the classy art deco night club; the neighborhood saloon, with its long lonely stretch of

bar. There are usually one or two street scenes, a row of glum brownstones, a downtown avenue seen through the plate glass windows of a restaurant (sure to be shattered in a sudden shootout). These studio settings are conventionalized, and for the most part, interchangeable. The city in the gangster story doesn't have the heightened presence that it does in many of the *noir* thrillers; it tends to be a neutral background, often lively, but tending toward an inconspicuous realism rather than an Expressionistic theatricality. Although the lighting is occasionally chiaroscuro,

The thirties gangsters were in some way sexually and emotionally damaged; (*below*) Little Caesar has an unhealthy, controlling attitude toward his hometown friend Joe (Douglas Fairbanks, Jr.); (*opposite, top*) Scarface (Paul Muni) has an incestuous attachment to his sister (Ann Dvorak); (*opposite, bottom*) Tom Powers (James Cagney), the Public Enemy, smashes a grapefruit into the face of his mistress (Mae Clarke), in a now-legendary gesture that indicates the character's scorn for women.

as in the finale to *Scarface* where the pursued hero has locked himself and his sister behind steel shutters, the visual texture of the gangster movie is flatter and less self-conscious than in *noir*. For the most part, the three leading directors of the classic gangster dramas—Mervyn LeRoy, Howard Hawks, and William Wellman—were working in a style of straightforward American realism, which was as direct and as economical as the narrative structure of their films.

As a storytelling mold, the gangster saga proved much less versatile than *film noir*. As it traced the hero's rise and inevitable fall, each gangster story was essentially the same story. The narrative format became so quickly a matter of formula that the genre lasted only a few years. By the mid-thirties, Cagney and Robinson switched to the other side of the law, and by the late thirties, the gangster and his world were subjected to parody in such films as *Brother Orchid* and *A Slight Case of Murder*. The remarkably brief life of the gangster picture may have been partly a matter of social realities, since the repeal of Prohibition removed the gangster's dependence on bootleg liquor and, as a result, the kind of underworld society depicted in *Little Caesar* was a matter of historical record by the end of the decade. In 1939, Raoul Walsh's *Roaring Twenties* provided a retrospective and nostalgic look at the gangster milieu; the film's elegiac tone, epitomized by Cagney's bravura death on the snow-covered steps of a church, was in sharp contrast to the unsentimental "high" gangster dramas of the early thirties.

Gangsters figure marginally in *film noir*, appearing as the central characters in only a few films, such as *White Heat* and *Key Largo*, which are themselves only marginally *noir*. In *White Heat* the gangster is played by Cagney; in *Key Largo* by Robinson. The casting certainly suggests a retrospective quality, yet the two stars are not simply offering a reprise, in the late forties, of the kind of performance that made them famous almost two decades earlier. In these two powerful films, Cagney and Robinson are playing diseased characters who have none of the enormous personal vitality of Little Caesar or Tom Powers. Like many of the protagonists of films more centrally connected to the *noir* tradition, their characters project mental and physical unhealthiness. Cagney's mobster has epileptic fits; Robinson's is the victim of uncontrollable shakes, and in each case physical disability indicates emotional paralysis: Cagney is tied to his mother, in what is probably the most perverse Oedipal relationship in the American cinema, while Robinson is a master sadist who takes special pleasure in humiliating his alcoholic mistress. Significantly, the underworld background in both films differs from that of the thirties crime dramas. *Key Largo* is set in Florida, on a remote island; the nervous, jagged movements of the gang in *White Heat* indicate that they are no longer a settled part of the American big city but are peripheral figures always on the run, hiding out in highway motels and mountain cabins. The settings are different because the gangsters are anachronisms, no longer supported by the rigid, hierarchical community that was shaped by the Depression-Prohibition era.

Played to the hilt by Cagney and Robinson as madmen floundering for survival, the gangster protagonists of these late films clearly lack the heroic thrust of their thirties counterparts. Cagney's intense performance as the bedeviled, mother-wrapped gang boss in *White Heat* may well be his greatest; the role offers him richer opportunities than the formularized gangsters of the thirties. The scene in which Cagney cracks up, when in prison he hears of his mother's death, is one of the bravura moments in American movies—no one who has seen it can ever forget it. At the end of *White Heat*, in a spectacular apotheosis, Cagney is blown up on the top of a gas tank.

Key Largo also has overtones that the original gangster stories downplayed. In Maxwell Anderson's heavy-handed script, the gangsters are treated symbolically. Though they may also have been interpreted as American icons, as upside-down incarnations of the American Dream, the thirties gangsters were primarily individuals, whereas Anderson's thugs are symbols of evil who must be destroyed in order to preserve democracy. After Humphrey Bogart, playing the film's reluctant hero-savior, mows them all down, his girlfriend (Lauren Bacall)

The nightclub hold-up, in *Little Caesar*. Like saloons in westerns, and like empty streets in *film noir*, nightclubs were among the visual fixtures of the gangster drama.

opens the windows of the dim hotel in which most of the action has been set, to let in a flood of holy, cleansing light.

In both these *noir* stories of gangsters, the relationship between the hoodlums and the straight characters is different from what it was in the thirties. The one-to-one connection between the kingpin mobster and the cop who's intent on capturing him no longer applies. In *White Heat*, computers, recording devices, and an array of technical gadgetry assist the police in tracking down the gang—police detection is now something of a corporate undertaking. In *Little Caesar*, the policeman is a fierce antagonist, obsessed with nabbing Rico. In *White Heat*, the cop is in disguise, masquerading as

Cagney's friend as he infiltrates the gang. His devious and dishonorable methods (Edmund O'Brien in a thankless role) contribute to the cynicism that pervades the film; the relationships in the old gangster dramas, both within the gang and between the hoods and the law, had a directness that is nowhere in evidence here. Psychotic and introverted, the gangster then survives into the *noir* period as a marginal relic, supplanted by the private eye and the bourgeois who slips into crime—characters distinctly less grand than the gangster in his prime.

As Expressionist motifs supplied *noir's* dark undercurrents, the Neo-Realist influence that appeared after the war introduced a documentary

Anna Magnani, in *Open City*, one of the pioneer
Neo-Realist dramas. The loose, seemingly spontaneous
quality of this shot, along with the grainy photography, the
natural lighting and the use of location settings,
epitomizes the documentary look of the Neo-Realist films.
Below: The visual textures of the Italian movies filtered
into *noir* in semi-documentary thrillers such as *Call
Northside 777* which, as the shot here (with James
Stewart) indicates, avoided the studied, theatrical style of
the Expressionist-inspired *films noirs*.

flavor into American thrillers. Quite unlike Expressionist artists, Neo-Realist directors intended not to distort or to refract reality but
simply (though this is never a simple matter) to
present it. The Italian directors associated with
the Neo-Realist movement—Rossellini, De
Sica, Visconti—turned to contemporary events
for their material, using the camera as a neutral
recording device. Their goal was to capture a
sense of the flow of reality, and such landmark
films as *Open City, Paisan, Shoeshine, La terra
trema, Bicycle Thief,* and *Umberto D* were notable
for their absence of stylistic flourish. The grainy
quality of their images, the natural lighting and

location photography, the frames packed with the background movement of the city, the uninflected camerawork and editing, the performers who seemed like (and often were) real people rather than actors, the scrupulous avoidance of aesthetic effects—these elements gave the stories of contemporary social realities a special force and freshness. In American films, the Neo-Realist influence was registered in an increase in location shooting, in documentary-like narration, and in a straightforward, utilitarian technique noticeably different from the Expressionistic *noir* thriller. The first crime films in the new semi-documentary style, *The House on 92nd Street* (1945) and *Call Northside 777* (1948), were produced by Louis de Rochemont, who transferred to fiction films the pace and texture that had marked his popular *March of Time* newsreels. In de Rochemont's films, sunlit, real city streets replaced the murky, artificial nightworld of the archetypal Fritz Lang *films noirs*. And instead of probing neurotic characters, the realistic *policiers* emphasized the process of detection. In *The House on 92nd Street*, a Nazi conspiracy is uncovered; in *Call Northside 777*, a journalist's tireless investigation saves the life of a man condemned to die for a crime he did not commit. Their style external and objective, the films move at an unbroken rhythm, containing few of the tonal or psychological shifts of the original *noir* dramas.

Moving crime into the real world and away from the tormented victims who dominated its early phase, the Neo-Realist influence modified the direction of *noir*. The central characters of the semi-documentary thrillers are staunch law enforcement officers, defenders and protectors of the status quo, who are less interesting than the damned figures in classic *noir* pieces like *Double Indemnity* and *The Woman in the Window*. Films on the order of *Call Northside 777* reduce the twisted characters, who are starred in Expressionist *noir* thrillers, to colorful but decidedly supporting roles.

Neo-Realism was really no help to *noir*. In its most provocative and absorbing form *noir* inhabits a twilight zone shakily suspended between reality and nightmare; it thrives on and indeed requires spatial as well as psychological dislocations, whereas the tendency of Neo-Realism is toward simplicity, directness, reportorial accuracy. *Noir's* richest offerings are oblique, deliriously slanted—anything, in short, but clear and direct. In opening the labyrinthine underground of urban crime and of the criminal mentality to the fully waking, daily world, in moving crime into real city streets at high noon, the semi-documentary thriller lacked the impact and originality, the special charged atmosphere, of *noir's* shadowy closed world. But fortunately, the Neo-Realist influence did not at any point entirely overtake the genre's Expressionist tendencies; and in many films in the late forties and early fifties (*Panic in the Streets, Side Street, The Naked City, D.O.A., The Window, Night and the City*), Expressionist motifs invaded location shooting, transforming the real city into moody echoes of the claustrophobic studio-created urban landscapes.

Italian Neo-Realism and the American hard-boiled school, however, do share a stance of presenting things as they are; both modes strive for a cool, unshockable tone. Similar elements between the two styles are revealed in *Ossessione*, Visconti's adaptation in 1943 of Cain's *The Postman Always Rings Twice*. Visconti presents Cain's sordid story of illicit sex and murder in a stark manner; the film's objective Neo-Realist technique complements Cain's stripped-down, hard-boiled prose. Visconti's camera watches with unblinking detachment as the characters meet their ironic fates. The film's relentless pacing, its grim location settings to which the passionate peasant characters seem inextricably bound, its rigorously unadorned style, match Cain's tough guy posture. As it filtered into the American crime film, though, Neo-Realist objectivity and toughness are less stylized than the hard-boiled manner of the Spade-Marlowe variety, and contained a social consciousness that the boys in the back room never aimed for. Visconti's film indicates that a Neo-Realist approach *can* complement a story of *noir* criminality; but by and large Neo-Realist tendencies did not provide a fertile background against which to "play" *noir* tensions.

Parallel shots from two versions of *The Postman Always Rings Twice*. Visconti's Neo-Realist *Ossessione* (with Massimo Girotti and Clara Calamai) has a true hard-boiled flavor, whereas the Lana Turner-John Garfield Hollywood adaptation is too polite.

Steamy Cain sexuality: Jack Nicholson and Jessica Lange, in Bob Rafelson's simmering 1981 version of *The Postman Always Rings Twice*.

4
The Crazy Mirror:

Noir Stylistics

Noir has been called a "sensibility," a sub-category of the crime film, a species of psychological thriller, a mystery with a private eye as its hero; but it has not often been called a genre. Its diverse story possibilities and its assimilation of several literary, artistic, and cinematic traditions have prompted critics to see it as an amorphous form, too loose and wide-ranging to be discussed in terms of genre. "*Film noir* is not a genre," writes Paul Schrader in "Notes on *Film Noir*." "It is not defined, as are the western and gangster genres, by conventions of setting and conflict, but rather by the more subtle qualities of tone and mood." "*Film noir* is not a genre, as the western or gangster film is," agrees Raymond Durgnat in "The Family Tree of *Film Noir*," "and takes us into the realms of classification by motif and tone." Durgnat parcels *noir* out among eleven thematic subheadings: 1) crime as social criticism; 2) gangsters; 3) on the run; 4) private eyes and adventurers; 5) middle class murder; 6) portraits and doubles; 7) sexual pathology; 8) psychopaths; 9) hostages to fortune; 10) blacks and reds; 11) guignol, horror, fantasy. For all its idiosyncrasy, Durgnat's tree metaphor is apt, as *noir* indeed has many branches—but its array of character types and

Lost in the maze: Rita Hayworth and Everett Sloane, in *The Lady from Shanghai*.

themes does not surely disqualify it from being a full-fledged genre.

A genre, after all, is determined by conventions of narrative structure, characterization, theme, and visual design, of just the sort that *noir* offers in abundance. *Noir* deals with criminal activity, from a variety of perspectives, in a general mood of dislocation and bleakness which earned the style its name. Unified by a dominant tone and sensibility, the *noir* canon constitutes a distinct style of film-making; but it also conforms to genre requirements since it operates within a set of narrative and visual conventions. Reviewers in the forties responded to the thrillers as something new in American movie-making, and spotted recurrent storytelling elements and visual motifs. *Noir* tells its stories in a particular way, and in a particular visual style. The repeated use of narrative and visual structures which soon became conventional, depending on a shared acknowledgment between the film-makers and the audience, certainly qualifies *noir* as a genre, one that is in fact as heavily coded as the western.

The typical *noir* story, to begin with, differs markedly from the Depression-era crime dramas. The gangster saga was simply told, in a headlong, straightforward manner, with the gangster himself remaining at the center of the frame. *Film noir* introduces a narrative method that, by contrast, is sinuous, oblique, often deliberately confusing. The gangster films never intended to puzzle their audiences; narrative or even moral ambiguity was not part of their repertoire, since the film-makers claimed they were fashioning simple, powerful statements to promote the idea that Crime Does Not Pay. The gangster film was really comforting to audiences of the time, in a way that *noir* certainly was not. On the one hand, audiences in the thirties could revel vicariously in the gangsters' exploits, enjoying the spectacle of the gangster challenging and for a time beating the system; and, on the other hand, the audience could be assured, with the gangster's inevitable demise in the final reel, that his illegal and violent methods really did not—and could not—work.

Noir offers no such comfort. It is impossible to derive from its dark stories either a sense of momentary uplift or the moralistic conclusions

provided by the gangster picture. The ideal metaphor for the world view that prevails in *noir* is the maze-like, many-mirrored fun house which Welles uses at the end of *The Lady from Shanghai*: the *noir* world is as filled with deception as Welles' bizarre set, and the multiple mirrored reflections of the film's duplicitous husband and wife are equally representative of the uncertain, shifting identities, the essential mysteriousness of personality, of an entire cross-section of *noir* characters. In the gangster drama, motivation and identity were fixed matters; if a character was playing a role (like Edward G. Robinson as a racket-buster posing as a gang member in *Bullets or Ballots*), we were let in on the deception. Characters in *noir* often assume several identities, and we are rarely alerted to their masquerades; we have to "read" a character through a thicket of contradictory clues.

The elusiveness and ambiguity that mark *noir* characterization, the cunning masquerades, the skillful performances that often frustrate the unwary anti-heroes, are all underlined by the genre's use of plots of labyrinthine complexity. *Noir* stories are often designed to stump the viewer. And they are presented, typically, in a non-chronological order. In a fractured time sequence, as flashbacks intersect present action, characters try to reconstruct the past, combing it for clues, facts, answers. "The past is a foreign country," says the narrator of L.P. Hartley's exquisite novel about time remembered, *The Go-Between*; "they do things differently there"—a truth which the fevered investigations into the past in *noir* bear out. In the *noir* thriller, time past retains its mysteries.

A representative example of the complex treatment of time in *film noir*, and of the pressure the past exerts on the present, is *The Killers*, an intelligent expansion of Hemingway's short story about a man who passively submits to his own death when two hired gunmen, like evil emissaries from his shrouded past, hunt him down in a small-town rooming house. Although Hemingway offers no explanation for the character's almost indifferent embrace of death, the film attempts to unravel the intriguing mystery of his submission. The search into the dead character's past is conducted by a dogged insurance investigator whose only clue is an

The fun-house mirror shattered, at the climax of *The Lady From Shanghai*: the characters' masquerade is over. (Everett Sloane, as the oily Mr. Bannister.)

insurance policy that the murder victim left to a clean-up lady in an Atlantic City motel. The investigator learns that Swede left the woman the policy because she prevented him from killing himself after his girlfriend walked out on him. From this single biographical detail, the claims man begins to penetrate the character's history. From a series of fragmentary interviews, he discovers that Swede was a boxer who fell in with a gang and who then took the rap for a woman. After serving his jail sentence, Swede returned to his old cronies at the time they were planning a big payroll heist. But his old girlfriend Kitty causes trouble for Swede once again, setting him up as the decoy in a double double-cross. Kitty runs off with the money and with the boss, making it appear that it was Swede who swindled them all. Shattered by her duplicity, Swede retreats from his criminal life, hiding out in a small town where he works at a gas station, lives in a dim furnished room, and

eats every night at the same diner (where the film opens as Swede's executioners, hired by the gang boss, await his arrival).

The film's splintered chronology, the flashbacks presented from multiple points of view, and the flashbacks within flashbacks, all have a crucial impact on both the mood and the meaning of the story. As the insurance man uncovers bits and pieces of Swede's background, he constructs different explanations for the character's self-sacrificial death, though only at the end of his search does he light upon the full truth. Till that point, his view of the character is fragmentary and clouded. Swede is one of the most elusive of *noir's* anti-heroes, Kitty is one of the genre's most masked spider women; and the film's own devious structure, its conflicting points of view, its choppy handling of time, reinforce the enigmatic aura that enshrouds the two main characters.

In *Out of the Past (Build My Gallows High)*,

The *femme fatale* (Jane Greer) returns, from *Out of the Past*, to plague the former detective (Robert Mitchum) who, like many *noir* heroes, cannot escape from his past.

Robert Mitchum plays a former private eye who has given up the city for a quiet new life in the country. But like Swede (and many other *noir* protagonists as well), he cannot escape the claims of the past. Out of the past comes one last assignment, a job that he knows is dangerous but also unavoidable. On the way to his fatal meeting with a gangland boss (Kirk Douglas), he calls on his sweet new fiancée and uncovers his past, revealing the secret other self that bedevils many *noir* victims. Like that of Swede, his fall from grace in his "other" life resulted from his infatuation with a woman. Following the long flashback, the present action contains ironic echoes of the past, as the doomed ex-detective is seduced once again by the charming, wicked woman he had loved and lost, and becomes hopelessly embroiled in a maze of double- and triple-crosses.

Reconstructing the past in fragments containing contradictory information, dramatizing the impact of the past on present action, the format of archetypal *noir* thrillers like *The Killers* and *Out of the Past* recalls *Citizen Kane*, the *locus classicus* for many *noir* patterns. *Kane's* framework—a series of colliding, incomplete recollections unified by an outside investigator's search for a single truth—served *noir's* complex time schemes. As in many crime dramas, the reporter's thrusts into the past in *Citizen Kane* only reinforce its elusiveness, its deep mysteriousness. We perceive Kane, as we do Swede, in subjective, illusory fragments.

Noir's recurrent use of a jumbled time sequence, its sometimes delirious flashbacks within flashbacks (as in *Sorry, Wrong Number* and *The Enforcer* as well as *The Killers*), support the characterizations, which are also, and often spectacularly, crooked rather than straight, devious rather than forthright. Like the handling of time, motivation and identity in *noir* are frequently oblique, confusing. A *film noir* can confound the audience even when it does not juggle past and present action. During production of *The Big Sleep*, Howard Hawks and William Faulkner, so the famous story goes, were said to have wired Raymond Chandler to ask him who killed the Sternwoods' chauffeur, to which Chandler responded by saying he didn't know. Whether or not this charming report is apocryphal is really beside the point, for it is true in spirit if not fact: the story of *The Big Sleep is* very hard to follow. Propelled by a series of criss-crosses, double-crosses, betrayals, deceptions, *noir* stories like *The Big Sleep* deliberately try to be knotted and sinuous.

In the fatally unstable *noir* world, voice-over narration often serves as an anchor. (Though even here, *noir* has tricks up its sleeve, as the narrator of *Sunset Boulevard* is dead: we see him floating face down in Norma Desmond's swimming pool, as we hear his voice on the sound track, telling us how he died. Both *Laura*

and *Criss Cross* begin with narrations by characters who are killed.) Usually reflective and commonsensical, the voice-over narrator is our guide through the *noir* labyrinth. Dick Powell in *Murder, My Sweet*, John Garfield in *The Postman Always Rings Twice*, Orson Welles in *The Lady from Shanghai*, Fred MacMurray in *Double Indemnity*, all speak in a brisk, straightforward way. Sometimes confessional, sometimes simply supplying information, their no-nonsense narration introduces a pointed contrast to the devious characters and tortuous plotting. The cool narrator talks about events which have already happened, while the image on the screen takes place in an ongoing present. The conflict between what we see and what the narrator tells us creates distance—his voice provides a frame in which the characters enact a drama that he knows the outcome of. Having survived a

Whether it is a gossamer fabrication, as in *Rope (below)*, or the real thing, as in *Side Street, Boomerang*, and *The Phenix City Story (following pages)*, and whether it is during the day or at night, the city in *noir* is a place of uneasiness and sudden violence — a cauldron of crime.

Two scenes from *Side Street*.

Above: Boomerang   *Below: The Phenix City Story*

nightmare, the *noir* narrator, for the most part, recollects the past in a matter-of-fact tone. Sometimes, his story is therapeutic, as he confesses to crimes; sometimes he speaks with relief, since he has escaped from a dragnet. But whether he is merely supplying background details or "coming clean," his cool tone has a hint of irony. Calmly, but with a trace of amazement, as if he can't quite believe what has happened to him, the narrator of *Double Indemnity* recalls the story of his fateful involvement with a *femme fatale*. From Death Row, the low-key narrator of *The Postman Always Rings Twice* tells his story of passion leading to crime. With a mixture of disillusionment and relief, the narrator of *The Lady from Shanghai* recalls his involvement with and escape from the mysterious heroine. Speaking in a voice of certain knowledge (he knows, after all, how things turned out), the tough *noir* narrator regards the characters like pawns on a chessboard as he moves them toward their grim, awaiting destinies. Voice-over narration, then, seals off the action from the world outside the film frame.

Like the measured, confining, voice-over commentary, other recurrent apsects of *noir* narrative style—the fractured time scheme, the shifting points of view, the maze-like storyline—are distancing devices which enclose the characters within the frame, and thereby underscore the genre's interest in alienation and entrapment. Cut off in some way from the normal world, *noir* characters inhabit a terrain of bleak and often terminal isolation, their remoteness from reality enhanced by the genre's stylized narrative techniques.

Noir's visual style is as highly inflected and as self-conscious as its storytelling methods. The central background for *noir*, as it had been for the gangster story, is the American big city. Presented in a variety of moods and designs, ranging from patently studio recreations in such films as *Scarlet Street* and *The Woman in the Window*, to the Expressionist overtones given to real city backgrounds in thrillers like *Night and the City, M, On Dangerous Ground*, and *The Asphalt Jungle*, to the more straightforward renderings in *The Naked City, Side Street, The Street with No*

Name, the city in *noir* is an inescapable image, its throbbing presence an integral part of the drama.

Powerful early *films noirs* were set in airless, fabricated environments; the city in these films, as in the German Expressionist dramas, consists of little more than a few deserted streets, their rain-swept emptiness illuminated by stray flashing neon signs. In *Scarlet Street*, there is no sense of life outside the frame; all exterior scenes are stripped of any sense of city density and rhythm. The film's unpeopled streets, the elongated shadows, the angular buildings that guard empty space like grim sentinels, recall the eerie night-time cityscapes in the paintings of Edward Hopper. *Scarlet Street* opens with a strange and rigorously choreographed street scene, with each of the pedestrians, from an organ grinder to a prosperous bourgeois and his wife stepping out for an evening's stroll, carefully planted in the frame. With its orchestration and its severely restricted movement, the scene is totally different in rhythm from the location shots in Neo-Realist films, where the movement of a real city is presented in all its randomness.

In other early *noirs* such as *The Maltese Falcon* and *The Big Sleep*, the city is mostly a matter of interiors. Both these archetypal private-eye stories admit the outside world in small doses, like the static shots of San Francisco glimpsed from the windows of Sam Spade's office. Eerily motionless and poised, "the city" here looks like a painting; it is inert, lifeless, far away.

Perhaps the most remote from physical reality of all the imaginary cities in early *noir* is the one in *The Blue Dahlia*. An apartment hotel, the Blue Dahlia nightclub, fragments of streets lined with blank-looking buildings, all seem cut off from the real world, suspended in a limbo of the Hollywood set designer's imagination. The film's world is posed and suffocating without a trace of natural daylight or nature, and therefore an appropriate frame for Raymond Chandler's contrived little thriller.

Many *noir* dramas combine studio simulations with the real thing, with sometimes noticeable lapses between the two. John Farrow's *The Big Clock* opens with a panoramic view of New York at night, its giant towers twinkling splendidly under the titles. After the credits, the camera pans to the right, zooming in on a particular building in the city. As the camera moves in through the window, the film shifts from the real world to one of studio fabrication. That descent from the outside world into a separate environment is used, unforgettably, in Hitchcock's opening for *Psycho*, where the camera moves slowly from a long shot of Phoenix at midday to a close-up of a darkened hotel window.

Crime dramas set in real cities have a denser texture than the austere studio pieces, though in location films, too, reality is heightened to create atmosphere. The city in *film noir* is never merely neutral, never simply a shapeless background. In both studio and location thrillers, it participates in the action, "comments" on the characters, supplies mood and tension. In the striking opening to *Possessed*, for instance, Joan Crawford wanders dazed through a real downtown Los Angeles. The deserted streets, the tall, silent buildings, the slanting, early morning light which casts elongated shadows are all an eerie projection of the tormented character. Through camera angles and lighting, the real city has thus been subtly transformed into a place of incipient nightmare. *The Asphalt Jungle* begins with shots of empty New York streets, with scattered newspapers blown about by the wind the only signs of movement in the early morning gloom. The film's kaleidoscope of the city at dawn is beautiful, but threatening, as if New York is ready to explode; the city's awesome canyons seem indifferent to human concerns.

In *Night and the City*, London is transformed into a menacing terrain of narrow alleys, winding, darkened streets, abandoned lots—a seething environment in which the haunted hero seeks refuge, with no success. The city's hostility is reflected in the sharp vertical lines that slice the frame, the harsh angles of buildings. Elegant London becomes a place crawling with waterfront dives and smoke-filled, cave-like rooms populated by oversized hoodlums. It is an inferno that mocks the hero's fate.

Panic in the Streets opens as the camera (mounted on a moving vehicle) hurtles through Bourbon Street, in the honky-tonk section of the French Quarter in New Orleans. The flashing neon signs, the clusters of people arranged in ominous formations, the gaudy strip joints, all suggest an atmosphere of potential violence. The city looks dangerous, infected, as indeed it will prove to be when in the course of the film it is threatened with an outbreak of bubonic plague.

The *noir* city—the great foul place—rumbles with danger and enticement. Bustling downtown areas appear as sinful and polluting. In *Phenix City Story*, recurrent shots of the dens of gambling and vice clustered on the city's notorious 14th Street, though pretending to be merely documentary, are in fact stylized portraits of evil. Phil Karlson has staged these panoramic views of his Sin City with all the exhilaration of a puritan fascinated by debauchery. The tangle of bodies, the blare of honky-tonk music, the swell of car horns, the nervously flashing signs create a dazzling visual and aural cacophony: the city as moral and sexual cesspool.

Orson Welles depicts a Mexican border town (actually Venice, California) in *Touch of Evil* as a hothouse of filth and corruption, its buildings and people rotting away in the steamy Mexican climate. In the famous bravura opening, Welles' camera cranes and tracks athletically through the thronged main street as the hero and his wife (Charlton Heston and Janet Leigh) move against the flow of traffic, creating visual tension that is echoed everywhere in the packed frame. This ugly Mexican community is the most pestilential of the *noir* cities.

In Max Ophuls' brilliant *The Reckless Moment*, Joan Bennett (as a proper upper middle class housewife drawn into a criminal milieu to protect her daughter's reputation) drives into downtown Los Angeles from her luxurious Balboa house. As she enters the inner city, the frame darkens and seems to contract; the streets, filled with grotesques milling about in threatening postures, are rife with danger for the prim, sheltered suburban matron. Going to the heart of the city to do business with a blackmailer, the character seems to be entering an inferno.

In *Edge of Doom*, the troubled hero (Farley Granger) walks through a seamy downtown on

his way to see a priest. Overrun with Bowery bums and prostitutes, its succession of beer halls and penny arcades and strip joints erupting in frenzy, the slum street seems to spring from within the character, his obsessions transformed, as it were, into a scene of mass disorder. The character's grim-faced processional through this urban phantasmagoria turns out to be the prelude to crime: he will kill the provoking and insensitive priest he is going to visit. After the murder, he walks back home through the blazing street. The loud, gaudy city in *Edge of Doom*, reflecting the hero's own chaos and bottled-up violence, thus frames his act of crime.

Drawing innocents into its dark byways, the city casts its net. Often in *noir*, a character

who enters the city, usually from a small town, is caught off guard. In *D.O.A.*, a hayseed insurance man (Edmond O'Brien) goes up from Modesto to San Francisco for a convention. After a night on the town, a whirlwind tour of the city's hot spots, he discovers that he has been fatally poisoned, and begins his death-watch through the city's underground to track down his murderer. In *Champion*, Kirk Douglas plays a poor boy from the sticks who becomes progressively corrupted as he penetrates the inner city's boxing syndicate.

In Stanley Kubrick's *Killer's Kiss*, set in a jittery midtown Manhattan, the heroine works at a dance hall at 49th and Broadway. As the camera pans the forlorn room, the dancers look like waxworks figures; they're more dead than alive, bowed down under the burdens of city life.

The city settings in the paintings of Reginald Marsh have the isolation and the brooding tension that hover over the city in *film noir*. *Death Avenue; Lunch;* and *The Subway*. (Courtesy Whitney Museum of American Art)

Marsh's *Ten Cents a Dance* has the casual, beckoning eroticism of *noir's femmes fatales*. (Courtesy Whitney Museum of American Art)

The *noir* city is often a place of extreme weather. It is sweltering, ripped apart by blistering heat in one film, an arctic outpost in another. Summer in the city is vividly etched in *Laura*. In the opening scene, the camera tracks through an elegantly appointed Manhattan penthouse as the hot summer sun streams through the large windows, throwing a shimmering light over the furniture and *objets d'art*. The few side streets and dingy tenements that represent the city in *Deadline at Dawn* seem to be drained by the heavy summer weather. Characters sweat profusely, peeling walls seem to be perspiring (as the men continue, in obedience to some curious outdated notion of propriety, to wear jackets and ties, their only acknowledgment of the stifling climate a loosening of their ties).

Laura and *Deadline at Dawn* suggest summer heat in studio settings; the real summer city, in such films as *The Window* and *The Naked City*, is equally brutal, with steam rising from potholes in the streets and fans circulating in pathetic battle against nature's unfriendliness. The merciless New York climate seems in these films a veritable catalyst to crime.

The image of the city as a place of terror and seduction, as a modern wasteland, an environment indifferent to people, a carnival edging toward disorder, has striking parallels in the work of artists of the twenties, thirties and forties. Anticipations and echoes of the *noir* city appear in the work of John Sloan, George Bellows, Franz Kline, Reginald Marsh, Edward Hopper, Martin Lewis. American artists who chose city scenes as their subject devised a style that blended American realism with Expressionism. Reminiscent of the work of caricaturists like Hogarth, Daumier, and Ensor, their city canvases often have a sharp, satiric thrust. In mood their work ranges from the austere images of isolation in paintings by Hopper to the bustling crowds by Reginald Marsh to the tense city scenes in the black and white lithographs of Martin Lewis.

Marsh, who worked from the late twenties to the late fifties, was centrally concerned throughout his career with New York, a city he loved and studied all his life. Marsh's characteristic treatment of the city, in his numerous Coney Island and Bowery scenes, is as a place of terrific energy. In his packed street scenes, muscular, sensual characters jostle each other in a spirit of Mardi Gras. But beneath the holiday pleasure, there is always the suggestion that the bursting scene is about to erupt into violence—the swelling crowds of pleasure-seekers are a potentially destructive force.

Ablaze with a nervous energy, a quicksilver intensity, Marsh's city, like the *noir* city, is a place of sexual promise and release. It glitters with temptation. In Marsh, as in *noir*, the visually striking city is a potent, galvanizing force, as beautiful as it is corrupt, as majestic as it is also putrid. Marsh's vision, again like that of *noir*, contains a raw poetry.

Noir's fascination with physically and morally battered characters has an equivalent in the photographic records of city life found in Weegee and Diane Arbus. The portraits by these two noted photographers are astringent documents of human wreckage, of life as it is lived on the edge, on downtown Skid Rows. *Noir* inevitably softened the extreme harshness of the two artists, but vestiges of their attraction to freaks appear throughout the canon, in grotesque supporting characters, in surreal cityscapes, in images of debasement, in an icy, insistent detachment from suffering.

The city as a cradle of crime and a cauldron of negative energy is the inevitable setting for *film noir*. Country settings appear infrequently, and usually as a counterpoint to the festering city. In *The Asphalt Jungle*, the hero's idea of the pure clean life is a farm with horses grazing serenely in the open rolling fields. Nicholas

Ray's *On Dangerous Ground* offers what is probably the most schematic opposition between town and country in all of *noir*. As it presents the daily activities of its beleaguered policeman, the first part of the movie is set in a virulent, blistering city. The protagonist's breakdown is played out against kaleidoscopic views of big city corruption. In the second part of the film, a stark, snow-covered rural landscape stands in eloquent contrast to the infested world from which the cop has had to escape to save himself. As he becomes involved in the lives of a blind woman, her emotionally disturbed brother, and an avenging father, he discovers that the country too has its dangers and pitfalls; but the film suggests that the overwrought cop is humanized by the country environment in a way that he could not be in the city.

Leaving the contaminating city for salvation in the country is a recurrent *noir* pattern. Burt Lancaster in *The Killers* and Robert Mitchum in *Out of the Past* retire from lives of crime to sylvan settings. A few *noir* movies— *They Live By Night, The Postman Always Rings Twice, Ace in the Hole,* and *Gun Crazy*—take place in rural locations. Some of these, though, like *The Postman Always Rings Twice*, merely transport a city mentality to an out-of-the-way setting. The film's two murderers are really city types at heart, with all the animal cunning and sexuality of characters who inhabit the city jungle. An exposé of yellow journalism, *Ace in the Hole* simply brings the mean streets to the country as a cynical reporter exploits a personal disaster (a man is trapped in a cave) in order to advance his own career.

They Live By Night and *Gun Crazy*, in contrast, are true countrified *noir* thrillers. Both films, dramatizing the adventures of couples who live on the margins of society, outside the law, are precursors of *Bonnie and Clyde*. Perhaps because of their rural settings, the films have a different narrative development than most *noir* pieces. Episodic, taking place in a greater number of locations than the usually claustrophobic *noir* thriller, the films have a picaresque flavor, though of a particularly dark tonality. They have a more open feeling in their outdoor sequences than in any of the more traditional

city-based dramas and *They Live By Night* even has a semi-romantic aura—its sweet, gentle outlaw couple are in love.

In Joseph Losey's *The Prowler*, the Mojave Desert is a novel and expressive *noir* setting. The parched landscape reinforces the barrenness of the characters, a corrupt policeman and his forlorn, pregnant wife, and proves to be as suffocating as the city environment. In *Leave Her to Heaven*, however, open country settings undermine *noir* tension. Photographed in color, the glamorous mountain retreats (that may accurately reflect the characters' social status) give the story a ladies' magazine gloss. The pristine scenery and the *House Beautiful* interiors soften the film's protrait of a psychopathically possessive woman and point up the fact that *noir* functions best when its settings are as idiosyncratic and neurotic as its characters.

The tenement, with peeling walls, rickety stairs, pools of shadows, blank brick walls and prison-barred fire escapes, is a recurrent *noir* setting. (Farley Granger and Adele Jergens, in *Edge of Doom*; Ruth Roman and Paul Stewart, in *The Window*.)

Like the western and the gangster film, *noir* uses the same kinds of settings over and over. Night clubs, hotels, tenements, police stations, offices, docks, corner luncheonettes and drug stores, factories, warehouses, crumbling mansions, boxing arenas, train stations, restaurants both shabby and luxurious are as integral a part of *noir* as private eyes and two-timing dames. Like the great city itself, individual locations are charged with menace.

Places in *noir* reveal character. The cramped tenements, the joyless middle-class apartments, the dingy furnished rooms that populate the genre carry the history of their inhabitants. Settings are chosen for thematic reinforcement. Cars and trains and boxing arenas figure prominently in *noir* stories because they provide visual metaphors of enclosure and entrapment. The packed, smoke-filled arena in such films as *Killer's Kiss*, *Champion*, *The Big Combo*, *Body and*

Trains, train yards, and train stations are familiar *noir* backgrounds. (Charles MacGraw, in *The Narrow Margin*; Glenn Ford, Broderick Crawford, Gloria Grahame, in *Human Desire*.) Trains, like cars, are means of escape that can easily become traps.

Soul and *The Set-Up* is an image of the fighter's destiny: the beating he gets within the tight, fixed "frame" of the ring reflects the kind of battering that is doled out to him in the outside world. Cars and trains are means of escape that can quickly become traps; they are tight, confined spaces from which there is no escape.

In addition to its symbolic use of ordinary environments, *noir* also relies on surreal and exotic settings: the unfinished highway, with roads dangling crazily in mid-air, at the end of *The Lineup*; the huge ferris wheel in which the climactic meeting takes place between Orson Welles and Joseph Cotten in the *The Third Man*; the mannikin factory in *Killer's Kiss*; the aquarium, the Chinese theatre, and the fun house in *The Lady from Shanghai*; the deserted warehouse at the end of *This Gun for Hire*; the ominous fairground, with its laughing fat lady and its fiendishly whirling merry-go-round, in *Strangers on a Train*; the sweltering greenhouse in *The Big Sleep*. *Noir* exploits the oddness of odd settings, as it transforms the mundane quality of familiar ones, in order to create an environment that pulses with intimations of nightmare. Whether in seemingly familiar or unusual surroundings, *noir* depends on settings that radiate menace and instability.

Bizarre backgrounds encourage the splashy visual set-pieces that decorate the genre. Usually involving a chase, a murder, a showdown, a release of tension or violence, a moment of madness, the *noir* set-piece is a showcase for the kind of baroque sensibility that most American genres have little use for. Defined by its bravura scale, these visual high points have a delirious humor, as if the film-makers are slyly ribbing themselves as well as the audience. The villian pinned against one of the Gothic spires of the Brooklyn Bridge at the end of *The Naked City*; Hope Emerson's grand entrance in *Cry of the City*, as she makes her way through a tunnel of doorways, turning on lights as she goes, to answer Richard Conte's insistent knocks (the scene is a virtuoso display of *noir*'s delight in chiaroscuro); the long take of the bank robbery in *Gun Crazy*, with the camera recording the action from the back seat of the killers' car; the equally long take of the heist in *The Killers*, where the

camera records the complicated maneuvers from a distance, in an unbroken chain of vertiginous angles and panoramic long shots; the villain's impalement on the spokes of a giant cuckoo clock in *The Stranger*; the high angle shot of a heist in *Criss Cross* (the extreme angle, which seems to turn the world upside down, evokes amazed laughter from audiences); Richard Widmark's bravura mad scene in *Kiss of Death*, where he pushes an old woman in a wheelchair down a flight of steps; Janet Leigh in *Touch of Evil* being terrorized in a creepy roadside motel by a brutal lesbian and her equally grotesque gang of thugs; Cagney on "top of the world," blown to bits by a gas tank explosion, at the end of *White Heat*; the similarly apocalyptic imagery at the end of *Kiss Me Deadly*, where Pandora's Box contains an atomic blast; Lee Marvin throwing scalding coffee in Gloria Grahame's face in *The Big Heat*; Constance Towers viciously beating up a john, and then taking off her wig (a scene that elicits howls of sadistic delight) at the opening of Sam Fuller's dotty *Naked Kiss*; the chase through the canyons of lower Manhattan, the camera perched at steep angles, in *Side Street*; the shootout between husband and wife, in the crazy mirror fun house, at the end of *The Lady from Shanghai*—a sequence that epitomizes the visual as well as psychological extravagance of the *noir* set-piece.

These privileged moments are isolated from the rest of the films in which they occur by their special intensity but not by their content: the best *noir* thrillers "earn" and can absorb these moments of visual and theatrical virtuosity; the violence and mania that are highlighted in these passages of kinky vaudevillian cinema flow directly from the *noir* milieu. But few *films noirs* can or even try to sustain the pitch of these italicized moments. Often, in fact, *noir* functions in a neutral, even deadpan range; instead of the energy that characterizes the set-piece, the films work for a flattened effect, an almost zombie-like verbal and visual mode.

The exotic *noir* setting, thick with danger and menace. A New Orleans house of pleasure, and *(following page)* a coffee warehouse, in *Panic in the Streets*.

The church as *noir* setting. Houses of worship offer no refuge for the *noir* outlaw: Farley Granger, in *Edge of Doom;* Humphrey Bogart, in *Dead Reckoning.*

Objects, things, fragments of decor loom as large as places in the *noir* iconography. Clocks, mirrors, staircases, windows and bedposts create images of entrapment and anticipate moments of doom. Characters in many films are caught behind window frames, imprisoned by bannisters. Stairs, windows, mirrors, as familiar a part of *noir* terrain as the saloon or the sheriff's office in westerns, are used to enclose frantic *noir* characters in frames within the frame. Reflections in mirrors and windows suggest doubleness, self-division, and thereby underline recurrent themes of loss or confusion of identity; multiple images of a character within the same shot give visual emphasis to the dual and unstable personalities that are rampant in the genre.

The closed world of the typical *noir* neurotic is reflected in the tight framing that is customary for the genre. Directors working with *noir* stories avoid openness and horizontality; the sense of space, the feeling for landscape that distinguish a Ford western or a Griffith epic have no place within the *noir* frame. Asymmetry, angularity, verticality are important compositional elements for *noir* thrillers; space is sliced up, it seems to close in on the characters as shapes converge over their heads, pressing them down to the bottom of the screen. The fractured image mirrors the characters' disintegration.

In *noir,* narrative continuity is typically achieved through tight cutting rather than a roving camera. Even tracking shots are used to create tension rather than the smooth, loose, flowing quality that such a movement often imparts. Close-ups abound, creating a sense of claustrophobia. The leisurely establishing shot, the generous long shot and the sensuous moving camera are of little use to *noir* design, and only undermine the tautness and concentration that the genre depends on.

Exaggerated angles are a regular, expected element of *noir* visual style. Extreme close-ups, low angles which distort the human face and figure, high angles and oblique, off-center angles appear with almost obsessive repetition. The high angle overhead shot, the most unheroic of perspectives, a visual signal of impending doom, may be the most frequently used camera placement in *noir.* Reducing the characters in size and underlining their vulnerability, the high angle shot places us in a superior position: we're looking down at the characters, aware of their fate before they are.

Noir stories are about departures and lapses from the normal world, and the films' deliberate visual styling enhances the kind of transformation from reality to nightmare that the narratives dramatize. The most well-known of *noir*'s visual inflections, its virtuoso lighting, is borrowed directly from the German Expressionists. Compulsively addicted to shadows, and to high contrasts between light and dark, the *noir* screen offers a cornucopia of patterns of chiaroscuro, as pools of shadow surround and sometimes overtake small centers of light. As the characters are menaced by a hostile world, so sources of light within the frame are attacked by an invading, pervasive darkness.

No white wall in any *noir* drama is free of shadows. Cast onto walls by sunlight filtering through venetian blinds or by artificial sources of illumination, shadows form spectral reflections of bannisters and human figures. Horizontal, barred, criss-crossed lines on walls create a prison-like aura, underlining the psychological and physical enclosure that is at the core of most *noir* stories. Isolated pools of light surrounded by velvety darkness; a face picked out from the encircling gloom by a harsh spotlight; lighting from below which throws an unearthly shine onto faces; severe vertical shafts of light bisected by menacing cross-bars of shadow; figures outlined in dramatic silhouette against a halo of light: these recurrent visual patterns are the signs of *noir*'s fascination with Germanic lighting. The films reserve their most bravura manipulation of light and shadow for climactic moments, for scenes of crime and passion, where chiaroscuro intensification is a signal of imminent and present catastrophe.

Noir's love of shadows—and the Hollywood know-how which can depict patterns of light and dark with the utmost technical

Reflections in mirrors and windows are a recurrent aspect of *noir* iconography. The double images suggest schizophrenia and masquerade. (Ida Lupino, below, and Robert Ryan, facing page, in *Beware, My Lovely*; Edward G. Robinson and Joan Bennett, in *The Woman in the Window*, above right. Following pages: Dick Powell, in *Murder, My Sweet* — p. 92; Dick Powell and Raymond Burr, in *Pitfall* — p. 93.).

skill and sensuality—supplied a few visual jolts to even the most uninspired and derivative storyline. The kind of visual coding and stylization that *noir* encouraged—indeed demanded—made it, for a time, a virtually foolproof genre. Among American film genres, *noir* has the most consistently high standards of visual design.

To create suspense and to enhance characterization, objects (like phones) and elements of decor (like paintings) are often given special emphasis in *noir* composition. The phone here is Sam Spade's, in *The Maltese Falcon*; the painting, which lends a spiritual quality to the suffering hero (Victor Mature), is from *Kiss of Death*.

Stairs in *noir* often lead to catastrophe: in *Sudden Fear*, Joan Crawford mounts to stairs to meet her husband (Jack Palance), who's planning to kill her; there's violence at the top of the stairs, in *The Naked City*.

Spiral staircases are a sure sign of chaos, as Burt
Lancaster discovers in *Brute Force*.

Frames-within-the-frame, a recurrent visual motif in *noir*,
underscore themes of enclosure and imprisonment;
characters in these shots occupy a fixed, tight space.
(Dennis O'Keefe, Marsha Hunt, in *Raw Deal*; Lucille Ball,
in *The Dark Corner*; Judith Evelyn, in *Rear Window*.)

Characters in *noir* are often caught in visual traps. *Counterclockwise from upper left*: Victor Mature is pinned against brick walls, in *Kiss of Death*; Francis L. Sullivan looks like a caged animal as he sits in his office, in *Night and the City*; overhead beams press down ominously on Jack Palance, in *Panic in the Streets*. Jean Wallace and Cornel Wilde *(opposite top)*, "framed" in *The Big Combo*; the ceiling seems dangerously close to Robert Ryan *(opposite bottom)*, in *On Dangerous Ground*.

High angle shots underline the *noir* victim's terror and helplessness: Robert Ryan on the run, in *Crossfire (Pages 100-101)*; David Wayne in flight from his pursuers, in Joseph Losey's *M (right)*.

Disorientation in *noir* is often suggested through extreme close-ups like that of Susan Hayward, in *Deadline at Dawn (opposite)*; through Wellesian low angle shots in which ceilings box in the characters: Don Taylor, in *The Naked City (below)*; Humphrey Bogart and Alexis Smith, in *Conflict (page 104 top)*; and through tilted angles, Humphrey Bogart, in *Conflict (page 104, bottom)*; Joan Crawford, in *Queen Bee (page 105)*.

Strongly influenced by German Expressionism, *noir* operates in a world of virtuoso contrasts between light and shadow: Orson Welles *(above),* in *The Third Man;* an elegantly choreographed shot, in *Panic in the Streets (opposite, right).*

Striking *noir* chiaroscuro (above): Mark Stevens and female shadow, in *The Dark Corner*.

Below, a recurrent *noir* design: venetian blinds which cast barred shadows onto characters. (Victor Mature, in *Kiss of Death*; Janet Leigh and John Gavin, in *Psycho*.)

Lighting from below makes actors look like waxworks figures (Alan Ladd and Howard da Silva, in *The Blue Dahlia*; Sydney Greenstreet and Humphrey Bogart, in *Conflict*.)

Caught in the spotlight: Joan Bennett, in *The Reckless Moment*; Richard Widmark, near the end of his ordeal, in *Night and the City*.

5
The Noir Director

Like the gangster film, the *noir* thriller established its conventions quickly. The low angles and theatrical lighting that embellish *The Maltese Falcon* soon became the common currency of the new genre. Because many *films noirs* have a similar look and sound—those same rainy abandoned city streets, those ominous flickering neon signs, that moody, lonely jazz score, that tight-lipped, he-man narration—critics have suggested that the genre offered a ready-made style to which any competent director could easily adapt himself. A common critical assumption has indeed been that *noir*'s hard-and-fast visual conventions tend to erase the eccentricities of individual style, and that *noir* dramas all look and "feel" pretty much the same.

Although there is some standardization—certain expected elements of narrative and visual style—the range of textures available to the *noir* director is in fact considerable. *Noir* has accommodated directors of a wide temperamental spectrum, from the absolute even-handedness and sobriety of Henry Hathaway to the baroque theatricality of Orson Welles, from the flat-footedness of George Marshall to the Germanic flourishes of Robert Siodmak, from the sanity of

Orson Welles on the set of *The Lady From Shanghai*, with members of the San Francisco Mandarin Chinese Theater.

Howard Hawks to the advanced neuroses of Sam Fuller. But the directors who achieved the greatest success in *noir* do share some technical as well as emotional predispositions.

Noir operates only within the confines of a small black-and-white screen, and therefore directors such as George Stevens, David Lean, D. W. Griffith and Cecil B. DeMille, who have an essentially epic vision and who favor large-scale stories set in vast natural landscapes, would never have attempted any hard-core *films noirs* even if their careers had intersected *noir*'s heyday. Directors for whom length and magnitude release their greatest strengths could obviously not be comfortable within *noir*'s constricted frame. *Noir* may well be the most unromantic and unsentimental of American film genres, and so directors with a basically open, generous, romantic temperament, with a benign view of the world—humanists like Ford and Renoir—could hardly thrive on the genre's bitter diet of cynicism and defeat. During Renoir's Hollywood period, working at RKO, a studio that specialized in dark films, he did try a piece in the *noir* vein, with predictably strained results. *The Woman on the Beach* is a flat and visually threadbare melodrama. It is possible that a director like Lang could have transformed its familiar elements—an unfaithful wife, a psychotically jealous husband, a studio-built seaside setting—into an atmospheric psychological thriller. There is no chance in the film for the constantly tracking camera, the elegant and complex deep focus, and the long takes of Renoir's masterpiece, *The Rules of the Game*. Forced to contract rather than to expand space, Renoir works in a minimalist style, with neutral medium shots and conventional angle-reverse angle cutting that are clearly uncongenial to him. The result is patchy, thin, curiously remote: a great director in alien territory.

Howard Hawks, Raoul Walsh, and Max Ophuls—other directors unsuited to *noir*—produced films which are more successful than *The Woman on the Beach* but which nevertheless show signs of strain. Hawks and Walsh, Hollywood's ultimate he-man directors, are more comfortable on the range than within the parameters of the *noir* city. For these two gregarious personalities, *noir* is too internalized and neurotic. Yet working against the grain, Hawks made *The Big Sleep* and Walsh *White Heat*, two of the most popular crime films of the decade.

Hawks is surely among the most proficient of studio directors; on assignment, he has worked in most of the major genres, acquitting himself professionally in westerns (*Red River*), screwball comedy (*His Girl Friday, Ball of Fire*), gangster stories (*Scarface*), even musicals (*Gentlemen Prefer Blondes*) and epics (the visually exciting *Land of the Pharaohs*). His one entry in the *noir* canon is a dead-pan classic, a cool, safe rendition of Raymond Chandler's intricate mystery story. Perhaps Hawks worked well in so many different areas because his "style"—a succession of neutral camera set-ups, flat lighting, conventional continuity cutting—is so unobtrusive. In its determined flatfootedness, *The Big Sleep* is almost an anti-*noir*, a display of impersonal Hollywood craftsmanship. Hawks is sure of his effects, he is skillful in handling his actors (he wisely places Bogart and Bacall at the center of the film), but *The Big Sleep* has no genuine feeling for the genre's possibilities.

Walsh's natural expansiveness is also uncomfortable with *noir*, though *White Heat* is a stronger piece than the overrated *Big Sleep*. Walsh's style is more open and direct than is usual for the genre; his pace is faster, his framing sidesteps customary *noir* claustrophobia, and he responds more warmly to his characters than a true *noir* director like Lang would. Certainly Cagney's crackpot gangster has more verve and expresses more feeling than the typical *noir* somnambulist.

Probably Ophuls' *The Reckless Moment* is the most successful *noir* made by a director at temperamental odds with the genre. In films like *Madame de . . .* and *Lola Montes*—stories about the rules of the game in high society—Ophuls was noted for the swirling, encircling movement, the wonderful darting rhythms of his camera. But Ophuls' craning, tracking, gliding, pirouetting movement, which would seem to suggest freedom and expansiveness, had an effect quite the opposite: the ceaselessly moving camera suggests time in its flight and underlines the impermanence of feelings and relationships as well as the inability of the characters to escape their pre-ordained fate. In his own way, that is, Ophuls was always as concerned with themes of entrapment as the directors of *noir*. For *The Reckless Moment*, a story about an average American matron's attempts against terrific obstacles to preserve her averageness, Ophuls changes his characteristic camera movement: there are no visual arabesques in this American *film noir*, no graceful, flowing rhythms. The film is choreographed in straight lines. Going downtown to challenge her daughter's no-good boyfriend, or meeting clandestinely with the blackmailer she almost falls in love with, the brisk heroine (Joan Bennett) moves in a direct, straight-ahead way, from her house to her car, from country to town, walking up and down stairs, charging "manfully" through doors and corridors. Ophuls' camera imitates the woman's movement, and the film is designed as a virtually uninterrupted series of lateral tracking shots, with not a single echo of the curlicues and twirls that defined Ophuls' celebrated *mise en scéne* for his stories of European sensuality. To portray this competent, no-nonsense American bourgeoise, Ophuls strips his work of its characteristic lushness.

Noir attracted directors noted, then, not for their warmth and rich painterly style but for their irony and distance, their unromantic tough-mindedness. And it is no surprise therefore that the best *noir* directors were German or Austrian expatriates who shared a world view that was shaped by their bitter personal experience of living in and then escaping from a nation that had lost its mind.

The group of expatriate directors who were to become the masters of the *noir* style began their careers during the heyday of the German Expressionist film, and they naturally brought to their American assignments a predilection for chiaroscuro and for stories in which brooding and solitary characters struggle against hopeless odds. (German art of the twentieth century, long before Hitler, was steeped in morbid subject matter, in themes of madness and death.) Their doom-ridden sensibility, partly a matter of artistic training and experience, partly perhaps an engrained national characteristic,

found an appropriate outlet in the crime films that developed into a Hollywood cycle in the immediate postwar period. The directors share a cynical view of human nature; good characters in their films are often presented as weak, unknowing, and defenseless against a pervasive corruption. In exile from a world gone mad, they are drawn to stories about man's uncertain fate, and about psychological obsession and derangement. The morbid, defeatist tendency of their work is checked, however, by an ironic humor: these Germanic directors have a mordant wit, a rich sense of life's potential for black comedy.

Their interest in emotional and social collapse is presented in a style notable for its glacial detachment. *Noir* at its most typical is not a wild-and-woolly attempt to dramatize the pitfalls and detours of its hapless characters; the people in the films may go mad, but the style in which their disintegration is recorded remains neutral. *Noir* attracts directors whose rigorously controlled and methodical work eliminates any chance for randomnesss, improvisation, spontaneous give-and-take. A vivid moment from Robert Siodmak's *Phantom Lady* indicates the kind of directorial calculation that is standard for the genre. The heroine follows a man onto an elevated train platform; she is tailing him to try to elicit evidence that will exonerate her boss from the charge of murdering his wife. As she stands on the platform, trying to conceal herself in shadow, a heavy black woman crosses in front of her, the resounding click-clack of the woman's heels causing the heroine to shudder. Coming from the outside world, from a reality that transpires beyond the frame of the story, the black woman does not, however, validate that external world; she is not introduced into the film for verisimilitude but to heighten tension, and her sudden appearance is as pre-planned, as precisely timed, as every other aspect of the film's action. This is a small gesture, to be sure, but a memorable one—a quintessential moment of *noir* contrivance, in which a passing stranger is conscripted into the film's fabric of calculated effects.

The stories of *noir* are like bad dreams, but the directors treat the events like *someone else's* nightmare, presenting personal apocalypse with deadly impassivity. *Noir* directors oversee their stories with Olympian detachment, for the most part watching pitilessly as lives unravel. The directors mean to unsettle the audience, to make it aware of its own vulnerability, but they are not interested in arousing conventional audience sympathy. There are no tears in *film noir*.

Of the four major Germanic directors of *noir*—Fritz Lang, Robert Siodmak, Billy Wilder, and Otto Preminger—Lang is the most consistently incisive. In temperament, he is the quintessential *noir* stylist, and from *Manhunt* in 1941 to *Beyond a Reasonable Doubt* in 1956, he contributed more well-crafted titles to the canon than any other director. Lang's earlier German films, ranging in style from the extreme ornamentation of *Die Niebelungen* and *Metropolis* to the muted texture of *M*, were constructed in the studio; and in all his work of this period, decor was molded to express the mood of the characters and the theme. Evoking the child murderer's paranoia and isolation, the studio-built city in *M* is a *created* environment of buildings, uncannily deserted streets, menacing storefront window displays, and a deathly silence pierced by occasional off-screen car horns and the heavily muffled sound of unseen traffic. The film's city is thus merely a faint echo of a real city.

Lang's work in America during the thirties continued to anticipate *film noir*. Directing for major studios, at a time when the studio's mass marketing methods were supremely powerful, Lang necessarily had to subdue his Expressionist tendencies. No American outfit would permit him to turn out a film as remote from the daily life of the audience as *Die Niebelungen* or even *M*. In dramas like *Fury* and *You Only Live Once*, Lang's style was noticeably chastened—the films certainly had a more earthbound look than his symbolic pieces for UFA—though they retained a distinct aura of Germanic gloom. Regardless of where he was working, Lang's output over a period of almost forty years reveals a remarkable visual and thematic continuity.

The director's *noir* titles—*The Ministry of Fear*, *The Woman in the Window*, *Scarlet Street*, *Human Desire*, *The Big Heat*, *Beyond a Reasonable Doubt* are a representative sampling—share strong thematic parallels. All concern victims of fate. From the hero of *The Ministry of Fear*, released from a mental institution and stumbling innocently into a network of spies, to the policeman in *The Big Heat*, who infiltrates the gang that killed his wife, the Langian hero is a marked man, hurled into a maze from which he struggles to escape.

A Lang film opens typically with a chance encounter—the hapless characters played by Edward G. Robinson meeting deceptive women in *Scarlet Street* and *The Woman in the Window*, Ray Milland in *The Ministry of Fear* walking into a fair and deciding to have his fortune told. Thrown into a dilemma of nightmarish proportions, he discovers a secret self, one containing unexpected possibilities. (The theme of the hidden or unexplored self, a favorite subject of German Expressionist films, continued to fascinate Lang throughout his career.) Lang's typical American heroes are seemingly average men who become deranged under the pressure of extraordinary circumstances. As he sets out to avenge his wife's brutal murder, the policeman in *The Big Heat* is unhinged. Taunted by a beautiful woman who pretends to be his mistress, the meek Christopher Cross in *Scarlet Street* proves capable of murder. Sedate Professor Wanley in *The Woman in the Window* begins to act like a shrewd criminal as he protects himself from the consequences of a murder he committed in self-defense.

Lang's response to his victims is one of detachment laced with a grim sardonic humor. He treats his characters like figurines, to be moved about according to the demands of his calculated master plan. His characters are specimens to be scrutinized and laughed at, rather than people with whom to sympathize.

Lang's deliberate pacing, his deep irony, and his interest in characters thwarted by fate, remain continuing facets of his work while his visual design undergoes progressive simplification, from the heavily decorative Expressionism of the twenties to the spare selective Hollywood realism of the fifties. Lang's Hollywood work is gradually subdued to the point where Expressionist inflection and abstraction sound but a faint echo. The real world is seldom admitted into the director's canvas, and where it is, in the

Most of Fritz Lang's films are set in the studio, where the director has maximum control over all elements of the *mise en scène*; but even when Lang, on rare occasion, ventures into the real world, as in this shot from *Human Desire* (with Glenn Ford and Gloria Grahame), he presents reality with distinctly Expressionist overtones.

few location sequences in his films (such as the train yard in *Human Desire*), it is subtly transformed into an environment bristling with terror. No matter what the dominant visual style of his work may be, then, Lang never loosens his grip.

In temperament, thematic interest and design, Lang is the pre-eminent *noir* director; but he never enjoyed the full Hollywood success of his compatriots Billy Wilder and Otto Preminger, who earned high reputations within the studio system, turning out films in a variety of styles that were commercially and often artistically successful. Lang seemed to be working more and more within the B category (*Human Desire* was released at the bottom of double bills), but in the long run his reputation has proved to be higher and more enduring than either Wilder's or Preminger's. All three direc-

tors, however, have received the kind of acknowledgment that Robert Siodmak, whose career parallels theirs, has not. At the end of the forties, after the initial phase of the *noir* cycle had ebbed, Siodmak had trouble finding work, and he returned to his native Germany, only rarely to be heard from again, and then with uncharacteristic film projects like *Custer of the West*. Was Siodmak so closely identified with *film noir* that he was unemployable once the genre had more or less run its course? From 1944 to 1949, in a remarkably brief span of time, he made nine memorable *films noirs*: *Phantom Lady*, *Christmas Holiday*, *The Suspect*, *The Dark Mirror*, *The Spiral Staircase*, *Criss Cross*, *The Killers*, *Cry of the City* and *The File on Thelma Jordan*.

Siodmak's work is notable for its physical and psychological compression; his characters, typically, are boxed into corners. The films have an edgy atmosphere, with less of Lang's directorial absoluteness and with a more flamboyant use of Germanic lighting and of Expressionistic transformations of physical reality. Some of the visual set-pieces in Siodmak are more striking than anything Lang would be likely to admit into his *noir* palette: the famous scene in the jazz club in *Phantom Lady*, for instance, where the extreme angles, sharp editing, and harsh lighting seem to be visual translations of the agitated music, and the climactic scene in *Christmas Holiday*, designed in the purest chiaroscuro, where the insane husband tries to kill his loyal masochistic wife. Lang's work is remarkable for its poise and detachment, its deadly irony; Siodmak's is at once less detached, and (except for *The Suspect*) less comic. Siodmak's visual range is greater than Lang's, the mood of his dramas generally more high-strung. Lang's stories are told in a linear fashion that parallels his simplified visual methods, whereas Siodmak films like *Christmas Holiday* and *The Killers* have an extremely intricate narrative development, their stories told in a series of fragmentary flashbacks, like boxes within boxes. In Siodmak, the past is often a maze that has to be penetrated, its mysteries uncovered only gradually, by means of a complex web of intersecting viewpoints.

The relative extremeness of Siodmak's style is reflected in his obsessive characters. The theme song of *Cry of the City* is "Never"; that of *Christmas Holiday*, "Always," warbled by a torch singer (Deanna Durbin) in love with a man (Gene Kelly) who has done her wrong. "Always" is an appropriate song for other Siodmak characters, too—like Swede in *The Killers*, for instance, who gives up after the woman he loves double-crosses him. Both these characters embrace their feelings of betrayal and abandonment, luxuriating in their bitterness. They don't want, or know how, to let go.

Sometimes, as in *Phantom Lady* or *Cry of the City*, the persistence of a Siodmak character leads to a positive outcome. In *Phantom Lady*, a secretary secretly enamored of her boss is determined to prove that he did not kill his wife, a crime for which he has been arrested. She sets out into the night-time city to track down the phantom lady, the nameless woman with whom her boss was out on the town the night his wife was killed. Showing the stubbornness that in-

fects most of Siodmak's characters, she moves ahead, donning a variety of masks, until she establishes her boss's innocence. In *Cry of the City*, a police lieutenant (Victor Mature) is determined to convict a wily criminal (Richard Conte) who is skillful in escaping his net. Relentless in his pursuit, the lieutenant, as Colin McArthur notes in *Underworld USA*, "hunts his quarry with an almost metaphysical hatred."

Siodmak's characters are nurtured by their obsessions. Their single-mindedness, their fierce grip on a hopeless love, give them a purpose and an identity; they desperately need their martyrdom to a usually lost cause.

Siodmak lets in more of the outside world than Lang does. Both *Cry of the City* and *Criss Cross* use real city streets as backgrounds; in both, there is a sense of a real city's tempo (New York in *Cry of the City*, Los Angeles in *Criss Cross*). Siodmak's cities, like his characters, seethe with unrest, promising imminent explosion.

Unlike Lang or Siodmak, Billy Wilder and Otto Preminger went on from their work in *film noir* to achieve true Hollywood celebrity. Both directors have enjoyed long, successful careers. After their early *noir* efforts, both turned, in the fifties and sixties, to other genres, Wilder to cynical, bittersweet comedies, Preminger to expensive epics. In his satires of American values and manners (*The Apartment*; *One, Two, Three*; *Kiss Me Stupid*; *The Fortune Cookie*), there are traces of Wilder's *noir* origins; in Preminger's elegantly constructed epics (*Exodus, In Harm's Way, The Cardinal*), there are virtually none.

Wilder's *noir* dramas contain the biting social comment, the stinging disapproval of the American way, that was to become his trademark. *Double Indemnity*, *The Lost Weekend*, *Sunset Boulevard*, and *Ace in the Hole* are all thrillers with a public focus. Lang and Siodmak concentrated on their characters; Wilder places his characters in a larger and more closely defined social context. His dramas are designed to make a telling social point, in a way that the claustrophobic work of Lang or Siodmak is not. Wilder sets out to attack his characters, setting them up, like the moralist he is, only in order to flay them for their shortcomings.

The Lost Weekend and *Ace in the Hole* blend *film noir* with social drama. The former is perhaps the most renowned of films about alcoholism; the latter is a fierce indictment of the sleazy practices of yellow journalism. *Double Indemnity* tells an archetypal *noir* story of passion and murder that contains a sly attack on American greed, as money rather than romance is the lure for the film's two conspirators. Wilder's stern disapproval of them makes them seem even nastier than the general run of *noir* villains. He treats their moral failings as representative of a generalized social condition—the film is a parable of American materialism gone sour.

Sunset Boulevard transfers *noir* psychology to a novel setting, the decaying mansion of a once-grand film star. Wilder's portrait of the megalomaniacal Norma Desmond (Gloria Swanson) is etched in acid; she is the embodiment of Hollywood's rotting foundations, its terminal narcissism, its isolation from reality. When Wilder returned, nearly thirty years later, in *Fedora*, to another study of a legendary screen star (the real-life model for Fedora was clearly Greta Garbo), his tone had softened; to Fedora, whose fate is equally as monstrous as that of Norma Desmond, he extended a measure of compassion. Set in lush Mediterranean villas, and filled with glowing sunlight, *Fedora* is a *film noir en couleur*. Like its famous forebear, it concerns the extortionate cost of fame, the crumbling of illusion, the depleting dependence of egocentric stars on their fawning public. In both films Wilder attacks the fabrications and deceits of the Hollywood system—biting the hand that feeds him, so to speak. But *Fedora* is a gentler film, the lingering backward look of an older man, himself a Hollywood monument, on the industry of illusion in which he has worked for more than half a century. *Fedora* has a generosity toward its protagonist that Wilder withholds from all his high *noir* characters, and certainly from Norma Desmond, the ultimate spider woman, a grotesque hibernating behind closed shutters in a swoon of alcohol and self-deception.

Hollywood, alcoholism, yellow journalism, the greed of the upwardly mobile American middle class—Wilder's *noir* pieces are themati-

A typically cool shot from Otto Preminger's elegant *Laura* (Gene Tierney and Dana Andrews).

cally ambitious, employing *noir* atmosphere to make cynical social statements. Since the fifties Wilder's work has retained the moralistic thrust of his earliest American work. He has remained a fierce satirist, excoriating people he disapproves of for the satirist's traditional purposes of correction and reform. Certainly Wilder has not been known for his amiability; his best work is hard, snappish, edged with stabbing humor. Although his later comedies echo the harsh tones of his *films noirs*, and although they are made with unfaltering control, for the most part they lack the visual elegance that distinguished his thrillers. Comedies like *The Apartment* or *One, Two, Three* are not much to look at. Their style is contained in the wit and the staccato pace of the dialogue (Wilder collaborates on most of his scripts with I.A.L. Diamond) and of the performers (James Cagney, Arlene Francis, Jack Lemmon, Shirley MacLaine).

Preminger's later work diverges even more

markedly than Wilder's from his *noir* origins. Of the four major emigré directors who earned their reputations in America in *noir*, Preminger's track record with the genre is by far the weakest. No Preminger *noir* has the authority of *Double Indemnity*, the concentrated power of *The Woman in the Window*, or the ominous atmosphere of *Phantom Lady*. Preminger's most successful *noir*, *Laura*, is nonetheless an elegant thriller, ripe with perverse sexual overtones, whereas his other genre entries—the lacklustre *Fallen Angel, Angel Face*, and *Where the Sidewalk Ends*—are disappointing. Preminger works best in an altogether different register. On such big films as *Exodus, Hurry Sundown*, and *Advise and Consent* (which have massive subjects like war, politics, religion, the founding of a modern nation), Preminger has a smooth, sweeping, and sometimes even majestic style. Compared to the flowing epic rhythm of *Exodus*, with its roving camera, its striking wide screen compositions and its handling of crowd scenes, a small-scale *film noir* by Preminger looks stiff. Preminger is most comfortable when his camera can explore wide open spaces as opposed to poking around a cramped *noir* environment; he thrives on the expansiveness and the essential objectivity of the epic frame. Preminger does, however, have a dryness and irony that serve *noir* well, and he has contributed two films that rate a high place in the genre's pantheon: *Laura*, one of the most popular thrillers of the forties; and an effective suspense drama, made long after *noir*'s heyday, the 1965 *Bunny Lake Is Missing*.

Laura is a cool piece of work, silken, remote, perhaps the most posh of all *films noirs*. From the opening shot, as the camera tracks discreetly through the swanky Manhattan penthouse of man-about-town Waldo Lydecker, the film has a powerful atmosphere of repressed sexuality. (*Laura* is set in the *haut monde* to which Preminger returns in his underrated *Bonjour Tristesse*—boredom and sexual dalliance among the rich attract him.) Except for Laura, the characters are unsavory. The twisted, possessive Waldo, who kills Laura (or thinks he kills her; that the victim is the wrong woman is the story's famous plot twist) because he fears he is losing her, is one of *noir*'s great psychopaths.

The crazed Pygmalion to Laura's Galatea, Waldo is played by Clifton Webb as an effete aristocrat. Whether consciously or not, Webb gives the character homosexual overtones, so that his obsession with Laura seems not entirely convincing, as if it's a cover-up.

Vincent Price plays a kept man, and like Webb, the actor has a prissy quality. The two of them seem like old-fashioned gay types, confirming in their bitchiness and superciliousness stereotyped popular notions of homosexual behavior. Their sexual uncertainty is here protected to some extent by the fashionable setting, as if the film-makers were counting on audiences' assumptions about how rich men are supposed to act. Price and Webb have some sharp exchanges; their tones are well-matched, which makes them a more likely pairing than Webb with Laura, or than Price with Laura's high society friend, played by Judith Anderson. Anderson's masculine presence completes the tone of sexual ambiguity that runs through the film. Playing a grande dame who keeps attractive young men, Anderson brings to the part her own natural assertiveness. Her deep authoritative voice emphasizes the character's dominating qualities, and her attempted control of Price echoes Waldo's "creation" of Laura. But her interest in Laura, while remaining implicit, is more convincing than her nominal attraction to the Price character.

The only "straight" characters are Laura and the detective (Dana Andrews) who investigates her "death." Even here there is an unhealthy undertone, as the detective is bewitched by Laura's portrait. He falls in love with a dead woman, or a woman he presumes is dead. Dead, she becomes an image of his ideal woman; alive, she is a person with a will of her own, and his enchantment diminishes.

The film's themes of sexual transference and obsession are presented obliquely, giving the drama a stealthy undercurrent. Preminger treats the loaded material quietly, in a matter-of-fact way. His fanciest touch is the visual linkage he makes between the detective and Laura's portrait, which hangs over the fireplace in her living room. Preminger works in a detached style, his camera for the most part maintaining a neutral distance from the actors. The film's un-inflected visual manner parallels the dry, reined-in performances: Gene Tierney and Dana Andrews look and sound like sleepwalkers; Clifton Webb, Vincent Price, and Judith Anderson introduce homosexual tints on the sly.

Except for the Chicago milieu in *The Man with the Golden Arm*, Preminger does not return to a *noir* mood until *Bunny Lake Is Missing*, which has all the razzle-dazzle, the visual high jinks, that he avoided in *Laura*. In this later thriller, Preminger uses the sweeping camera work he had developed for his epic subjects. The film is filled with visual bric-a-brac: an active camera, peering into corners and trundling through doors and up and down stairs; bizarre angles, and lighting from below which throws disfiguring shadows onto faces. A thriller about a missing little girl, who may or may not exist, the film is crammed with eccentrics: Martita Hunt as a daffy schoolmistress, Noel Coward as a surpassingly seedy landlord, and Carol Lynley and Keir Dullea—the Veronica Lake and Alan Ladd of the sixties—as the mysterious, icy-looking brother and sister who seem to have misplaced Bunny Lake. The only sane character in sight is the droll inspector, played by Laurence Olivier. The film has a dotty sense of humor that at times seems to betray the *noir*

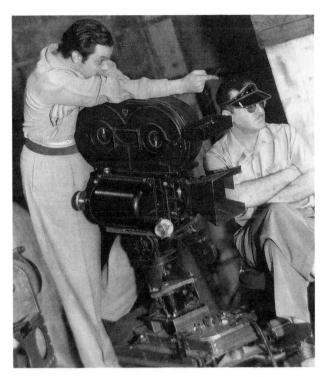

Orson Welles and his cinematographer Gregg Toland, on the set of *Citizen Kane*.

genre. It is both cranky and grandiose, and in its visual openness and fluency it indicates Preminger's essential discomfort with the claustrophobic style that dominated the forties cycle.

Noir intersected the careers of several major American directors. Some of these, starting out in the forties, did their strongest work in the *noir* mold; others went on to other kinds of films, retaining elements of style developed during their *noir* apprenticeship. In visual style and thematic concerns, *noir* had a strong impact on a wide range of American directors, from Orson Welles, Stanley Kubrick, Joseph Losey, Elia Kazan, Jules Dassin and Don Siegel to cult figures such as Nicholas Ray, Sam Fuller, Joseph H. Lewis and Phil Karlson. Although their work varies in quality, all of these directors have interesting and unusual temperaments; they are powerful visual stylists whose essentially dark sensibilities are well suited to *noir*'s brooding themes.

Of this roster of notable names, Orson Welles made the greatest contribution to *noir* stylistics. Welles' connection to *noir*, like his connection to

Glacial Carol Lynley and Keir Dullea, in Preminger's striking post-*noir film noir, Bunny Lake is Missing*.

virtually everything else in the history of American film, is that of bold innovator rather than intelligent follower. He is the only American director whose contribution to *noir* equals that of the German expatriates. Among its many other claims to landmark status, *Citizen Kane* also exerted an enormous influence on both the visual and narrative patterns which were to coalesce into the recognizable *noir* style.

Released in 1941, *Citizen Kane* appears at the head of the *noir* cycle, in the same year as *The Maltese Falcon*. Perhaps it, rather than Huston's thriller, should be considered the primal American *film noir*. *Kane*, of course, is not a crime film and thus stands apart from *noir* in this important respect; but in the way it tells its story, as well as in its visual idiom, the film contains many of the crucial elements that were to define *noir* technique. With its journalist assuming the role of the investigating detective, and its quest for the meaning of Rosebud substituting for the whodunit motif of the traditional murder thriller, *Kane* is constructed like a mystery. The film's

splintered structure—the divergent points of view of the people whom the journalist interviews, the interweaving of past and present, the series of flashbacks—anticipates the narrative labyrinths of many of the richest *films noirs*. And the film's celebrated compositions, in which the frame is divided into fragments of light and shadow, also clearly point toward *noir*. *Kane* was the first major American film steeped in the shadowy universe of the German Expressionists; like the Germans', Welles' infatuation with theatrical lighting is used to indicate the mysteries of personality: the film's shadows corroborate Kane's inner darkness. Welles' delight in exaggerated angles—the famous low angle shots which distort the characters' appearance—also became a standard part of *noir* syntax.

Although Kane is a titanic figure, a man of destiny, he is often placed within the frame in such a way as to suggest confinement and limitation. Low angle shots, which magnify Kane's physical stature (even in his twenties, Welles was of Falstaffian proportions), also contain ceilings

Meticulous Wellesian composition: deep focus, balance, Germanic lighting. (Ruth Warrick, Ray Collins, Dorothy Comingore, and Orson Welles, in *Citizen Kane*.)

Many elements of Welles' *mise en scène* in *Citizen Kane*—such as low angles with ceilings and high contrast lighting—became regular features of the *noir* style.

which seem to weigh down on the character and to diminish him. Cutting him down to size, the low ceilings provide an ironic counterpoint to Kane's dominant personality. In the cavernous rooms of his mansion, the character is overwhelmed by his environment, framed by a door in the rear of the image, for instance, as if he is a wax figure on display. Welles' careful placement of all his actors within the frame restricts their freedom; they seem to move only at the director's bidding, and the orchestration, together with the pervasive images of visual entrapment, gives the film the claustrophobic quality of the *noir* thrillers that follow.

Welles is clearly indebted to German Expressionism, but he avoids its extreme stylization, eliminating abstract settings, exaggerated acting, and nightmarish distensions of time and space. More stylized than the average American film—than *any* major studio American film up to this time—*Kane* is not a dream film, altogether remote from a recognizable world. Welles is careful to balance Expressionist elements with techniques such as depth of field, the long take, and overlapping dialogue which enforce a sense of reality.

When Welles later made films that were clearly in the *noir* vein, he was returning to a style his own seminal work had helped to forge. Thus, *The Lady from Shanghai* in 1947 and *Touch of Evil* eleven years later are unmistakably by the same man who had directed *Citizen Kane*. These two full-fledged *noir* dramas fall short of *Kane*, but Welles treats them in the same bravura style. Welles used a *noir* style for nearly everything he worked on, refracting both Kafka and Shakespeare, for instance, through a *noir* prism. His versions of *The Trial*, and of *Macbeth* and *Othello*, have the feel of *film noir* in their calculated imagery of nightmare and entrapment, their delirious angles, their bizarre settings and circumambient shadows.

Welles is the most exuberant of all directors drawn to *noir*. Temperamentally, he sits at the opposite end of the *noir* spectrum from Fritz Lang. But his work shares many similarities with Lang's. Welles has a nostalgic streak, a longing for an idyllic past (a prominent motif in both *Kane* and *The Magnificent Ambersons*) that

the dour Lang does not reveal; but beneath the sentimental echoes and the stylistic pyrotechnics, Welles' vision is as dark as Lang's. Welles is drawn to powerful and power-seeking figures like Kane, Macbeth, Mr. Arkadin, the sheriff in *Touch of Evil*. But his men of destiny are ultimately defeated by destiny, cut down by the very excesses of personality that elevated them to positions of power. Kane ends up a hollow, defeated man, alone in his fortress, yearning for a long-vanished innocence, and puzzled about the meaning of his accomplishment. The character's dissolution is vividly shown in the scene where he walks through his castle in a daze, after his second wife has left him, his stooped frame reflected in a huge mirror in an infinitely regressive series of images. None of Welles' larger-than-life heroes survives. Like most *noir* protagonists, they are overwhelmed by a combination of forces, their own deficiencies of character magnified by the impact of a battering and merciless fate.

Welles' vision is as doom-ridden as Lang's. Almost the only "happy" ending in Welles' work is the one in *The Lady from Shanghai*, where the narrator, who has been victimized by a beautiful woman, escapes with his life. Surely it is no accident that this one character of Welles' who survives is the most modest and gentle protagonist in the Welles canon, the one character who does not challenge the order of the universe.

In visual style, Welles is certainly more athletic and extroverted than Lang, but both directors control reality, shaping it to their own preordained aims. Sharply curtailing the randomness of the real world, both men adopt a stance of God-like omnipotence over the worlds they mold on film. The pre-eminent American director of *noir*, Welles is the most flamboyant of *noir* stylists. But beneath the self-intoxication of his celebrated bravura manner, he is transfixed by themes of despair and defeat.

Welles continued to use low angle compositions throughout his career, as evidenced in this shot. (Tony Perkins and Madeleine Robinson, in *The Trial*.)

A Welles deep focus shot. (Charlton Heston and Welles, in *Touch of Evil*.)

Dassin, Losey, Ray, and Kazan began their careers in the late forties after the revolutionary visual and narrative style of *Citizen Kane* had been fully absorbed by *noir*. Losey and Dassin reversed the history of the German directors by becoming expatriates. To escape the blacklist, Losey settled in England; Dassin moved from France to Greece. Except for brief visits, neither has returned to America. Losey achieved his greatest success in his collaborations with Harold Pinter, Dassin his greatest notoriety (though not his highest achievement) in his films with his wife, Melina Mercouri. Unaffected by the blacklist (Kazan was a cooperative witness), Kazan and Ray remained in Hollywood. *Noir* was an ideal testing ground for all four directors, and the variety of their offerings, both texturally and thematically, is decisive proof against the argument that *films noirs* are all alike.

Ray and Losey served their apprenticeship at RKO, a studio particularly receptive to *noir*

films. Both made a number of movies, in the late forties and early fifties, which were either fully or marginally *noir*—odd, personal pieces that announced their stubborn and non-conformist temperaments. The two strong-willed men adjusted the *noir* idiom to their own ends, offering variations on what had become, by 1947—the year of their debut as film directors—generic conventions.

Ray's two most notable dark films, *They Live By Night* and *On Dangerous Ground*, defy traditional *noir* motifs. Both films are shot through with a sentimentality and romanticism that represent a daring reversal of the characteristic *noir* tone. The close-up of the two lovers which opens *They Live By Night*, and the lush musical theme are radical departures from the urban vistas with their thrusting skyscrapers blazing in the night sky and the cacophonous jazz that customarily announce the *film noir*. Ray's fugitive lovers are fragile and less neurotic than the usual couple-on-the-run: compare Ray's outlaws to the psychopathic couple in *Gun Crazy*. Ray's characters really care for each other, and an undercurrent throughout the film is the suggestion that Bowie (Farley Granger) and Keechie (Cathy O'Donnell) would be an ideal average pair if only Bowie had not been born to a life of crime. Scenes of the two dancing at a nightclub, walking in the park, celebrating Keechie's pregnancy, and the last, lingering close-up on Keechie, recording her stunned reaction to Bowie's death, have a strongly sentimental flavor. The film's bittersweet, rueful tone, which sets it apart from any other *noir* drama, is supported by shrewd casting. Farley Granger and Cathy O'Donnell do not fit the *noir* stereotypes of hardened criminal and tough moll; they are young innocents caught, as the opening states, in a world they did not create. They are adrift in alien territory. Bowie is obviously ill-suited to a life of crime, even though that is the only kind of life he has known; and Keechie is drawn into his world because of her feelings for him. They are too weak to break out of the mold that has been set for them by their elders. Granger's fresh-faced, juvenile lead ingenuousness, ironically at odds with the cutthroat gang leader the newspapers and radio bulletins report him to be, and O'Donnell's sweetness and stillness, make them unique outlaws in the crime film canon.

Another element of the film that sets it apart from the *noir* mainstream is its rural environment. The action takes place entirely in the country, on the open road or in small towns. A leitmotif throughout the film is a high angle moving shot of the runaways' car on the open highway. Visually, the shot is more panoramic than almost anything else in *noir*, yet its insistent repetition suggests enclosure, as if the speeding car is hurtling the characters to their doom.

Ray also uses a rural setting for the unusual *On Dangerous Ground*. Here, a country landscape—snow-covered, isolated, coldly beautiful—provides a startling contrast to the festering city in which the film opens. The film's protagonist is a policeman on the verge of a crack-up; the pressures of his job, and of the tough city environment in which he must func-

tion, have pushed him beyond the point of endurance, releasing his latent capacity for violence. Ordered to go for a rest in the country, he becomes involved in a different kind of criminal case, at the end of which he is a man transformed. The country people he gets to know, a blind woman and her troubled younger brother, soften him, and in the course of his country exile he gradually sheds the city-based manner of a psychotic tough. Reversing *noir's* usual interest in dramatizing defeat, this story of emotional renewal is even more sentimental than *They Live By Night*. Ray dares to make corny *films noirs* that celebrate the healing powers of romantic love.

Cutting across several different genres, Ray's subsequent work maintains a remarkable thematic consistency. Most of his pictures—*Rebel Without a Cause, Wind Across the Everglades, Johnny Guitar*—are about outsiders and rebels; the Ray hero does not fit into the pattern of an established community. *Noir* encouraged the director's preoccupation with loners, and with hostile, conformity-ridden groups. The genre, though, was not simply a launching point for Ray, a prelude to later achievement, because his earliest work is among his strongest: his essential style was full-grown at the very beginning of his career, with *They Live By Night*.

Noir proved for Jules Dassin, as it had for Ray, the inspiration for his strongest work: *The Naked City, Brute Force, Thieves' Highway,* and *Night and the City*. Although Ray's work does not show steady growth (his last film was the lacklustre and uncharacteristic *55 Days at Peking*), it still has a marked continuity, with remnants of *noir* visible in nearly all his films, whereas Dassin's career has dramatic changes, in quality as well as style. After he left America, Dassin seemed to be a director without a country. Even in his *films noirs*, though, Dassin was a chameleon as he moved from the predominant Neo-Realism of *The Naked City* to the intense Expressionism of *Night and the City*. At both ends of the *noir* spectrum, however, he works with a tautness and intensity not evident in most of his later films. New York in *The Naked City*, London in *Night and the City*, and the prison in *Brute Force* are powerfully rendered backgrounds which reflect the entrapment of the films' heroes. In its hyperactive transmutations of London into a web of alleys and underground dens, its fevered chiaroscuro, its angular, fragmented images, and in Richard Widmark's bravura performance of a born loser—"an artist without an art," another character calls him, in a memorable phrase—*Night and the City* may well be the definitive *film noir*. (Borde and Chaumeton chose a picture of Widmark, glassy-eyed, frightened, a cigarette dangling from his lips, for the cover of their pioneer study of *noir*.)

Dassin's crime films have terrific energy not evident in his later work after he begins to use Melina Mercouri and when, starting with *He Who Must Die*, he is drawn to allegories. When Dassin casts himself as a collaborator on Christian and classical myths, as in *Phaedra, He Who Must Die,* and *A Dream of Passion*, his work turns arty and bloated. Early on in his peripatetic career, when he made *Rififi* in France in the mid-fifties, he drew on his experience in *noir*; and his expertly constructed drama of a bank heist is cited by Borde and Chaumeton as the only pure example of *film noir* in France. But a later return to America, and to *noir* terrain, with an updated version of *The Informer (Up Tight,* 1968) set in a Chicago slum, lacked the bite for which Dassin had been noted twenty years before. Dassin's four vivid *films noirs* remain high points from which the rest of his career represents a curious falling away.

Joseph Losey's history has geographic and political parallels with Dassin's. But unlike Dassin, Losey's *films noirs* do not represent his best work. For Losey, in a way that was not true for either Ray or Dassin, *film noir* served primarily as an apprenticeship, and his achievement in the genre was only an anticipation of mature works like *The Servant, Accident, Mr. Klein,* and the supreme *The Go-Between*. Losey came to his first film assignments from a background in political theatre; in the thirties, he worked for the Federal Theatre on several Living Newspaper dramas, and in 1947 he directed the world premiere of Brecht's *Galileo* with Charles Laughton. He approached his first films with an earnest social consciousness derived from his left-wing associations. *The Boy with Green Hair,*

Jules Dassin on the set of his two best pictures, both exemplary *films noirs, Night and the City* and *The Naked City (opposite)*.

The Dividing Line, M and *The Prowler* are *films noirs* with a distinct social thrust; they are thrillers that assault the status quo and that, in the kinds of emblematic American communities they portray, contain references to the contemporary witchhunt for communists. The protagonists of *The Boy with Green Hair, The Dividing Line* and *M* are social outcasts tracked mercilessly by a community of bigots which cannot tolerate any departure from a bland norm. *The Boy with Green Hair* is an antiwar fable whose real focus is an indictment of small-town narrow-mindedness, the profound inability of the rigidly conformist town to accept difference. The boy's green hair outrages the town fathers in the same way that the presence among them of a communist or a homosexual or a Jew would; in order to preserve its purity, the WASP community must expel the boy.

The hero of *The Dividing Line* is a victim of

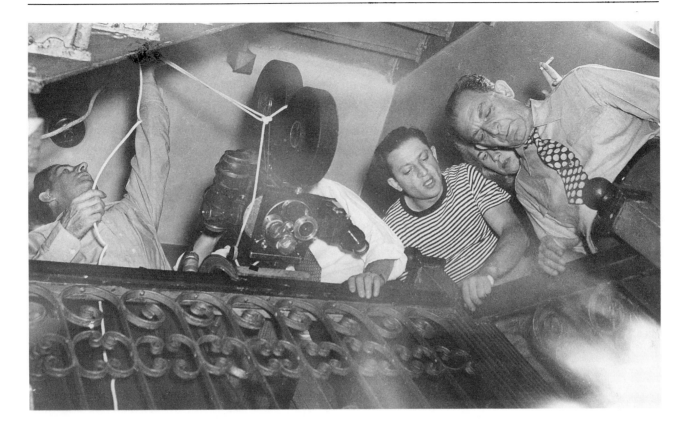

racial prejudice—the "line" of the title separates the white part of town from the Mexican ghetto. Through a chain of unhappy circumstances, the protagonist is accused of both rape and murder, and forced to run for his life from a mob of wrathful whites. In its social analysis and political sympathies, the film is far too pat; but it is nonetheless an interesting experiment in adapting the *noir* manhunt theme to an explicit social purpose.

M and *The Prowler* are less schematic than either of Losey's earlier pamphleteering statements, although here too *noir* conventions are brushed with social overtones. *M* adapts the story of Lang's classic German film to a dilapidated downtown Los Angeles, where it does not entirely work: the underground criminal network that seemed so natural a part of the shadowy, studio-built German city is an alien presence in Los Angeles, even in the rotting, colorful Bunker Hill section (since torn down) that Losey uses. To avoid obvious echoes of Peter Lorre, Losey chose the quintessentially

middle American and sympathetic David Wayne to play the child-murderer. Losey wanted to stress the fact that the character needs to be helped rather than prosecuted, and he harnesses the material's thriller elements—the efforts of the police and the gang to track down the child-murderer—to a final plea for greater understanding of the mentally disabled.

A story of greed and passion leading to murder, *The Prowler* is closer to *noir* conventions than any of Losey's other early work. Recalling Cain's *Double Indemnity* and *The Postman Always Rings Twice*, it concerns an extramarital affair—in this case, between a rapacious cop and a bored housewife—which leads to crime. Yet there are variations on this standard *noir* theme: the wife is far from the lethal spider woman of the Cain mold, the man is the aggressor here, and he plans to murder the woman's husband without her knowledge or approval. Sympathetic and sexual, the woman is a rare *noir* character. Because she wants a child her impotent husband cannot give her, she allows herself to be seduced

Typically claustrophobic *noir* framing, in this studied shot from Joseph Losey's first-rate *The Prowler*. Peering in through the window, the policeman (Van Heflin) is visually identified as both an outsider and a voyeur.

by the fast-talking policeman, the prowler of the title. At the end, after she has discovered her lover's treachery, she bears his child in a remote desert cabin where the couple hide out to escape social censure. The desert setting, the child motif, the woman's aching loneliness, the implicit criticism of the crooked cop's lust for status and money, for the trappings of the American Dream, that runs throughout the film—these elements attest to the freshness and originality of Losey's vision.

From the early fifties, when he was forced to leave Hollywood, to the early sixties, when he collaborated with Harold Pinter on *The Servant*, Losey was demoted from a promising director of American thrillers to a modest status in the British film industry. During these lean years, when he was offered a series of routine melodramas (all with *noir* overtones), Losey continued to create closed worlds on film and to explore settings for symbolic reinforcement of character and theme. As he developed and mas-

tered a taut style, he never forgot his *noir* training. Almost all his films are variations of *noir* themes of enclosure and paranoia: his settings (the houses in *The Servant, Secret Ceremony, Boom*) continue to evoke *noir* isolation in their separateness from an outside world. The recent *Mr. Klein* is directed with a steely control that proclaims Losey's indebtedness to the closed, clammy *noir* vision.

For Kazan, as for Losey, *noir* was a prelude to greater achievement. Kazan directed two notable *noir* thrillers, both in the semi-documentary style popular in the late forties. *Boomerang* and *Panic in the Streets*, both filmed on location, concern manhunts, and are filled with moody lighting and studied compositions that invest the real city settings (a small town in Connecticut in *Boomerang*, New Orleans in *Panic in the Streets*) with Expressionist intensity. Kazan presents New Orleans as steamy and exotic, a hothouse of sex and violence that looks like the perfect setting for *A Streetcar Named*

Elia Kazan introduced elements of lighting and composition used on his early *films noirs* into non-*noir* dramas like *A Streetcar Named Desire* (with Vivien Leigh and Karl Malden) and *On the Waterfront* (with Marlon Brando and Eva Marie Saint).

Desire, the film Kazan directed in 1951, a year after *Panic in the Streets*. Like *Streetcar*, later Kazan films such as *On the Waterfront, East of Eden,* and *Baby Doll* have vestiges of *noir* visual style in their high contrast lighting, their smoky environments, their scrutinizing close-ups, their occasional odd camera placement (the tilts in *East of Eden*, for instance, that punctuate the father-son confrontations). But Kazan is finally too impassioned for the somnambulist *noir* style; he is too exuberant to be contained for long within the *noir* frame and world view. Pushing his performers into emotional explosions, Kazan is more comfortable with the heady mix of sex and poetry in the plays of Tennessee Williams than he is with the taut, measured rhythms of the typical *noir* screenplay.

Kazan is a romantic, and his best films, which have heroes who overcome obstacles and which usually end in some kind of emotional resolution, are essentially optimistic and therefore anti-*noir*. The bravura acting—triumphs of Actors Studio naturalism—in Kazan's richest and most characteristic work violates the containment of the hard-boiled manner. Kazan ranks among the greatest directors of actors in American films, but within the *noir* canon he is a marginal figure.

Films noirs were low-budget and therefore often considered, by both studios and exhibitors, to be B entries. Although they were often the best work that the studios were producing, the front offices did not think of the crime dramas as warranting major promotion efforts, and most of them were given a modest release. Some directors, like Kazan and Losey, who began their careers on *noir* dramas, went on to projects that were clearly A in both budget and prestige, while other directors, who had no interest in or pretensions to "class," flourished at the B level, in the Hollywood equivalent of the pulp jungle. B directors like Sam Fuller, Joseph H. Lewis, and Phil Karlson worked in a variety of genres, turning out programmers to fill in the slots at the bottom of double bills, though it was primarily their *films noirs* that have earned them their cult reputations. *Noir* tapped their own dark sensibilities, releasing images that are

among the quirkiest in the American cinema. Their *films noirs* are stories of misfits, and of criminal corruption, presented in idiosyncratic styles. The work of directors like Fuller and Lewis was relegated even lower in the studio pecking order than a Siodmak (which might boast Stanwyck or Laughton as its star) or a Lang. They were clearly second-feature directors handed scripts from the bottom of the barrel. As a matter of routine, they were given B unit crews and actors. And yet it is precisely in the tension set up between the half-baked scripts and the pulp directors' genuine feeling for the medium that their work achieves its vitality, its eccentric signature. The formulaic scripts permitted a maximum of directorial intervention; and it was with the delighted discovery of the kind of personal stamp that low-class, high-strung directors were able to give their work that French critics began their celebration of the American B film and their formulation of the *auteur* theory. *Films noirs* by Fuller and Lewis were thus primary examples, cited by adulatory French critics, in substantiating the validity of the *politique des auteurs*.

Sam Fuller is probably the kinkiest of all B *auteurs*. Chronologically, he entered the *noir* field at a late date, well after the cycle had reached its post-war maturity. His most powerful *noir* is *Pickup on South Street*, released in 1953. Making his movies when and how he wanted to, Fuller produced three notable post-*noir films noirs*: *Underworld USA* (1960); *Shock Corridor* (1963); and the notorious *Naked Kiss* (1965). In their freewheeling approach to genre conventions, the films are all characteristic of Fuller's work.

Pickup on South Street is an especially ripe example of Fuller's methods. The basic story line, involving a search for a valuable object, is standard, recalling the archetypal pattern of *The Maltese Falcon*. In this case, the prized possession is a document containing atomic symbols which spies are attempting to smuggle to the Russians—this allows Fuller an excuse to embroider the thriller frame with some typically wacky right-wing Americanism. Fuller also bends *noir* formulae in his treatment of characters. Its political simple-mindedness aside, the film shows

The tilted angle in this shot from *Pickup on South Street* (with Jean Peters and Richard Widmark) captures the tension and energy that are hallmarks of Samuel Fuller's direction.

real affection for its leading players: a petty thief conscripted into patriotic action (Richard Widmark); a near-prostitute who is an innocent messenger (Jean Peters); and, most of all, a streetwise woman who earns her living as an informer (Thelma Ritter). Fuller endows these people, who live on the margins of the city, with greater human dimension than is usual in *noir*. Compared to such *noir* landmarks as *Double Indemnity* and *The Woman in the Window*, *Pickup on South Street* is a warm-hearted film. Perhaps the peak moment is Thelma Ritter's death scene. Fuller holds the camera on her as she reminisces about her life on the streets, defining her code of honor in a way that recalls Sam Spade summing up his ethic to Brigid O'Shaughnessy. Fuller is unusually generous as he keeps his camera in place for the long and frankly sentimental scene, an odd touch in a film noted for its speed and energy.

Fuller's athletic camerawork also counters

noir convention. The film is almost constantly in motion, as the camera nervously tries to keep abreast of the action with a series of jiggling tracking and crane shots. The pattern of the movement differs from the utterly controlled methods of Lang or Wilder. Fuller seems to work from a spontaneous impulse, and the location shooting has a sense of improvisation, an immediacy, that separates it from the directorial calculation typical of *noir*. Scenes on the subway, and a climactic shootout on a subway platform, place the action in a palpably real environment: New York in the summer, an inferno of waterfront dives and steamy, crowded streets. The emphatic local color is carried over into the dialogue, which is packed with underworld lingo. *Pickup on South Street* is a brilliant example of the way an idiosyncratic director can redeem ordinary material. Out of a sub-*noir* story, Fuller has fashioned a punchy valentine to the big city underworld, with petty hoods and bag-lady informers stirred to their finest hour as they vanquish the communist threat.

Everything that Fuller touched, whether it was a war story or a western or a deep-sea adventure, he stamped with his own unmistakable signature, with a raw energy that animates his crude reactionary themes. It is not possible to talk of Fuller's career in terms of progression or decline because his cranky, kinetic style is as apparent in his first film, *I Shot Jesse James* (1949), as in one of his most recent, the vividly-titled *Dead Pigeon on Beethoven Street* (1975). Fuller is a law unto himself, Hollywood's great primitive, whose *films noirs*, true to form, are not quite the same as anyone else's.

The careers of Joseph H. Lewis and Phil Karlson do not exhibit the same consistency or the same stubborn individuality as Fuller's. Neither managed entirely to overcome the burdens of shoddy formula scripts, or to forge a strong personal style, until *noir* assignments offered them visual and thematic challenges. Lewis's breakthrough came in 1946, with the distinctly lower-case but visually arresting *So Dark the Night*; Karlson's, in the fifties, with *Kansas City Confidential* and *The Phenix City Story*.

So Dark the Night is an ideal example of the opportunities for visual expressiveness which *noir* offers. The film is about a high-powered detective forced by his boss to take a vacation. Trouble follows the detective. A young woman he meets during his country holiday is murdered, and the detective launches a characteristically intense investigation. Early on, we realize that he is looking for himself. Lewis presents this absorbing but hardly unusual study of schizophrenia with a calculated visual design, the character's psychological schism telegraphed through a series of mirror shots and reflections as well as a consistent frames-within-the-frame motif. Space is broken up by doors, windows, beams, railings, bars, low ceilings. Visually trapped within the image, the detective never occupies space that is open and clear; he is pushed into the frame, photographed behind windows and doors, as space seems to close in on him. This sense of encumbrance is magnified

Mise en scène in the films of Joseph H. Lewis emphasizes the physical entrapment of his characters: Nina Foch framed behind a barred window, in *My Name is Julia Ross*; Peggy Cummins and John Dall, at the rear of a claustrophobic diner with slanted walls that seem to be closing in on them, in *Gun Crazy (opposite)*.

as he comes closer to confronting his doubleness. The way Lewis presents a tormented, self-divided character is certainly not original, but it reveals a genuine flair for telling a story through visual means.

More adaptable than Fuller, Lewis shifts his own style to accommodate the style of his characters and their setting. The detective in *So Dark the Night*, on the surface, is sedate and implacable, a man of absolutely sober deportment; and the film's own measured manner echoes the character's. The fugitive couple in *Gun Crazy* have a very different rhythm. The woman, who goads the man into a life of crime, is wildly impulsive, forever on the run; to capture her

essential spirit, Lewis adopts a more expansive style than the one he used for the earlier film. He gives *Gun Crazy* a nervous, jagged movement.

After *Gun Crazy*, the flexible director returned to routine B work, where he remained for the rest of his career. Lewis clearly lacks Fuller's scrappy individuality, but he certainly knew how to enhance underdone scripts. And when, for once in his career, with *Gun Crazy*, he was given a script that demanded little directorial embroidery, he made a true genre classic in an unforced, masterly style.

Phil Karlson had somewhat better luck than Lewis. He began in the same bottom-rung position, forced to churn out a string of commodity entertainments. He served an undistinguished apprenticeship until, with *Kansas City Confidential* in 1952, he stepped out of the factory line-up to show the kind of directorial presence of which cults are made. Karlson's *noir* style, unlike Fuller's or Lewis's, has documentary overtones; he

works best on exposés of criminal corruption (*Phenix City Story*, *Walking Tall*) which pretend to a kind of cinematic journalism in their hard-headed, crusading manner. *Phenix City Story* begins, unforgettably, with a series of interviews by Los Angeles newscaster Clete Roberts with real people who experienced the crime wave that inundated their town. The interviews give the film the stamp of journalistic immediacy. In his strongest dramas, Karlson's style is crisp, alert, seemingly objective. As he has risen in the studio ranks, though, Karlson has eliminated a knottiness that gave his pieces of the fifties an added jolt. Made on an A budget, *Walking Tall* is a smoother and much less forceful portrait of mob rule than *Phenix City Story*. Both films reflect Karlson's right-wing belief in countering violence with greater violence. Like Fuller, he is a true political reactionary who responds to crime as a stain on the American landscape. Karlson has a vigilante mentality. In

Phenix City Story, he creates an environment of true horror in which decent family people are victimized by a ruthless, anonymous mob force. Karlson constructs such a powerful case against the syndicate that the unleashing of vigilante ferocity seems an inevitable and even defensible reaction.

Don Siegel's career parallels Karlson's, but his promotion from B to A status, with a string of hits starring Clint Eastwood, has proven more decisive and enduring. Like Karlson, Siegel has untied the knots from his style as he has moved up in the studio hierarchy. In early films like *Riot in Cell Block 11* and *The Lineup*, Siegel was a nervy and self-conscious stylist; in later films like *Escape from Alcatraz* he is an immaculate craftsman turning out smooth popular thrillers. *The Lineup* is a fast-paced action drama, with one of the great *noir* psychopaths as its central character, the amoral idiotic killer named Dancer (played by Eli Wallach with a wicked gleam in his eye). Siegel has retained his interest in psychotic characters (as in the brilliant and underrated *The Beguiled*, in which Clint Eastwood is a wounded Confederate soldier held prisoner in a house of hysterical women). But the gothic traces in his work, and the attraction to bizarre personalities, have been steadily reduced as Siegel has become a more bankable director. It is no accident that poker-faced, tight-lipped Clint Eastwood, the hard-boiled hero of the seventies, is Siegel's favorite actor. In his archetypal role as Dirty Harry, Eastwood is a cop who flaunts the law in order to conquer evil; the character thus fulfills the vigilante urge announced in Karlson's work with more efficiency than any Karlson hero would be likely to manage. In concentrating on Dirty Harry and his successors, Siegel shifted his focus from the psychotic *noir* villain to the figure of the loner cop who also lives on the edges of society but who is working nonetheless to uphold rather than to subvert its structure.

Eastwood is a good film actor who communicates through a minimum of means and who invariably plays private characters. "What was your childhood like?" asks a fellow inmate of the Eastwood loner in *Escape from Alcatraz*. "Short," he snaps back with characteristic terseness. Eastwood is a man of few words and much action. Over the years he has refined his style in a way that matches Siegel's—both work now with absolute assurance and economy. Their collaboration is probably the closest equivalent in current Hollywood film-making to the hard-boiled style of the forties. Both Siegel and Eastwood have the kind of control, the leanness, the self-consciously masculine pose that Hemingway and other writers and performers of the tough guy school were aiming for. Siegel's A budget crime dramas in color (*Madigan, Dirty Harry, The Killers, Coogan's Bluff*) represent an updating of *noir*, though they have a visual smoothness that was never a part of the forties cycle. Siegel's eye for the eccentric detail which transforms reality (as in *The Lineup*) all but disappears in the blandly rendered location settings of his recent work. As he has gained in status and technical assurance, Siegel has become a less flavorful director than he was in the beginning of his career, when he made tough, energetic, lopsided stories of dangerous loners.

Among directors who "rose" from *noir* to prestige projects, Stanley Kubrick made the most astounding leap. His early thrillers—*Killer's Kiss* (1955) and *The Killing* (1956)—are so self-consciously steeped in *noir* conventions that they look like an anthology of genre stylistics.

The Killing, a brilliantly paced story about a racetrack robbery, is the work of a professional filmmaker; *Killer's Kiss*, that of a talented amateur. In story and visual style, the latter is almost a parody of *noir* motifs. Its down-and-out hero is a boxer (that recurrent occupation of the *noir* loner) who becomes involved with a woman who lives across the courtyard. She is trying to break away from her psychopathically jealous lover, who tries to kill the hero—but the lover's henchmen corner the wrong man. The film concludes with the obligatory chase through off-beat urban settings. Clearly derived from other movies rather than from life, *Killer's Kiss* has a ready-made, hand-me-down quality.

Visually if not thematically, the film is rewarding. With the eye of a born film-maker, Kubrick effectively captures an atmosphere of urban seediness. The film's settings are carefully

Don Siegel graduated from low-budget thrillers like *The Lineup* (Eli Wallach, with gun, on an unfinished highway in San Francisco) to A budget projects like *Dirty Harry* (Clint Eastwood and Andy Robinson) which retain remnants of the director's original *noir* style.

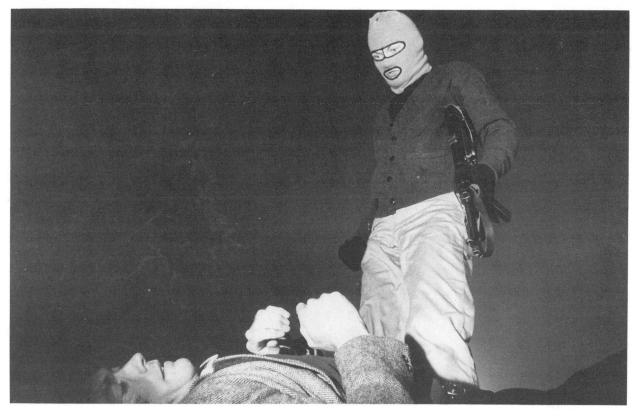

The schizophrenic Hitchcock criminal: Robert Walker, at home, and *(below)*, about to commit murder, in *Strangers on a Train*.

chosen: a shabby Bronx apartment house where the hero and heroine peer at each other through their facing windows, a smoky gym where the boxer trains, a dance hall where the heroine works, a bizarre mannikin factory where a climactic fight is staged, the old Pennsylvania station where the film begins and ends. True to *noir* tradition, the story begins at the end, and is told in a flashback, with the beleaguered hero serving as the narrator of his own downfall. Kubrick's settings and *mise en scène* reinforce the aura of defeat that trails the down-at-heels hero as the director frames his character through windows or places him against the intricate, prison-like architectural details of the old Penn Station.

Regardless of genre, all the director's later films have the kind of control, the manipulation of reality, that is typical of the *noir* thriller—his work remains as calculated as his two early crime dramas. *2001: A Space Odyssey*, his greatest achievement, is a long way from the small-scale canvas of *noir*, but it shares with *noir* a bleak vision of human destiny, a sense of man as the victim of forces he is unable to control, and a style of complete detachment. Both the theme and the style of *2001* stress pre-ordainment: Kubrick's commanding control is as absolute as the monolith's power over human destiny.

Noir proved an appropriate training ground for Kubrick. And in the classically immature and embryonic *Killer's Kiss*, Kubrick's essential qualities are on full display: his interest in enclosure and entrapment, as a visual style and as a theme; his tight control over all elements of the *mise en scène*; his emotional detachment.

Since he is neither a German expatriate with a penchant for Expressionism nor an idiosyncratic American, Alfred Hitchcock, the most renowned director of thrillers, does not belong to any group prominently associated with *noir*. Hitchcock, in fact, is seldom labeled as a *noir* director—certainly he is not linked with the genre to the same degree as Fritz Lang or Robert Siodmak or early Jules Dassin. And yet, as he continued working in that narrow vein of the thriller that he has made distinctly his own,

Hitchcock is pre-eminently a *noir* stylist: *Shadow of a Doubt, Rope, Spellbound, The Paradine Case, Strangers on a Train, I Confess, Rear Window, The Wrong Man, Vertigo,* and *Psycho*, are richly, demonstrably *noir*.

Like the traditional *noir* director, Hitchcock maintains a decided distance from his characters, looking down on them as they become entangled in the nets he carefully spreads. His typical posture is one of amusement—what fools these mortals be—as he masterminds the often catastrophic fates that confound his protagonists. Awful things happen to them—the Hitchcockian world is a series of traps for unsuspecting victims. Like Lang and his compatriots, Hitchcock watches dispassionately, though with more deadpan humor than the Germans could summon, as a terrible pre-ordained destiny overtakes his characters. That same dry humor and unflappable detachment, that same deadly matter-of-factness (part of Hitchcock's familiar persona of a droll, imperturbable Englishman) are present everywhere in the films.

Two neurotically fixated Hitchcock heroes: *(above)* Gregory Peck with Ingrid Bergman in *Spellbound*; James Stewart with Kim Novak *(page 141)*, in *Vertigo*.

The director is attracted to stories in which average people are undone. In his films, the normal waking world is covered with quicksand; sometimes a character's fall is occasioned merely by grisly coincidence—the "wrong man" theme that appeals to Hitchcock's nasty and mordant sense of humor. Sometimes a character conspires in his own undoing rather than being the passive recipient of a malevolent fate. Many of his characters are victims of circumstance, like the unlucky musician in *The Wrong Man* who is accused of a series of crimes because, as it turns out, he has the ill-fortune to resemble the real criminal. Through this chance fact, his routine life is brutally disrupted: he is thrown in jail; his wife has a nervous breakdown. The priest in *I Confess* is implicated in a murder. Circumstantial evidence points overwhelmingly to his guilt, yet he cannot reveal the real murderer who confessed his crime to him in church because to do so would betray his priestly vows.

It is always dangerous for Hitchcock's characters to step beyond normal boundaries. When the tempted secretary in *Psycho*, a model of cheerfulness and efficiency, decides to steal money from her boss, she becomes a doomed character. In Hitchcock, to borrow Robin Wood's useful formulation, the night world often invades and gradually overtakes the day world; dark forces penetrate the most seemingly ordinary characters and settings. In *Rope*, a dead body is buried in a casket the two murderers use as a table on which to serve their dinner guests. The elegant apartment setting, with a view of the Manhattan skyline, seems an incongruous context for a pathological crime. The bland small town, the acme of *Saturday Evening Post* Americana, that harbors the Merry Widow murderer in *Shadow of a Doubt*, the courtyard in *Rear Window*, the peaceful Northern California community in *The Birds*, are all atypical backgrounds for dark deeds. The eruption of crime in a seemingly innocuous setting—the gunshot that interrupts the concert in *The Man Who Knew Too Much*—is one of the manifestations of Hitchcock's sardonic humor.

The recurrent violence that disturbs outwardly calm settings parallels Hitchcock's belief that we are all potential criminals, that lying in wait, beneath our civilized masks, is a dark, leering, other self. Many of Hitchcock's characters are therefore seen in a kind of double focus, as variations in a variety of keys on the Dr. Jekyll-Mr. Hyde formula, with Norman Bates the most dramatic example in the canon: a pleasant repressed young man on the surface, a sex maniac within. Psychological as well as visual doubleness echoes throughout the films. The doubleness within is often mirrored in an external way, as one character takes on the qualities or completes the actions of another: Hitchcock's much-discussed "transference of guilt" motif. But the transference extends from the characters within the drama to the audience so that, in more manipulative ways than in most crime films, we are made to root for the criminal. Who doesn't want sweet, put-upon Marion Crane to get away with stealing in *Psycho*? It is easy to identify with Charlie's protection of her uncle in *Shadow of a Doubt*, even when she has found out he is a murderer. Or to sympathize with the tennis player's secret desire to get rid of his nagging girlfriend so that he can marry a senator's daughter (in *Strangers on a Train*). Through sly means, Hitchcock often implicates us in the criminal action; and our response to the guilty characters reflects the criminal psychology that the film dramatizes—our identification with the criminal indicates our own dark undercurrents, the possibilities of our own unexplored selves.

As he manipulates audience involvement, contriving our sympathy for undeserving characters, suggesting our complicity with criminals, Hitchcock himself remains immune, overseeing with Olympian aloofness the dark games he has devised. He resembles the *noir* director not only in his detachment from the nightmares he depicts but in the absolute control of his work. His autocratic methods are perhaps more well-known than those of any other director. Before filming begins, Hitchcock has planned the film down to the last movement of the camera. There is no "fat" during production, no room for improvisation or spontaneity; everything moves in strict accordance to the director's tight master plan. Hitchcock's often-quoted witticism, that actors are (or at least

should be treated like) cattle, is true in spirit if not in fact: certainly no actor, with the possible exception of the sly Judith Anderson as the grotesque lesbian housekeeper in *Rebecca*, has ever been allowed to upstage Hitchcock. Moving and speaking in obedience to his commands, his actors are the puppets to his master puppeteer; Hitchcock is as dictatorial with them as he is with every other element of his *mise en scène*. As a result, actors in his films always seem to be a little dazed, their voices monochromatic, their gestures a little muffled, as if they have just been awakened from a trance and are not entirely sure of where they are. It has often been noted that Hitchcock is drawn to bland, icy blondes—non-actresses like Kim Novak or Tippi Hedren, or good actresses like Eva Marie Saint or Grace Kelly who resemble sleepwalkers when Hitchcock uses them. Hitchcock obviously favors women who are reserved and who will not resist his control. Relegating his performers to essential but nonetheless subsidiary roles in the film's orchestration, Hitchcock is the true star of his own movies.

Like many *noir* directors, Hitchcock often conceives of his films in terms of set-pieces. Sometimes, when he has a weak script, as with *Foreign Correspondent*, the film consists of practically nothing but a series of sequences intended to display the director's ingenuity. But in all the most successful Hitchcock films there are particular scenes which serve the plot but which also stand on their own, as clever manipulations of film technique that startle the audience. Two of his most fully realized works, *Strangers on a Train* and *Psycho*, are ablaze with set-pieces: in *Strangers*, memorable high points include a murder reflected through the victim's glasses, Griffith-like cross-cutting between a tennis match and the killer's frantic efforts to retrieve a lighter from a drainpipe, and a merry-go-round that whirls crazily out of control; in *Psycho*, the brilliantly edited shower scene, an explosion of Eisensteinian montage, the vertiginous angle as Norman Bates carries his mother down to the cellar, the cross-cutting between the sister's search through the Gothic house for Mrs. Bates and the tense confrontation in the motel office

between Norman and the murdered victim's fiancé. All of these passages involve a rigorous and self-conscious use of editing, camera movement, and camera placement that demonstrates Hitchcock's virtuosity. Just as he controls his actors and his audience, the Master loves to play with film, molding its properties to suit his own ends.

Like all *noir* directors, Hitchcock is attracted to stories of confinement. After an accident, the photo-journalist in *Rear Window* is a wheelchair recluse whose only recreation is spying on as much of his neighbors' lives as he can see through the windows on the other side of the courtyard. *Rope* takes place entirely within an elegant New York penthouse. For this stage-bound drama, Hitchcock devised one of his most ingenious technical solutions, filming the action in a series of long takes, with the few cuts masked by the camera moving in on dark objects that fill the entire frame. *Dial M for Murder*, another adaptation of a claustrophobic play, is set for the most part in an apartment and in the outside hallway. Many of the films take place in an environment that is physically limited. But even in the films that venture beyond confined interiors, the ones set against colorful backgrounds (San Francisco in *Vertigo*, Morocco in *The Man Who Knew Too Much*, New York in *The Wrong Man*, Montreal in *I Confess*, Washington, D.C. in *Strangers on a Train*, Havana in *Notorious*), Hitchcock's canvas is not expansive. The pressure of events forces the characters into hiding; assailed by the unexpected at every turn, they become paranoid, withdrawn. Even wide-open spaces in Hitchcock are dangerous—in a flat open field in *North by Northwest*, a plane materializes to attack the dazed hero. And even in the superficial *To Catch a Thief*, the French Riviera in which the story is set is not a glorious holiday backdrop but a place of lurking threats and potential pitfalls.

Hitchcock's camera choreography is more complex than the tight, static set-ups typical of *noir*. There are virtuoso displays of camera movement throughout the canon: the camera encircling the lovers in *Vertigo*; the camera retreating down the stairs and away from the scene of a murder in *Frenzy*; the gliding, roving camera in *Rope*, its movement breaking up the static space in which the action unfolds. But the utter calculation of the movement prevents it from having an open, liquid quality, a fluency that would be foreign to *noir*. Even when he indulges in movement that is seemingly sweeping and expansive, Hitchcock's work is taut, intentionally mechanical.

SF-7

6
The Noir Actor

Actors are often prized for their naturalness. Some actors become stars because they are exotic, because they are strikingly different from the everyday, but most of what we see in American films is meant to pass for realistic behavior that audiences can easily identify with. Yet all acting, no matter how real it attempts to be, involves some degree of stylization. Supremely realistic performers like Gary Cooper and James Stewart, who may pretend to be nothing more than the guy next door, nevertheless have a carefully groomed manner.

Acting, like directing, demands choices which contain elements of simplification and abstraction; and acting in genre films increases the amount of stylizing the performer needs to bring to his part. Genre storytelling is streaked with codes that have been worked out over the course of time. Characterization in genre pieces also depends on a kind of shorthand, so that roles are defined quickly by such matters as dress (the western convention in which good guys wear white and villains are garbed in funereal black) or environment (the dance-hall hostess in her saloon, the gangster in his newly acquired white-on-white apartment). Genres depend on audience familiarity, and actors performing genre roles often have to do less filling-in with

Deadlier than the male: Joan Crawford in *Sudden Fear*.

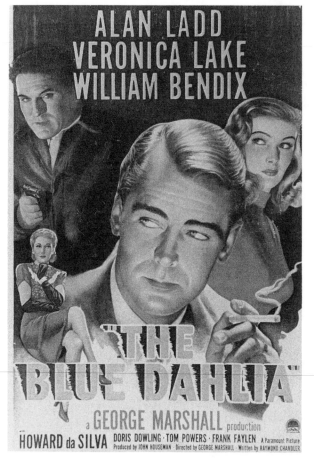

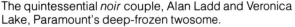
The quintessential *noir* couple, Alan Ladd and Veronica Lake, Paramount's deep-frozen twosome.

the kind of realistic detail that might be more naturally introduced into a non-formula picture.

The most consistently stylized acting in American genres is in *film noir*, which is itself, along with the special case of the musical, the most stylized Hollywood genre. If *noir* stories often seem like a bad dream, the acting in *noir*, fittingly enough, is somnambulistic. The performers most closely identified with the genre have masklike faces, their features frozen not in mid- but in *pre*-expression. Performing in a constricted area both physically as well as emotionally, the *noir* actor has a glacial presence. He does not open up the frame, claiming screen space for himself, but plays close to the chest, remaining a figure in the *noir* landscape, one element in the film's overall composition. Actors with expan-

sive personalities are unlikely to appear in *noir*. When on occasion they do, like an overly emotive Bette Davis in *Beyond the Forest*, they all but dismantle the tight *noir* frame. Actors who either overact, or who project a basically sunny disposition, appearing to be at ease with themselves and the world, are not *noir* material; and if by chance this masterful kind of personality shows up—like Charlton Heston in *Touch of Evil*, for instance—he plays a masterful character (one of the few in the canon).

The *noir* actor is an icon. More often than not, he is embodying a type, and he creates his effects with means that are both vivid and sketchy as he provides something of a visual shorthand for a full-dress character. Because he is part of the decor, conforming to the all-important *noir* mood and ambience, he is kept on a short leash, his actorly enthusiasm constantly checked. True bravura performances in *noir* are therefore rare. Cagney in *White Heat* and Robinson in *Key Largo* perform with an all-out intensity that the genre normally discourages, and it's significant that both actors date from an earlier movie tradition, one that encouraged a dynamic style. The typical *noir* performer is tighter, emotionally stingier than Cagney or Robinson at full blast.

The quintessential *noir* couple is the utterly deadpan Alan Ladd and Veronica Lake, *noir*'s answer to William Powell and Myrna Loy. In *This Gun for Hire, The Glass Key,* and *The Blue Dahlia,* the two players perform the same kinds of roles, with no variation in pitch or temperature. Their faces barely move. Their dry, tight voices, monotonous in rhythm and intonation, lack any music or coloring. And the similarity of their chiseled features and Nordic complexions adds to the general eeriness. Their unblemished beauty has a manufactured quality; they look like a mogul's idea of what American movie stars should look like. And, with all this, they are both very, very good—perfect icons, in fact, for the world of forties *noir*. Their dazed, mannikin-like quality is exactly right for *noir*. Lacking the strength and force of character of stars like Gable or Garbo, they make convincing victims, suggesting, beneath their masks, a weakness and vulnerability that the *noir* stories require of them as they get pushed about by bizarre turns of fortune. Neither star could withstand the stresses of Hollywood fame; both were alcoholics, both died relatively young. Lake's film career was finished by the end of the decade. Ladd managed to hold onto a career of sorts through the fifties, despite the fact that his own private torment began to appear in his sagging, wasted appearance. Had he lived, he might have developed into an interesting character actor, whereas Lake passed to a point where her Hollywood celebrity was unrecoverable. In middle age, Lake looked nothing like her forties image, the immaculate frozen beauty as much a memory as her trademark peek-a-boo hair style.

In *noir*, Ladd and Lake acted in a rigorously minimalist vein; their presence alone commanded our interest and attention. Neither occupied much screen space. Part of their appeal was in their essential stillness, their sculptured quality. Lake speaks in a tough voice that is a hair's-breadth away from sounding merely common. Ladd has one of the flattest voices on record, quieter and softer than Lake's, more "feminine," and in this way suggestive of the kind of sexual reversal which cuts across *noir*. Their scenes together are at the opposite end of the acting spectrum from the wit and sparkle, the generous give-and-take, of the running screen battles between Spencer Tracy and Katharine Hepburn—Lake and Ladd perform as if from the end of a tunnel, phoning in their lines from remote control. Their somnolent delivery, together with the invariably dim or flickering light in which they perform, begins to take on a sinister quality. And yet some human responses are observable beneath the apparently thick-skinned veneer. Something close to good nature even manages to surface, particularly at the ends of their films, when tensions between them are resolved and they go off together. Lake proves to be good for her co-star: she is his helpmate, urging him to serve his country (in *This Gun for Hire*), and aiding him in solving the murder mystery (in *The Blue Dahlia* and *The Glass Key*).

In *This Gun for Hire*, the film that made him a star, Ladd plays a cold-eyed, dead-voiced killer who seems to have no moral restraints. Hiding out in shabby rented rooms between assignments, he is a dangerous loner, his capacity for menace engrained in Ladd's mask-like face, stiff movements, and parched voice. But by the end of the film, the character softens under Lake's influence; his violent impulses are used to thwart a Nazi conspiracy. At best, though, he is a reluctant, inverted anti-hero, far removed from the dynamic villains of the gangster films. In *This Gun for Hire*, he is extremely well cast as a pained, convoluted character who remains as much a mystery to himself as he does to us.

Lake's work is not as layered as Ladd's; but she is very sly, very sexy. She is one of a series of forties leading ladies with a deep voice and an ambiguous sexuality. Although the scripts often treat her as so much embroidery, as a mere handmaiden both to the put-upon hero and to the tortuous plot, she has a direct, dominating quality. She cracks wise, in the style of thirties sharpshooters like Rosalind Russell, but unlike the thirties dames she lacks a touch of dizziness. She is all business as she trades quips with her male sparring partners. Her voice and her bearing have a sharpness, an angularity, not easy to warm to; she is tough, and no mistake about it. Snapping out her lines in a gravelly, hard-edged voice that already had the whisper of the alcohol that was to destroy her life, she is the perfect partner for Ladd. This polar couple defined *noir* style early in the decade. Not every *noir* performance was pitched in the same severe key, or was so strictly confined to the same narrow register, but the stylized work of Paramount's deep-frozen twosome anticipated the somnambulistic mode of the forties thriller.

At the time, Ladd and Lake were enormously popular, perhaps unimaginably so now that their stylized non-emoting seems rather specialized, an acquired taste. *Noir* certainly needed the kind of screen presence that they had,

but it also needed actors who were more than authoritative icons. It needed stars who could also act, as demonstrated by the careers of the undisputed king and queen of *film noir*: Humphrey Bogart and Barbara Stanwyck. Their work spans the period, setting standards and creating models for other performers to emulate. Both began their careers in the thirties, though they didn't fully come into their own until their startling work in early *films noirs*— Bogart in *The Maltese Falcon*, Stanwyck in *Double Indemnity*.

As Sam Spade and then later as Philip Marlowe in *The Big Sleep*, Bogart caught the particular flavor of Hammett's and Chandler's hard-boiled style. Like Ladd and Lake, Bogart works in a restricted area, with few inflections and minimal movement. His tough guy style is tense and tight-lipped, yet surprisingly agile, arrived at without any visible effort. His features fixed in a perpetual frown that modulates into scorn and cynical disbelief on the one hand and into a kind of bemused irony on the other,

Veronica Lake, the archetypal forties dame, wisecracking, deadpan and sexually ambiguous.

Searching for the gang that killed his wife, Dick Powell in *Cornered* sheds some of the poise of his impersonation of Philip Marlowe in *Murder, My Sweet*.

Humphrey Bogart, the perfect *noir* icon, the compleat forties tough guy.

Bogart hardly moves facial muscles. As Spade and Marlowe, dealing with an assortment of criminals, oddballs and misfits, he remains detached and wary, especially of pretty women who tell a lot of stories. He keeps his feelings to himself. The detectives may be tempted by women and by money, but they really can't be bought. As Bogart plays them, the private eyes are men of principle, men with their own code of honor whose cynicism masks their essential integrity. It is the moral certainty which emanates from Bogart, and the sense of shrewdness in his judgment of others, that more than anything have been responsible for the actor's mystique. Bogart became a cult hero at Harvard, where students at the Brattle Street Cinema responded to his honesty and knowingness.

With his stiff face and taut voice, his rhythmed recitation (accented by the famous lisp) of the roguish Hammett-Chandler dialogue, Bogart works in a monochromatic style. His delivery is as lean as his physique. For him, less is certainly more. And yet the actor's pared down, straight-ahead, no-fuss manner communicates a subtle range of feeling, from waggish humor to romantic interest. Throughout both key films, there are chinks in the tough guy armor, moments when the actor drops the rigor mortis mask. The private person beneath the investigator's facade is revealed in a delightful scene in *The Maltese Falcon*, where, after Spade laces into Kaspar Gutman (Sydney Greenstreet), laying it on thick, he kicks up his heels in glee on his way to the elevator, pleased with his own performance.

Bogart had the perfect face for *noir*, a face filled with character. Though he tried, Bogart could not conceal worry or regret or the sadness that always seemed to gnaw at him. His mask is thus different from the idealized ones of Lake and Ladd, from which all human concern seems to be erased. In contrast to their unblemished facade, Bogart has a frankly homely face—a mug—and he doesn't look at all like anyone's stereotyped concept of a movie star. Ravaged and sad-eyed, he looks positively unhealthy. With a few minor adjustments, Bogart can easily appear sinister, a quality which was exploited for most of his early career at Warners, when he played heavies. Curling his lip in a perpetual sneer, furrowing his brow in scorn or menace, the early Bogart looked surly and dyspeptic. The startling originality of his presence, though, was not realized until 1941, in both *The Maltese Falcon* and *High Sierra*, a swan song to the thirties gangster in which he played a sentimental con infatuated with a crippled girl and loved in turn by a mature and self-effacing woman (Ida Lupino). In both these roles, his innate decency collided interestingly with echoes of the snarling, embittered characters he had played as second banana to Edward G. Robinson's emphatic tough guys in crime dramas of the thirties. The result is wonderfully shaded, with the integrity and humanity of his Spade and Roy Earle qualified by an underlying harshness. Bogart balanced astringency with a fleeting sentimentality and romanticism in a way that no other actor ever has.

Bogart, then, has the face of a man of enormous feeling kept in check—he is clearly a man with churning insides beneath the still mask. His gaze is direct yet wary; the scornful twist of the lips does not belie the sense of honor that turns him into a hero no matter what kind of role he is playing. The face hard yet vulnerable, the cold gazing eyes human and wounded, Bogart is the archetypal *noir* loner. His posture is tensed, hunched; he rarely moves. Our characteristic view of him is seated at a table, the inevitable drink nearby, cigarette in hand, as he stares out at the world dispassionately yet with intimations of a seething tension within. His means of expression are limited, practically to the point of abstraction, yet he radiates complexity.

Bogart's loner status is modified or challenged only by women who can talk back to him, giving as good as they get. His ideal sparring partner, of course, is Lauren Bacall. In *To Have and Have Not, The Big Sleep, Dark Passage,*

Appearances are deceiving in this shot from *Thelma Jordan*, as Barbara Stanwyck, the meanest woman in *film noir*, clings to Wendell Corey for support.

and *Key Largo*, they are a more human but no less stylized *noir* couple than Ladd and Lake. The quintessential Bogart-Bacall relationship occurs in *The Big Sleep*, where their feelings for each other are expressed through mutual baiting and a slicing, edgy wit. They resemble the sparring couples in Restoration comedy whose attraction to each other is measured by their caustic humor, a mark of their shared response to the fools who surround them. Like the Restoration gallants terrified of sentiment and disdainful of sentimentality, Bogart would be unable to tolerate a weepy woman; he would expose her as pitilessly as he does Brigid O'Shaughnessy. He appreciates a sarcastic dame like Bacall who carries herself, in many ways, like one of the boys, rather than standing on ceremonies, expecting deference and courtliness where none are likely to be forthcoming.

The perpetual bachelorhood and final flight from involving alliances of the Hammett-Chandler private eyes match Bogart's own aura of stubborn independence. His most famous role is that of the wary private investigator who stands coolly outside and above the criminal action. But Bogart tried other kinds of parts within the *noir* canon, playing characters distinctly not in control. As he moves from the patented Bogart, the distrustful Sam Spade and Philip Marlowe, to the role of a victim in *Dark Passage*, of a criminal in *Conflict*, and of a crackpot in *In a Lonely Place*, Bogart covers the *noir* spectrum. His gallery of *noir* neurotics is a notable achievement, though the cynical, honorable characters in *The Maltese Falcon* and *The Big Sleep* will always be his most forceful image. Bogey cracking up or being villainous looks like an impersonation, no matter how skillfully conceived, and audiences are likely always to see the "true" Bogart as Sam Spade or Rick Blaine (in *Casablanca*), tough guys who keep their distance but who end up doing the right thing.

In *Dark Passage*, he is accused of two crimes he did not commit. After escaping from prison, his character has plastic surgery, emerging from the operation looking like Humphrey Bogart—only to become entangled in another web of incriminating circumstantial evidence. In both cases, he has been set up as the fall guy by a ferociously jealous woman (Agnes Moorehead). In *Conflict*, he is another *noir* archetype, the murdering spouse. The character concocts an elaborate scheme for killing his frigid wife, while all the time his own deception is being watched by a clever analyst (Sydney Greenstreet). *In a Lonely Place* presents him as a Hollywood screenwriter who has temperamental explosions. Accused of killing a young woman, he is presumed guilty because of his erratic behavior. He even alienates the woman (Gloria Grahame) who provided his alibi and who falls in love with him. His tantrums frighten her to the point where she begins to suspect he *is* guilty, even though she knows better.

In these three films, as *noir* victim, conniver, and neurotic, Bogart was playing against the strong persona he had created earlier in the decade, that of the self-contained hero. Bogart, of course, is an accomplished actor with a flexible range, but there is a sense of strain—a sense, precisely, of "acting"—in his portrayal of characters who lose control. As Sam Spade or Philip Marlowe, Bogart's work is seamless; but as the unbalanced screenwriter, the fiendish husband, the unlucky former con, he is on stage. The neuroticism of these later Bogart performances, though, was suggested in the private eye characters, as even in his most protected tough guy stance the actor had dark undercurrents. He invariably invested his characters, even the most seemingly adjusted ones, with a strong neurotic potential.

The actor whose record in *noir* most closely approximates Bogart's is Dick Powell. Powell earned a reputation in the thirties as a song-and-dance man. He had an engaging, lightweight personality and a mellow singing style. By the mid-forties he was eager to change his image, and he sensed that the current *noir* phase offered an appropriate opportunity to do so. He played Philip Marlowe (before Bogey did, in fact) in the 1944 film version of *Farewell, My Lovely* (the title was changed to *Murder, My Sweet* because the producers thought the original title, especially with Powell starring, might lead audiences to expect a musical). Raymond

Chandler later said that Powell came closest to his own idea of Marlowe. If anything, Powell is even dryer in the part than Bogart, erasing entirely the crooner's geniality that had made him a popular fixture in Warner musicals. The only echo of the earlier Powell is the actor's physical grace—he has a dancer's flowing ease. Powell's voice is flat, his face taut and frozen in the masklike *noir* vein, and he plays Marlowe as a blunt, no-nonsense professional. His work is wonderfully tight and economical; he is guarded and sardonic, but he falls short of projecting Bogart's aura of absolute integrity. Beneath the straightforward he-man manner are flashes of shiftiness: this Marlowe might use *any* methods to crack the case.

Like Bogart, Powell fits so snugly into Marlowe's character that the audience is unaware that he is acting: his is the kind of style that conceals style. As Chandler's private eye, he is *noir's* perfect tough guy, yet the toughness is never insisted on, it is simply there as a natural part of the character. Powell as Marlowe has a rough time of it: he is hit over the head, duped by a devious woman trying to hide from her notorious past, drugged, locked up, suspected of murder by the police. Through it all, Powell remains a model of the Hemingway code of grace under pressure, his irony a shield against constant mischance.

Murder, My Sweet was among the most favorably received of all *films noirs*, and Powell decided to stay within the *noir* mode for the rest of the decade. From the hired professional detective of the Chandler film, he switched to playing a more impassioned investigator in *Cornered*, where he is cast as an ex-soldier tracking down the gang responsible for killing his wife. Here, his search is not that of the disinterested sleuth but the personal quest of a man bent on vengeance; his performance is therefore more high-strung than in *Murder, My Sweet*. In *Pitfall*, Powell becomes a *noir* victim, playing a strait-laced insurance man (recalling Fred MacMurray in *Double Indemnity*) who makes a fatal choice to double-cross the company for which he has worked loyally.

Like Bogart, then, Powell covers the *noir* keyboard from detached investigator to weak-minded bourgeois who slips into crime. His work is spare and subtly stylized, regardless of the kind of character he is playing, though like Bogart, Powell is at the top of his form as the ironic observer, maintaining a skeptical distance even from his own misfortunes as he trades cracks with his adversaries the police, and with the low-down, two-timing dames that he is wise to.

Bogart's achievement in *film noir* is matched by that of Barbara Stanwyck, the genre's undisputed first lady. Stanwyck's persona, however, is not as variable as Bogey's; she has such a powerful screen presence that she is simply not convincing as anything other than a *noir* spider woman, ensnaring men in her web. In *Sorry, Wrong Number*, she plays a bedridden woman whose husband is plotting her murder. In prospect, the role is certainly uncharacteristic, but she plays it with such force that audience sympathy shifts to her downtrodden, would-be killer. Stanwyck turns this potential victim into a virago, and though her only weapon in her isolated Sutton Place apartment is her bedside phone, she uses it with the authority of a general dispensing orders to his men.

Her face frozen in a perpetual mask of scorn, Stanwyck is *noir's* ultimate Gorgon. She is hardly more mobile than Veronica Lake, and she is far more intimidating. Her posture is as rigid and defensive as her taut face and voice. She has no curves, no flowing lines; everything about her presence is sharp, angular, hard-bitten. Her greatest *noir* role, that of the murderous wife in *Double Indemnity*, is the embodiment of menace: a woman who dispenses death without any feelings whatsoever. She plays Phyllis Dietrichson—a grotesque in woman's clothing, a character conceived by men who hate and fear strong women—with an icy, poisonous sexuality that is unsurpassed in the *noir* canon.

With a smile like a surgeon's incision and a voice of steel, Stanwyck brutalizes men. She is often cast against softies, tantalizing genial Fred MacMurray in *Double Indemnity*, skillfully courting and deceiving weak-willed Wendell Corey in *The File on Thelma Jordan*, dominating Burt

Noir's masochistic *femme fatale*: pumpkin-faced Gloria Grahame, with Lee Marvin, in *The Big Heat*, after he has thrown coffee in her face; and with Robert Ryan, in *Odds Against Tomorrow*.

In *noir,* women for the most part are either devouring fiends, or else supportive wives like Jane Wyatt (with Dana Andrews, in *Boomerang*) or Coleen Gray (with

Victor Mature, in *Kiss of Death*) who seem to function only as adjuncts to their embattled husbands.

Lancaster (in his passive, *noir* victim phase) in *Sorry, Wrong Number*. And in *Clash by Night*, she is a knowing woman of the city who returns to her small home town and marries a sweet-natured and gullible man (Paul Douglas) while carrying on an affair with a loner (Robert Ryan) whose nastiness and selfishness match her own.

Stanwyck's powerful women were a new element in American films. Following her lead, the genre presented a string of dominating females whose toughness may well have reflected a change of status produced by the war; but *noir*, characteristically exaggerating and distorting the realities of American life, had no use for a straightforward presentation of the newly enfranchised woman. The genre portrayed female strength as brazenly sexual, madly aggressive. Filtered through *noir's* transforming lens, the decade's New Woman became the *femme fatale* in whose presence no man was safe.

Noir is the product of men, and the recurrent, indeed obsessive image of women as ravenous, castrating, demonic creatures is after all a male fantasy. What woman in her right mind would create a character like Phyllis, who

is the product of the woman-hatred of James M. Cain transcribed through that of Billy Wilder and Raymond Chandler (collaborators on the screenplay of *Double Indemnity*)? The role of women in *noir* reveals male fantasies at a time when women in large numbers not only ventured beyond the home but also ran the home. As figments of male anxieties, women in *noir* deploy their power almost exclusively in sexual terms. The genre's three most striking *femmes fatales*—Stanwyck in *Double Indemnity* and Joan Bennett in *Scarlet Street* and *The Woman in the Window*—have nothing to do except to brandish their sexual allure in order to destroy men. The Bennett characters float around the city, their sexual attractiveness kept at the ready, a lethal force lying in wait for the repressed, unsuspecting males played in both films by Edward G. Robinson. The *noir femme fatale* has no occupation; sex is her full-time job.

Stanwyck is the most vivid of all the temptresses in *noir*, the most relentless and unsparing. Yet other actresses who made notable impressions as *noir's* cracked version of the New Woman are very much in the Stanwyck mold:

Ida Lupino (in *The Man I Love*) was one of the few actresses in *noir* to transcend stereotype: she was neither a black widow nor a simpering wife.

Joan Crawford in *Mildred Pierce* and *Sudden Fear*; Lauren Bacall; Lizabeth Scott in *Dead Reckoning, Pitfall*, and *A Stolen Face*. With their set expression and low voices, all project hardness and sexual ambiguity; at times, their sexual presence is exaggerated, at other times ridiculed. These *noir* anti-heroines often seem to be mocking the men who fall into their net: Joan Bennett's taunting laughter at a woebegone Edward G. Robinson in *Scarlet Street*, when she tells him that her "love" for him has been a mockery, echoes throughout the canon. There is something fatally missing in these firm-jawed, grim-faced women who regard men (and the world in general) with faintly concealed distaste.

In Joan Crawford's case, at least, the on-screen hardness mirrored her true personality. Child-torturer and castrating wife, Crawford was a vicious woman. The toughness and fundamental meanness that spilled over into her screen image is especially apparent in the archetypal Crawford vehicle, *Sudden Fear*, where she plays a scorned woman who discovers her husband's plan to murder her and who then sets out with a brutal will to ensnare him and his paramour. The single-mindedness, indeed the diabolical ferocity with which she goes about catching her enemies, bespeaks a will of iron. Like Stanwyck in *Sorry, Wrong Number*, Crawford converts a potential victim into an avenging tyrant; these women cannot bear to lose, and the men who fall into their devouring, annihilating embrace are to be pitied.

Women in *film noir* are presented in a narrow range. Either they are masked malevolence in the Stanwyck-Crawford vein or desperately conventional housewives, like Jane Wyatt in *Pitfall*, or Teresa Wright in *The Steel Trap*, whose primness drives their husbands not to drink but to crime. In *noir*, sunny, bland housewives are covert castrators. In *The Reckless Moment*, Joan Bennett is a housewife fiercely determined to

One of the most vivid of *noir's* spider women: Gloria
Swanson as Norma Desmond, ministering to William
Holden, in *Sunset Boulevard*.

keep up appearances. When her daughter acci-
dentally kills a no-good boyfriend in a heated
argument, Bennett acts quickly on her own to
preserve the family name by covering up the
crime. Her zeal for defending her middle class
status is so powerful that she trafficks fearlessly
with an assortment of criminals. This otherwise
conventional American matron proves as wily
and as emasculating as *noir's* most determined
femmes fatales.

Positive images of women are indeed rare in
the *noir* canon. Ida Lupino plays two of them: a
torch singer in *The Man I Love* and a blind
woman in *On Dangerous Ground*. Lupino projects an intelligence and emotional generosity
that are just right for the singer, a wise woman
of the city who solves everyone's problems but
her own. The film operates on the male fantasy
that such a knowing woman is destined to be
unlucky in love. At the end, in the kind of
romantic and sentimentalizing touch that pre-

vents the Raoul Walsh film from being a full-
fledged *noir*, Lupino is alone, looking up
tearfully at the moon. Like many of the forties
actresses, Lupino has a tough veneer, but she
also radiates warmth and vulnerability. Her astringency and common sense cut across the
maudlin role of the blind woman in *On Dangerous Ground*. In this film, as in the earlier *High
Sierra*, she plays a character whose loyalty and
capacity for love help to regenerate an embittered hero. Lupino thus provides an unusual
note in *film noir* in her portrayals of women who
are truly supportive and yet who have a sense of
their own worth as well—women who are not
mean and who are also not fools.

Sweeter, more pliant than Lupino, Cathy
O'Donnell in *They Live By Night* and *Side Street*
and Coleen Gray in *Kiss of Death* and *The Killing*
are other likable heroines. O'Donnell and Gray
may well be the only actresses in the genre who
are pleasant without being either sticky or hypo-

critical. Both are good at playing nice, normal women who fall for hard-luck guys, and who remain loyal once their men slip into the *noir* quicksand.

But *noir* has little interest in wholesome characters, male or female, and its footage is packed with a variety of sexual psychopaths rather than with women like Lupino or O'Donnell. The *noir* mauler is not always as hard-bitten as Stanwyck or Crawford, but she is always just as dangerous. Sweet-faced Gene Tierney plays a soft-spoken obsessive in *Leave Her to Heaven* who aborts her child and watches her husband's brother drown. The healthy-looking Peggy Cummins moll in *Gun Crazy* incites her man to a spree of looting and killing. Although Joan Bennett's attractive ladies of the evening in *Scarlet Street* and *The Woman in the Window* really care for and rely on the dapper heels played in both films by Dan Duryea, they end up wrecking the lives of men they enchant.

Then there are the *femmes fatales* whose essential quality is not meanness but mystery. In *The Lady from Shanghai* and *Gilda*, Rita Hayworth clearly lacks the hardness or authority of Stanwyck. Her lush femininity shades off into vagueness: who *is* the lady from Shanghai? The question runs throughout the film, preoccupying the narrator-hero as well as the audience. Victim rather than instigator, Hayworth always seems a little puzzled. She has a come-hither quality, a willingness to share her acting space. Yet beneath the vaporousness, the little-girl-lost mask, she too is poisonous. Yvonne De Carlo in *Criss Cross*, Ava Gardner in *The Killers*, Jane Greer in *Out of the Past*, and Gloria Grahame in *Crossfire, In a Lonely Place, The Big Heat, Human Desire,* and *Odds Against Tomorrow* also share something of Hayworth's moral ambiguity and sexual mystery. We are never sure until the climax exactly how to "read" them. Their opaqueness, like Stanwyck's utter rigidity, is a measure of their dangerous sexuality. In *Criss Cross* and *The Killers*, Burt Lancaster is obsessed by inaccessible women. De Carlo in *Criss Cross*, and Gardner in *The Killers*, both curvaceous and womanly, play elusive temptresses with a sneaky sense of humor and a gleam in their eye, their every gesture fraught with double meaning

as they dispense baffling mixed messages to the hopelessly smitten Lancaster. Unlike the hatchet-faced Crawford or Stanwyck, Jane Greer's dragon lady in *Out of the Past* is charming—hence especially insidious. When she materializes, dressed in white, on the street of a lazy Mexican town, she looks like the hero's daydream come to life, and decidedly not like the nemesis that she really is.

Gloria Grahame likewise introduced a new shading to the fatal woman type, playing her not as a victimizer, a cruel tyrant, but as a victim, whimpering and aching and even good-hearted. Grahame has a timorous, appealing, little girl quality; thin-lipped, squeaky-voiced, slit-eyed, pumpkin-faced, wrinkling up her nose and face like a mouse, she is found hiding in smoky tenement rooms waiting for her men. Abused and humiliated in her search for love, she is *noir's* pre-eminent masochist, the inevitable cast-off moll. In a scene that recalls Cagney smashing a grapefruit in Mae Clarke's face, Lee Marvin hurls scalding coffee at Grahame in *The Big Heat*. A bad girl who means well, a real hard luck dame, Grahame brought a note of pathos to *noir*. No one else projected quite the same combination of traits—dumb, sullen, devoted, available, hungry, above all steamy.

Whether hard or soft, mannish or womanly, all of *noir's* fatal women seem to move in a dreamlike landscape. They are projections of male fears and fantasies who seem merely to be simulating human action. These women are acted in a remote, compressed, semi-abstract style. In *The Woman in the Window*, a painting of a beautiful woman inspires Professor Wanley's fantasies; yet all *noir* temptresses have the remoteness of a painting seen in a window. And to embody their dreamlike otherness, the actresses who impersonate them perform in a cryptic stylized manner, sleepwalking through masculine nightmares.

Noir offered many opportunities for the character actor, just as it did for the "character" director. Richard Widmark, Jack Palance, Victor Mature, Robert Ryan, Clifton Webb, Richard Conte, Francis L. Sullivan, Peter Lorre, Sydney Greenstreet and Edward G. Robinson all had the

All *noir* temptresses have the remoteness of the painting of the woman in the window. (Edward G. Robinson and Joan Bennett, in *The Woman in the Window*.)

most rewarding roles of their careers playing an array of *noir* weaklings, misfits, dictators and victims. *Noir* capitalizes on the actors' unusual qualities, of face and voice and physique. The performers all project an unsettling sexuality; playing either sexual tyrants or outsiders, they suggest anything but wholesomeness.

In his excellent performances in *film noir*, Edward G. Robinson made extravagant departures from his gangster image. Yet in playing a repressed and very sedate professor in *The Woman in the Window* and a meek husband in *Scarlet Street*, he suggests *noir* menace beneath the characters' masks as law-abiding citizens. Victims of ironic circumstance, both characters commit murder, and Robinson, with the image of the thirties gangster trailing him, and his own swarthy, dyspeptic appearance, captures the characters' underlying rage, their capacity for twisted passion and violence. In *Double Indemnity*, he plays a shrewd claims investigator for an

insurance company, a character who is married to his job and who pursues his research into questionable claims with zealous persistence. Even when he is impersonating seemingly normal characters then, Robinson radiates emotional unhealthiness. There is something not quite right about his professor, his Sunday painter clerk, his claims investigator—and it is precisely that hint of imbalance that *noir* requires. His characters look like people to whom something bad or unexpected is going to happen. As the professor and the clerk, he is clearly a born victim, yet there is a residual underlying strength that lingers about the actor's persona; and the embattled imagery of strength and weakness, of ferocity and meekness, splendidly highlights the theme of the divided self that runs throughout *noir*.

Sydney Greenstreet, Peter Lorre, and Francis L. Sullivan do not possess Robinson's double-edged quality, his suggestion of violence

A memorable contribution to *noir's* gallery of sexual grotesques: Clifton Webb as the effete killer, in *The Dark Corner*.

held in reserve, of a private rage underlining a benign public mask. In appearance and manner, they are clearly heavies, and so their work, good as it is, does not have the shading and subtlety of Robinson at his best. Within a narrower range, though, they are unbeatable. So odd and singular in appearance, the three actors have a menacing sexual presence, a factor which is exploited in *The Maltese Falcon* where Greenstreet and Lorre are playing homosexuals as conceived by Dashiel Hammett, who had an old-fashioned notion of them as decadent exotics living in an unreal, perfumed world. Lorre is swarthy, small-boned, jittery, always on the verge of hysterics; Greenstreet is elegant, cosmopolitan, seemingly in control—and unmistakably malevolent. He radiates world-weariness and cynicism; he is out for the kill even when he is supposedly sympathetic, as in *Conflict*, where he is a psychiatrist who ensnares wife-killer Humphrey Bogart. Francis L. Sullivan has Greenstreet's oiliness. As the maniacally jealous nightclub proprietor in *Night and the City*, he is photographed from a low angle that emphasizes his enormous bulk, with lighting from below casting ominous shadows across his face. Looking like some kind of caged beast, he is observed frequently through the bar-like windows of his office.

As the effete killer in both *Laura* and *The Dark Corner*, Clifton Webb is a memorable addition to *noir's* gallery of sexual grotesques. In both parts, Webb plays a cosmopolitan dandy whose passion for unattainable women leads him to commit murder. Webb has a civilized, indeed an over-refined veneer, which, in Hollywood iconography, is suspicious; in the anti-intellectuality that has always plagued American movies, well-bred aesthetes are usually morally and sexually questionable. Webb's manner targets him as at best a dubious character. In both films, as a man-about-town and a patron of the arts, he turns out to be among the sickest of all *noir* villains. The films could acknowledge the decadence of Webb's aestheticism, but could not, in the forties, link it to homosexuality. Webb embodied an old-fashioned idea of what homosexuals were supposed to be: dandified, affected, superficial, addicted to fine living, concerned excessively with fashion and with appearance. The lingering suspicion about Webb's sexual persona is filtered into the films by casting him as a character who cannot control *heterosexual* impulses. Obsessed by Laura, whom he feels he has created and whom he wants to control utterly, he is impelled to kill her. In *The Dark Corner*, he is likewise driven to crime to preserve the waning interest of his young and beautiful wife. Both films place him—by the force of his monomania, his psychotic jealousy and possessiveness—beyond acceptable heterosexual patterns. In these two virtually identical roles, Webb is made quite a despicable character; covertly, the films reveal a fear of as well as a strong hostility toward the sexual outsider.

Like Webb, Farley Granger projects sexual ambiguity. In *Rope, Edge of Doom, They Live By Night, Strangers on a Train*, and *Side Street*, he plays moral weaklings who slip into crime; his characters are too forlorn or too soft to withstand temptation. With his quiet voice and weak face he makes a perfect *noir* victim, the eternally dazed man in a net, retaining an essential sweet-

Farley Granger, *noir's* pre-eminent pretty boy victim, with Cathy O'Donnell, in *They Live By Night*.

ness and innocence despite what happens to him. In both *Rope* and *Strangers on a Train*, he is the passive partner in a masked homosexual relationship, dominated by John Dall in the former and Robert Walker in the latter, who flirt with him and are obviously drawn to him sexually, though Granger seems unaware of their interest. *Noir's* pre-eminent pretty boy (and a more capable actor than he is usually given credit for being), Granger in film after film is victimized by his beauty. In his sexual helplessness, he is exactly the opposite of the ravenous women who populate the genre.

Granger is the most visible of the weak men *noir* used recurrently. Affable Fred MacMurray in *Double Indemnity*, fuzzy Wendell Corey in *Thelma Jordan* and dazed Dana Andrews in *Fallen Angel* and *Where the Sidewalk Ends* seem to invite sexual manipulation. Gullible, evidently not in control, perplexed, the screen image of actors like Andrews and Granger pales beside that of their vivid leading ladies, or the dominant males, who lure them into crime.

Richard Widmark, Jack Palance, Robert Ryan, and Richard Conte, who clearly do not

project the sexual indecisiveness of Webb or Granger, are deeply hard-boiled. Anything but dandies or preening ladies' men, they suggest a powerful heterosexual impulse gone amiss. In one of the best-remembered scenes in *noir*, Richard Widmark, in *Kiss of Death*, pushes a woman in a wheelchair down a steep flight of tenement steps while he cackles in insane delight. The actor plays the part of an ex-con who tracks an informer (Victor Mature) with wild intensity, covering the screen with the nervous, pent-up energy of a caged panther. With his stabbing voice, his clipped delivery, his madman's mirthless laugh, his strange regional accent, the hard angularity of his face and his steely eyes, Widmark is truly terrifying. He plays the character as a mass of twitches, with a restlessness and a wired tension that counterpoint Mature's inevitable sleepwalker's stolidity. The two actors perform beautifully opposite each other: Mature, with his taut, deadened face, his stiff movements; and Widmark, with his gyrating thrusts and lunges. Widmark claims the space around him like a boxer moving in on a punching bag, while Mature seems closed in, as if he is separated from the world by a glass partition. Mature is ideally cast as the saintly masochist to Widmark's macabre sadist. The role of the informer who yearns to go straight taps a soulful quality that Mature has, a propensity for noble suffering, while the part of Udo calls on Widmark's hyper-edginess. *Kiss of Death* contains Mature's finest performance; Widmark went on to fill other extraordinary *noir* roles, as a fierce racist in *No Way Out*, as a pickpocket in *Pickup on South Street*, and, most memorably, as the embattled con artist in *Night and the City*. In that film, he gives what is perhaps the archetypal rendition of the neurotic *noir* victim, a self-destructive overreacher forever on the run. His eyes pleading and terrified, a cigarette dangling at his lips, Widmark endows the two-bit hustler with a heroic vitality. Performing with a sustained energy unsurpassed in *noir*, Widmark palpably conveys his character's mounting desperation, his struggle against impossible odds. Jumpy, erratic, damned, Widmark adds a demonic rage to the role, his nervy, hyped-up acting perfectly matching Jules Dassin's power-

Fated to play villains: saturnine Jack Palance, terrorizing Joan Crawford, in *Sudden Fear*.

ful direction, which transforms elegant London into a city of fear.

Widmark's portraits of doomed characters—his eyes ablaze, his face set in a sadist's leer, his body hunched, as if in readiness for attack—leave such a strong impression that it is difficult to accept him in normal roles. He is mediocre as a health inspector in *Panic in the Streets*—playing an average family man who is determined to track down villains who may be carriers of bubonic plague, he is so adamant and astringent that he seems to be quoting from his gallery of *noir* psychopaths. Widmark's cruel handsomeness, with its promise of decadence, makes him seem out of place in everyday roles. The actor has not been seen to good advantage since the *noir* cycle ended.

Careers of other *noir*-bred actors—character tough guys Jack Palance and Richard Conte—suffered similar eclipse in the mid to late fifties. Both actors slipped into low-budget crime dramas that were clearly not of *noir*

calibre. But in their heyday, which corresponded to *noir's* prime, both made exemplary villains. Palance, by appearance, was fated to play heavies. His saturnine face conveying menace and ill-will, he positively radiates the imminence of dark deeds. He is a man who inspires discomfort. As the two-timing husband who plans to murder Joan Crawford in *Sudden Fear*, and as the murderer unknowingly carrying bubonic plague in *Panic in the Streets*, he is oily, sinister, reptilian. Those deep-set dark eyes, that smarmy, sibilant voice, that scowling visage accented by the prominent cheekbones, all carry the threat of catastrophe.

Richard Conte had more flexibility than Palance—his swarthy Italian handsomeness could be both menacing and appealing. In *Call Northside 777*, he is convincing as a victim of circumstance who is given a life sentence for a crime he did not commit. Playing this beleaguered character with a fetching gentleness, he offers a striking contrast to his definitive *noir*

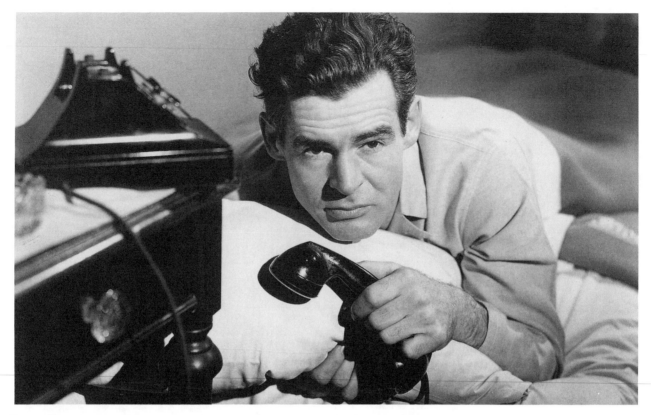

Robert Ryan, who played tormented *noir* misfits, in two of his strongest performances, as the psychotic cop in *On Dangerous Ground*, and as the intruder in *Beware, My Lovely* (with Ida Lupino).

criminals, the desperate man on the run in *Cry of the City* and the racketeer, crazed by jealousy and ambition, in *The Big Combo*. Conte has a rugged charm, no matter what kind of part he plays; he is believable as a romantic hero in a way that neither Widmark nor Palance could ever be. In *Cry of the City*, he uses his appeal on a number of willing female victims. Whereas Widmark and Palance seem to want to destroy women, their capacity for sadism immediately apparent in their evil grinning masks, Conte is more winning but no less dangerous. He is a cunning manipulator of women, turning into a tyrant when he fails to get what he wants.

Unlike Widmark or Conte or Palance, Robert Ryan went on to enjoy a distinguished post-*noir* career, although his string of characterizations within the genre remains his strongest work. As the rabid anti-Semite in *Crossfire*, the violent cop in *On Dangerous Ground*, the psychotic intruder in *Beware My Lovely*, the racist bank robber in *Odds Against Tomorrow*, the hulking lover in *Clash by Night* and *The Woman on the Beach*, Ryan was unfailingly powerful, investing his tormented characters with a brooding intensity that suggests coiled depths. Cut off from the world by the strength of their feelings, his characters seem to be in the grip of torrential inner forces. They are true loners. Ryan's work has none of the masked, stylized aura of much *noir* acting—he performs with an emotional fullness that creates substantial, complex characters rather than icons.

Noir also launched the careers of three performers who are decidedly leading men rather than character actors and who went on, after their introduction in *noir*, to long careers as major stars: Burt Lancaster, Robert Mitchum, and Kirk Douglas. Certainly these actors are not identified with *noir* to the extent that Widmark or Conte or Ryan are, but they began their careers playing quintessential *noir* types, and although they broadened their range beyond that normally allowed to actors in crime dramas, they retained traces of the *noir* image. This is especially true of Robert Mitchum, whose recent work as Philip Marlowe in *Farewell, My*

A reprise of the hard-boiled hero: Robert Mitchum as Philip Marlowe, in the 1978 remake of *The Big Sleep*.

Lovely and *The Big Sleep* is a resurrection of the forties tough guy. In these roles, which carry more than a hint of self-parody, Mitchum is the *noir* sleepwalker interpreted, like everything else in these films, with an exaggeration bordering on satire. Mitchum as Marlowe is the ultimate somnambulist, his eyelids so heavy they require a visible effort to be held halfway open. His voice muffled, his bloated face and body drooping in middle-aged fatigue, Mitchum looks and sounds drugged. Frozen-faced and frozen-voiced, he himself seems like a reconstruction, a waxworks image of the real Robert Mitchum. Yet the actor's famous irony still manages to cut through the weariness, and remnants of his innate nobility surface now and again to give his work fleeting integrity. Mitchum carries the notion of cool to self-effacing extremes, and only an actor of his fame and proven stature could get away with this tired carbon-copy version of a once-vivid original. Mitchum has simply settled for being a *film noir* icon, evoking a bygone movie genre by his mere presence.

In his *noir* heyday, in *Out of the Past*, and later in *The Night of the Hunter* and *Cape Fear*,

In *film noir*, Burt Lancaster played masochistic
anti-heroes, as in *Criss Cross* (with Stephen McNally,
above, and Yvonne De Carlo, *opposite right*). The actor's
early image is very different from his later tyrant figures,
like the powerful columnist in *Sweet Smell of Success*
(with Tony Curtis, *opposite bottom*).

Mitchum made a powerful impact. In *Out of the
Past*, playing one of *noir's* fated victims, he is a
private eye who cannot escape the claims of his
past, when he made the mistake of falling into
the web of one of the genre's most charming and
deceitful spider women. In *The Night of the
Hunter*, he plays, unforgettably, a greedy,
lecherous preacher. In *Cape Fear*, he terrorizes a
dull bourgeois couple enacted by Gregory Peck
and Polly Bergen. In each of these roles,
Mitchum is both crafty and menacing. Even at
his meanest, he has a glint in his eye, and his
threats are laced with a droll humor and a lopsided warmth, revealed especially in his rapport
with children. He is superb with the children in
The Night of the Hunter, seducing them with his
convincing show of paternal affection. Mitchum
works nonchalantly, with a seeming minimum
of effort and an absence of any visible technique.

He is among the least hard-working of star performers.

Kirk Douglas, on the other hand, is too
impassioned and eager for *noir*, and he scored
only qualified success in the genre. He is too
young to fill out the role of the ganglord—
Mitchum's nemesis—in *Out of the Past*, though
he is suitably intense as the misused fighter in the
marginally *noir Champion*, the film that really
launched his career. Unlike Mitchum's, his
expression is alert. Entirely lacking Mitchum's
arrogant coolness and devastating sexual assurance, Douglas is a strenuous actor, whose expansiveness, heat and energy place him outside
the *noir* range. He has the dimensions of the
larger-than-life hero; he was fine as Ulysses, in
an otherwise inferior fifties version of Homer's
epic, and superb as Spartacus. More at home
with the panoramic scale of epics and westerns,

Douglas chafes at *noir* confinement.

Burt Lancaster, by contrast, has never been more interesting than in his early *noir* roles. In *The Killers, Criss Cross*, and *Sorry, Wrong Number*, he enacts weak men who are seduced by clever, castrating women. Lancaster has the build of a gymnast, and with his flashy smile and open-faced handsomeness, he has the look of an all-American—a winner. But his *noir* characters have a powerful urge toward annihilation as they court romantic disaster. The roles thus exploit dark undertones lurking beneath Lancaster's healthy grin; his victims are voluptuous masochists, yearning for defeat and death. The tangled combination in Lancaster's early persona of beauty and perversity makes a striking dramatic impact. Lancaster in *The Killers*, lying in wait in the shadows of his empty room anticipating the arrival of his executioners with a kind of exaltation, provides one of *noir's* great moments.

If his early parts tapped a vulnerability and sickly passivity, his later roles, with a startling iconographic reversal, emphasize an extreme hardness. In his post-*noir* career, Lancaster made his mark playing commanding figures, heroes cut to wide-screen size, yet his most compelling later work—the malevolent energy of his Elmer Gantry, the monomania of his power-hungry general in *Seven Days in May*—carries overtones of *noir* pathology. There is often a frightening quality in the actor's obsessive, powerful characters—a quality not quite human. He is especially sinister in the late *noir* drama, *Sweet Smell of Success*, where he plays a tyrannical gossip columnist determined to shield his sister from reality. Wielding authority with satanic power, his eyes hidden behind dark glasses, his set expression radiating contempt, his voice icy and cutting, Lancaster as this maniacal, incestuously fixated character is truly chilling.

7

Down These Mean Streets. . .

Narrative Patterns

The investigator, the victim, and the psychopath are the central figures in *noir's* basic story patterns. Investigators of many kinds—private eyes, sleuths, policemen, journalists, private citizens—are the protagonists of the manhunt film. The victim, accused of a crime he did not commit, or slipping into crime because of a momentary lapse, or because he is seduced by an alluring woman, or because he is sick of his wife, or because he is in a financial hole and needs money fast, is the quintessential *noir* anti-hero, around whom the genre's most ironic stories are framed. The psychopath is the dark underside of the *noir* victim—far gone before the film opens, he remains trapped in an ongoing nightmare. The stories which focus on the pathological criminal, probing and exposing his mania, are the grimmest in the canon.

All *noir* stories share a number of features, and character types overlap from one kind of narrative to another—victims and psychopaths occupy the same stage with hard-boiled private dicks; but usually one of the three basic character

A cavernous New York street: on location for *The Naked City*.

types dominates the action. The films with an investigator as the central character are different from the ones which present crime from the point of view of criminals; the distance from which crime, *noir's* central nervous system, is observed influences a film's style and flavor. Stories told from the vantage point of a private eye, or some other impartial outsider who is paid to solve a murder, to find the missing person, to expose a gang, tend to have an objective tone, their dry quality paralleling the investigator's own detachment, his essentially disinterested search for the truth. But the investigating hero can be portrayed in a variety of emotional tones, from the utter coolness and poise of Bogart's Spade and Marlowe to highly-strung questers, such as Edmond O'Brien in *D.O.A.* (who wants to find out who poisoned him and why) or Glenn Ford in *The Big Heat* (tracking the gang that killed his wife), who have a strong personal investment in cracking the case. In stories built on the victim pattern, the distance between the central character and the central crime narrows, and the films, often sharing the point of view of their collapsing protagonists, have a more complex, fevered texture than the cool private eye manhunts in *The Big Sleep* mold. In "victim" movies (*Side Street, Double Indemnity, The Woman in the Window, Sunset Boulevard, The Window, The Wrong Man*), crime invades bourgeois insularity, penetrating its self-protective boundaries. Caught off-guard, ordinary, lawful citizens are either pushed into crime against their will or discover their criminal potential as the films shift from ironic detachment to more subjective views of encroaching chaos. Stories of inveterate criminals (*White Heat, Touch of Evil, Night and the City, Night of the Hunter*) adhere more closely than the private eye or victim dramas to the Expressionist's nightmare world. These films veer, typically, from a detached view of madness to occasional hallucinatory renderings of the psychopath's disordered mind.

Films starring the professional investigator come the closest in spirit to the classical detective story. Private eye stories are constructed like puzzles in which the investigator questions a series of suspects in order to find out whodunit.

"My name is Philip Marlowe, private detective," announces Robert Montgomery at the beginning of *Lady in the Lake*, going on to provide a fair summary of the genre's ground rules: "You know, someone says follow that guy. Find that female. And what do I get out of it? . . . You'll see it just as I saw it. Maybe you'll get it, maybe you won't. You have to be alert, things may creep up on you."

Traditionally, the investigator is hired to find a missing person, and before he knows it, "things creep up" on him. His client has lied to him; his eternal adversaries, the police, think he did it; women throw themselves at him. He is hurled headlong into a world where almost no one speaks the truth. But through it all— through the assorted bribes and seductions which assault him—the investigator (Sam Spade, Philip Marlowe) retains his integrity. He cannot be bought or fooled. At the end he dispenses justice, sending Brigid O'Shaughnessy off to jail; he has earned his money, even if the case has not turned out the way his client intended it to.

The original request for finding the missing person leads the private eye into a maze. The stories are complicated, with as many twists and turns as the tales which that brilliant tale teller Brigid O'Shaughnessy fabricates for Sam Spade. "I'm a liar, I've always been a liar," Brigid confesses, in one of her moments of disarming candor—and she is speaking, in effect, for virtually the entire cast of characters of private eye dramas. The people the detective talks to are ready and often quite competent liars and it is his job to gauge their reliability. The private eye has to be a shrewd judge of character.

Narrative construction is remarkably similar in the best of all private eye *films noirs: The Maltese Falcon, The Big Sleep, Lady in the Lake, Murder, My Sweet, Kiss Me Deadly, The Glass Key.* All the pictures are arranged as a sequence of interviews between the private eye and witnesses and potential suspects which lead, after a string of false clues and the investigator's mistaken judgements, to a final, surprising revelation. The stories are deliberately hard to follow; we are supposed to be as baffled as the inquirer. *The Big Sleep's* reputation as having an all-but-impossible-to-follow storyline is justified, as the film *is* a maze, as circuitous and convoluted as the most devious *noir* liar.

A close look at another Chandler-based mystery, *Murder, My Sweet*, indicates the web-like narrative pattern typical of the investigation drama. Arrested by the police, who have accused him of multiple murders, Philip Marlowe explains how he wound up where he is when the film opens, battered and blindfolded and subjected to a tough police grilling. It all started when he was working late one night at the office . . . He glances up from his desk to catch the reflection of a looming figure in one of his windows. It is Moose Malloy, who is just out of prison and who wants Marlowe to find his girl Velma. After some prodding, Marlowe agrees to go with Moose to a joint called Florian's, where years ago Velma was a dancer. No Velma there anymore, of course, and no Florian either. But Marlowe seeks out Mrs. Florian, a boozy, rumpled dame—"with a face like a bucket of mud"—who doesn't want to talk much, though her vague memories of Velma arouse Marlowe's interest. Finding Velma, he figures, is going to be the kind of challenge he enjoys.

The search for the woman is set aside at this point when another client claims Marlowe's attention. Lindsay Marriott is an obvious dandy, who, apparently by chance, has selected Marlowe to be his companion when he delivers money to some crooks in return for jewelry that they stole from a Mrs. Grayle. The whole set-up smells fishy to Marlowe—Marriott is no more credible as a client than Moose. The rendezvous with the thieves is to take place at night, off an open highway out of town. Marlowe disregards the signs of danger, and goes off into the night with Marriott. At the meeting place he is knocked unconscious. Some time later he is awakened by the voice of a woman peering anxiously down at him, asking "Are you all right?" and then fleeing into the night. Marlowe then discovers that Marriott has been killed.

At his office, a woman reporter arrives to ask questions about the murder. Marlowe suspects that she is not a journalist and calls her bluff. She turns out to be the stepdaughter of Mrs. Grayle, the woman whose jewels were stolen. Marlowe calls on Mr. and Mrs. Grayle at their mansion, and sizes up the situation quickly, almost as quickly as Mrs. Grayle makes a play for him, which is as soon as her rich, feeble old husband leaves the room. Their tête-à-tête is interupted by the arrival of Jules Amthor, a spiritualist with a local reputation as a smooth-talking swindler. Marlowe has been eager to meet Amthor because the cops have told him to lay off the guy. (Amthor appears the moment after Mrs. Grayle has pronounced him a man of great mystery and inaccessibility.) Shortly after this first meeting with Amthor, Marlowe finds himself shot up with dope and lying in a bizarre hospital presided over by Amthor, a self-confessed quack doctor.

At this point, all the pieces of the puzzle have been introduced. All the important characters are on stage, and what remains is for Marlowe to sort out identities and relationships. What is the connection between plot number 1 (the search for Velma) and plot number 2 (the stolen jewels, the murder of Marriott, the Grayle ménage, and its mysterious links with Amthor and his thugs, among whom is Moose Malloy)? After further roughing up, and more hassles with the police, Marlowe pieces it all together. Mrs. Grayle is Moose's Velma, risen mightily in the world and determined to wipe out her past. Thus, a mean, determined woman, it turns out, as it often does in Chandler, is responsible for everything: Velma, or, as she is now known, Mrs. Llewellyn Lockridge Grayle, staged the robbery (working with Amthor) and killed Marriott, thinking he was Marlowe. In the climactic showdown, Velma, Moose, Amthor, and old Grayle are all killed, leaving only Marlowe and the stepdaughter to await the arrival of the police.

Stories in the private eye dramas tease the audience by presenting characters and events in a deliberately garbled, roundabout way. Marlowe takes on a second case just as the first one gets started, and we are left dangling, wondering about Velma, having become interested in what happened to her after Marlowe's interview with the slovenly Mrs. Florian. Except for the hard-core mystery addict, the puzzle-solving seems more trouble than it is worth. The tricky, criss-

Call Northside 777 conforms to the classical pattern of the story of investigation: the crime (a masked man shoots a policeman); the manhunt (a reporter, James Stewart, questions the star witness); and the solution (the date of the newspaper in the photo determines a man's innocence or guilt).

cross plotting exists for its own sake, as a witty exercise in stage-managing, rather than as a means of deepening characterization. With almost no will of their own, the characters are at the mercy of the writer's juggling skills, tossed into the stew and stirred about to little purpose except to create confusion. In *Murder, My Sweet* and *The Big Sleep*, the fun is not in the delirious plotting but in the dialogue and atmosphere. The wittiest and most appealing moments in these two films are the male-female games played by Bogart and Bacall, and by Bogart and Dorothy Malone (as a prim bookseller who turns out not so prim after all), and by Dick Powell and Claire Trevor (as the duplicitous Mrs. Grayle). In these scenes, the films crackle with Chandler's droll, sexy, grown-up humor.

The investigation framework has a greater potential impact when the quester is personally involved in the case. The private eye, after all, is a hired professional, an outsider. Like the archetypal western hero, he does what he has to do; and solving the case is his badge of honor. He may use devious methods, he may well resort to violence, but he is not a criminal. He keeps his distance from the underworld, and from his own underworld as well. He is a detached, essentially disinterested figure, and his fundamentally objective view of crime is engrained in the more or less detached style that is the mark of the private eye story.

The private detective film is the best-known of the *noir* story types. For most moviegoers, *film noir* may well summon up the image of Bogart in a trench coat and fedora asking tough dames and hoods with punched-in faces a lot of questions. But of the various narrative strains that qualify as *noir*, the private eye prototype is the least rewarding thematically, because in it the hunter and the hunted occupy

clearly separate places. One of the provocative ideas in *noir* is that a potential criminal is concealed in each of us: the private eye story does not acknowledge that complex, dark, and secret other self that surfaces in other kinds of *noir* dramas. The private eyes may be vulnerable, but Spade and Marlowe and their sort tend toward emotional invulnerability, which makes them less interesting characters than the hunter who is personally involved in the puzzle-solving and who has an ambivalent, unresolved relationship to the crime he is investigating. Because Marlowe is not genuinely concerned about finding Velma except to satisfy his manly code of professional competence, the search remains something outside of him. He is shaken up, doped, beaten, lied to, but at the end he is the same person he always was and always will be. And so the story, twisting and eventful as it is, lacks a dynamic connection to him. He remains a person to whom things happen.

But Marlowe is certainly an attractive character; he is an enduring popular culture hero for good reason. The most interesting character in *Murder, My Sweet*, however, the one most capable of surprising us, is Velma turned Mrs. Llewellyn Lockridge Grayle. Painted and perfumed, she is a fabricated, self-created woman; and she performs her part with style. She is the catalyst, but in terms of the narrative development she is merely one of a number of people Marlowe questions and whom we see from his jaundiced view—she is a figure in the tapestry. How much more provocative a story it would be if told from her point of view, as her delicately balanced world is invaded by Moose, a figure from the past, and by the snooping private eye.

Psychologically then, the professionally conducted investigation is the least challenging of the *noir* narrative patterns. The essential detachment and objectivity of the form made it the obvious story line for *noir* in its so-called semi-documentary phase. In such films as *Boomerang, Call Northside 777, The House on 92nd Street,* and *Street with No Name,* the framework of professional investigation is taken into the real world. The milieu is not the enclosed and fictional one of the byzantine Hammett-Chandler narratives,

but true-life settings taken from the files of the FBI and newspaper headlines. In these dramas, investigations are not conducted for their own sake, but as a means to a serious and socially-minded end: to uncover a network of communist spies; to save an innocent man from execution; to alert America to the spread of organized crime. "The story you are about to see is based on fact," a title announces at the beginning of *Boomerang.* "In the interests of authenticity, all scenes, both interior and exterior, are in the original locales and as many actual characters as possible have been used." "This story is adapted from cases in the espionage files of the FBI," we are told at the beginning of *The House on 92nd Street.* "Produced with the FBI's complete cooperation, it could not be made public until the first atomic bomb was dropped on Japan."

Investigators in these case-history reconstructions remain personally disinterested. They are professionals doing a job. Yet they are fired by goals higher than Marlowe's—higher, that is, than interest and pleasure in cracking a case. These hunters are patriots, crusading journalists, lawyers determined to defeat a corrupt political machine, FBI men bent on toppling a crime syndicate. In these hard-hitting problem dramas, *noir* emerges from the fictional labyrinth to become a form of propaganda: the crime thriller as social pamphlet, as journalistic exposé, as contemporary crusade.

The narrative structure of these semi-documentary films is much the same as that of the private eye whodunits: an outside investigator confronts a maze. The plotting is as complicated and gnarled, as the crack questioner grills a series of witnesses. In *Call Northside 777,* James Stewart is a journalist whose boss sees a suspicious ad ("Call Northside 777") which offers money for information about an eleven-year-old case. Skeptical, the reporter thinks the ad is a fake. He traces the 777 number to a cleaning woman, who has worked for eleven years to accumulate the $5000 reward money she now offers because she believes that her son Frank, who was convicted of murdering a policeman and is serving a life-term in prison, is innocent. The reporter is unpersuaded, but gradually he sees that Frank may well be the victim of circumstantial evidence, and Stewart becomes determined to see that justice triumphs. After his laborious reconstruction of the past he is convinced of the condemned man's innocence.

Fact is stranger than fiction, as the reporter saves the condemned man in a spectacular variation on the last-minute rescue. The case is decided by the date on a newspaper which appears in the rear of a photograph taken at the time of Frank's arrest. Both Frank and Wanda, the woman who accused him of murdering the policeman, are in the picture, as they walk up the stairs of the police station. Wanda swore in court that she did not see Frank until December 23, the day she identified him in the line-up. If the newspaper is dated December 22, as the reporter suspects it might be, Wanda's credibility is suspect, and the district attorney has agreed to a new trial. The man's fate then rests on whether a new process of photographic enlargement is powerful enough to reveal the date of the newspaper. Typical of the film's emphasis on technology, the climax involves a documentary detailing of the photo blow-up process. The crime is solved not in the *noir* nightworld that the private eye inhabits, but by science.

Call Northside 777 contains the intriguing "wrong man" theme, but undercuts its potential by presenting the action from the reporter's rather than the condemned man's perspective. Visually and thematically, the film's emphasis is on the processes of investigation and discovery rather than on the wrong man's paranoia and entrapment. Skillfully constructed and well acted, the film downplays character in favor of documentation, which leads to a dramatic dead end.

The manhunt theme works most interestingly when the investigator, unlike the reporter in *Call Northside 777*, or the private eye is connected to the crime not through his job but in some personal way. Here is where *noir* comes into its own, introducing themes of true moral and psychological complexity. *Cornered, The Blue Dahlia, Black Angel, Phantom Lady, Deadline at Dawn, D.O.A., The Big Clock, The Big Heat* are stories of manhunts conducted by investigators with personal motives. In *Cornered*, Dick Powell is a soldier who embarks on a mission of

vengeance as he tracks political criminals who killed a woman to whom he was married for only twenty days. As a veteran combing the underground of postwar France and Brazil, Powell encounters as much trouble as when he was Philip Marlowe, except this time his search takes on a desperate quality as the character becomes progressively unhinged. *Cornered* is not as well made as *Murder, My Sweet*, but its thematic focus has more potential than Chandler's whodunit. In *The Blue Dahlia*, Alan Ladd is another soldier facing a postwar trauma. He returns home to an unfaithful wife, who is murdered soon after his arrival. As the obvious suspect Ladd quickly leaves, forced into hiding, "cornered" like Dick Powell as he undertakes his own search into his wife's murder.

These two hunters, spurred by personal involvements, are more high-strung and more vulnerable—more complex—than a cynical private dick or a liberal journalist doing a bang-up

The investigator with a personal motive: Edmond O'Brien (with Beverly Campbell) hunts for his own murderer, in *D.O.A.*

job as he takes on the American system of justice. The emotional instability of the Powell and Ladd characters adds an edge to the films, as the psychological distance between hunter and hunted, between tracker and quarry, menacingly narrows.

In *D.O.A.*, the investigator is dying of poison, and so his search to find his killer is quite literally a race against time. Here is *noir* irony at its blackest. The investigator in *The Big Clock*, as a victim of circumstances, is forced for much of the film to conduct a search for himself. The quest motifs in both these underrated dramas, with Edmond O'Brien investigating his own death, and Ray Milland superintending a fake search for himself, raise the kind of provocative psychological questions that the more straightforward pattern of the private eye stories do not. Is O'Brien's poisoning an oblique comment on the kind of deadly life he has led? Does Milland's entrapment in the building in which he works as a hotshot magazine editor have a more than

literal significance? O'Brien is a small town insurance man who leaves home to go to a convention in San Francisco. There his ordeal begins. He attributes his poisoning to a night on the town; like all small towners in *noir*, he regards the city as a place of excitement and possibility, but also one of danger and even of possible annihilation. In the course of his frantic search he learns that the roots of the fatal poisoning came from an event that occurred in his home town of Banning: he had notarized a bill of sale that would convict a woman and her lover of having murdered her husband.

Their alibi is that the husband killed himself over a business failure, but the affidavit spoils their case, and so they poison O'Brien, an innocent bystander caught in a ghastly *noir* fate: if only the murder victim had not, by chance, come to him to sign that note. But has there also been something unhealthy about his utterly routine life in Modesto, and has he come to the city as much as anything to escape the marriage

The wrong man theme: Ray Milland in *The Big Clock* and Jack Carson (opposite), in *Mildred Pierce* certainly look guilty, but they are only victims of circumstance.

demands of his loyal and conventional secretary? One of the film's many ironies is that his last desperate search involves him in his life more forcefully than he has ever been before. Tracking down his killer just before he dies—discovering the reason for his death—turns out to be the triumph of his life.

Similarly, the hero's search and entrapment in *The Big Clock* provide telling comments on his character. A go-getting magazine editor whose specialty is finding missing persons is all but enslaved to a dictatorial boss (Charles Laughton) and to a nagging wife, which, in *noir*, is a certain sign of disaster. To break his routine, he agrees to go out for a drink with the boss's conniving mistress, who casually suggests a blackmail scheme against the boss. The editor wants no part of the deal, or of her. Laughton kills the woman in an argument, after she has taunted him with the news that she has gone out with a "Jefferson Randolph." The boss had glimpsed a man leaving her apartment, just as he had arrived, and he employs his henchmen to

find this "Jefferson Randolph" in order to pin the murder on him, little suspecting that the wanted man is in fact his ace editor and chief spy. Milland/"Jefferson Randolph" ends up trapped in the building that houses the Laughton publishing empire, cowering in the shadows of a massive clock tower. The story is told in flashback, as Milland muses that only twenty-four hours ago his life was in perfect order. His ironic search for himself forces him to question the possibility of his own moral guilt, and he feels convicted. As his life seems to close in on him, he casts a cold eye on his marriage and his job, by both of which he feels trapped.

At the end, his ordeal over, he is relieved to return to normal. *The Big Clock*, with its cop-out ending, is a well-made thriller with interesting psychological overtones, not a deep character study of the man in the grey flannel suit. But the investigation here approaches a search into the self, sketching in the beginnings of that journey into the heart of darkness that is at the center of the *noir* vision. *The Big Clock* dramatizes

"I'm backed into a dark corner and I don't know who's hitting me": the *noir* victim's theme song, spoken by Mark Stevens in *The Dark Corner*, as a private eye who's been set up as the fall guy for a crime he did not commit.

the precariousness of the normal everyday world—one of the central themes in the victim stories that constitute a second cluster of *noir* narrative patterns.

"There goes my last lead. I feel all dead inside. I'm backed into a dark corner and I don't know who's hitting me," says Mark Stevens as the beleaguered protagonist in *The Dark Corner*, speaking for an entire gallery of *noir* victims. In such films as *The Dark Corner*, *Dark Passage*, *The Wrong Man*, *Ministry of Fear*, *Edge of Doom*, *Cry of the City*, characters are accused of crimes they did not commit, their lives subjected to wild reversals and inversions. Cornered, framed, set up as the patsy and the fall guy, these victims are the playthings of a malevolent *noir* fate.

In *The Dark Corner*, Stevens, a private eye, is set up as the murderer of his ex-partner Jardine by Clifton Webb, who is pathologically jealous

because Jardine is having an affair with his young wife. Webb hires a thug (William Bendix) to trail Stevens, and to make Stevens think Jardine wants to kill him. In *Dark Passage*, Humphrey Bogart has been sent to jail for a murder he did not commit. He escapes from prison, takes on a new identity with the help of plastic surgery, and becomes once again the fall guy for a murder. With his new face, he is a wanted man all over again, living a fugitive existence in which every knock on the door induces terror. Both times he was framed by an insanely jealous woman (Agnes Moorehead) who killed his wife and then implicated him in the second murder.

In *The Wrong Man*, Henry Fonda, making a routine visit to check up on an insurance policy, is arrested because the women in the office think he is the man who recently held them up. The innocent man bears a striking physical resemblance to the robber, who turns up only after Fonda and his wife live through a prolonged nightmare.

Cry of the City, *Edge of Doom*, and *Beyond a Reasonable Doubt* introduce further ironic variations on the wrong man theme. In *Cry of the City*, Richard Conte, who has been condemned for killing a cop (in self-defense) is framed by a crooked lawyer for a jewel robbery that he did not commit. He escapes from jail, confronts and kills the lawyer who set him up, and then spends the rest of the film on the run from a plodding cop (Victor Mature). Branded for a crime he did not commit, the Conte character becomes a true criminal, enmeshed in a web from which there is no way out. In *Edge of Doom*, Farley Granger, who has killed a priest to whom he has gone to ask for money to bury his mother, is picked up by cops in an all-night diner and hustled off to the police station, to be questioned about another crime of which he is innocent. Fritz Lang's *Beyond a Reasonable Doubt* submits the wrong man theme to what may well be its darkest reversals. A journalist agrees to go along with his boss's notion that an innocent man can be condemned. Their plan is to build an airtight case against the journalist (for killing a chorus girl), and then, after his conviction, to reveal their charade. But the editor is killed in a car accident and the journalist is caught by their

"They came at me from all sides," says Vera Miles, as the wife of a man (Henry Fonda) wrongly accused of committing a series of robberies, in Hitchcock's deeply *noir The Wrong Man*.

clever scheme and convicted of murder. The final twist is that he really *is* guilty (the woman he killed had been blackmailing him).

In such films as *Scarlet Street*, *The Woman in the Window*, and *Mildred Pierce*, the characters wrongly convicted for a crime clearly *have* the capacity to be murderers. In *Scarlet Street*, Johnny (Dan Duryea) takes the rap for killing Kitty Collins (Joan Bennett), when it is Chris Cross (Edward G. Robinson) who is the murderer. But there is no question that Johnny is a violent man—we first see him beating up Kitty—and that he has all the makings of a murderer. His arrest and execution for a crime he did not commit represent a perverse kind of justice.

In *The Woman in the Window*, Duryea and Robinson enact another grim variation on the theme of the transference and exchange of guilt. Professor Wanley (Robinson) kills a man in self-defense. The murder victim's bodyguard (Duryea), who has been blackmailing the terrified professor, is gunned down by the police, who mistake him for the murderer. The story has been a bad dream, imagined by the professor while he has dozed off after dinner at his club; yet has the dream revealed something about himself, about his latent criminal capacities? In the dream, he kills a man in self-defense and then, again in self-defense to protect his name, proceeds to act and plot like a criminal covering his tracks, as his nemesis, Duryea, blackmails him. Duryea's character would certainly be capable of murder—the odor of foul deeds emanates from him—and it is one of the film's many ironies that we are relieved when the wrong man is shot for a murder he was not responsible for. Yet is the professor entirely innocent?

Mildred Pierce willingly assumes the wrong man role, claiming she killed her husband in order to protect the real murderer, her daughter Veda. But everything about Mildred—her possessiveness, her intense identification with and attraction to her daughter—suggests that she would be capable of almost anything, including murder, to win her daughter's approval. Veda pulled the trigger, but Mildred's smothering, indulgent attitude has contributed to the girl's crazed act, the ultimate outburst of a spoiled child not getting her own way.

Stories in the wrong man mold depend on coincidence. Henry Fonda just happens to look like a robber; Mark Stevens just happens to have an ex-partner who is having an affair with a woman whose husband is insanely jealous. To be at the receiving end of nasty chance is to induce not only paranoia, a conviction that the world is a dangerously uncertain place, but also to arouse feelings of guilt. The wife in *The Wrong Man* begins to feel that she has in some way deserved her horrible fate, that what she

takes to be her own moral unworthiness has invited the affliction that has overtaken her.

The line between guilt and innocence in many *films noirs* is blurred; the "wrong" man turns out to be guilty in one way or another. Accused of violent crimes, the victim is forced to examine his own outlaw potential. Among *noir*'s wrong men, Henry Fonda stands out because he is clearly *not* capable of the hold-ups of which he has been accused. The true criminal is only his *physical* double; in this case, the enemy does not reside within, but is a matter of purely blind chance, of dumb accident. And this kind of external threat is as unsettling and corrosive as the villainous alter ego that remains an ever-present possibility throughout the "innocent" victim stories.

Once *noir*'s wronged men have been singled out by a dark and capricious fate, they are hurled into an abyss, their lives fatally disrupted, their personalities inevitably stained and transformed. Their entrapment may spring from guilty *thoughts* more than guilty deeds, and from an

The wrong man cornered: Farley Granger (*below, left*) being given the third degree about a murder he is innocent of, in *Edge of Doom*; and Arthur Kennedy in *Boomerang*, as he is hurled into a *noir* nightmare (*below, right* and *opposite*).

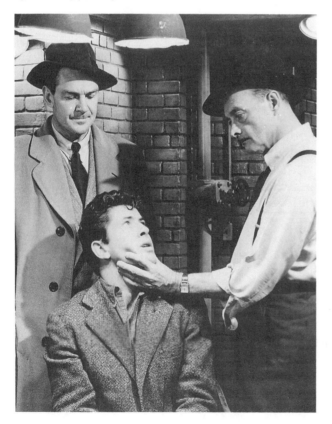

unconscious masochism; the wrong man may be a born victim, a crisis-oriented personality led to expect disaster. At least glancingly, then, the wrong man stories deal with the possible connections between the victim's neurotic character traits—his burden of guilt, his leanings toward schizophrenic behavior, his innate capacity for violence, his pent-up rage—and his present misfortune, his accidental bad luck.

"Every time we get up, something comes along and knocks us down again," says Vera Miles, at the beginning of *The Wrong Man*, before the chance encounter that is to destroy their lives has occurred. This could well be the epigraph for all the victims in *noir*, for all the characters who are defeated by circumstance.

Most of the wrong man stories conclude with at least a token restoration of the moral order. The real villains are apprehended, while the technically innocent are allowed to return to their normal lives. But the stories imply a world in which good is decidedly not rewarded and evil remains unchecked. Henry Fonda impris-

oned for crimes he did not commit and Vera Miles in permanent residence in an insane asylum would be too subversive even for Hitchcock to consider as a serious story possibility. Nonetheless, the triumph of darkness underlies the material: these stories of innocence betrayed are unsettling.

In the wrong man stories, the victims do not appear to earn their misfortune. But in another, closely related *noir* mold, rather than being stick figures wounded by the random and ferocious finger of destiny, the characters are victims of their own past actions. In *Out of the Past*, *The Killers*, *Kiss of Death*, and *The Woman on Pier 13*, characters are convicted by who they once were, in a past they have tried to overcome. Once their history catches up with them, they are as helpless as the wrong men. In *Out of the Past*, Robert Mitchum is a former private eye who has left the big city for a small town, where he runs a gas station. In the dark past, he was hired by a gambling kingpin to find a woman. He found her, fell in love with her, was betrayed by her, and then tried to forget her. When the gangster sends messengers to find him, to call him out of "retirement" for one last gig, the pressure of the past is as fateful as in a Greek tragedy. Repeating the past, he becomes involved once again with the *femme fatale*, and is sucked into a complicated criminal scheme that results in his death. In *The Woman on Pier 13*, an ex-communist, now a thriving capitalist, is blackmailed into working for the party. His past entrammels him, as he sinks deeper into the communist world, which is depicted as a criminal underworld, with hoods meeting clandestinely in garages and abandoned waterfront warehouses. Unable to escape or to deny his past, the ex-communist is a fated *noir* victim.

In *Kiss of Death*, Victor Mature is an ex-con who goes straight. Caught and sentenced for his role in a jewel heist in the Chrysler Building, he is released from prison after he agrees to testify against his cellmate (Richard Widmark). He installs his wife and child in a quiet, tree-lined neighborhood in Queens and is all set to lead a regular life when, through a technical fluke, his nemesis escapes prosecution. But even before his nasty turn of fortune, Mature was a marked

No way out: Victor Mature, an ex-con, can't escape his past, in *Kiss of Death*; in *No Way Out* Richard Widmark and Linda Darnell, like characters in a naturalist novel, are victims of heredity and environment.

man—*noir* tells us again and again that a man cannot escape his past, and surely an ex-con will be haunted all his life by what he once was and might become again.

The spectral past is only one of the many means of entrapment for the *noir* victim. In *No Way Out*, the characters cannot escape the pressures of environment and race. In *The Dividing Line*, the hero is victimized because of race prejudice. In *Ace in the Hole*, the main character feels trapped by a job. Pressures of both job and environment combine in the several *films noirs* set in a boxing milieu, where the fighter becomes a symbol of *noir* victimization. In all the films where characters are pressed by circumstances, there is no way out as the protagonists stare mutely at lives of absolute dead-ends. "I used to live in a sewer. Now I live in a swamp. I've come up in the world," says an embittered Linda Darnell, playing white trash in *No Way Out*. "You never get out of Beaver Canal," she says. "The stink never gets out of you." In *Ace in the Hole*, Kirk Douglas is a newspaperman who has been stuck for a year in Albuquerque. "Where's the big story that's going to get me out of here?" he asks. Then he hears about a man trapped in a cave and he sees the story as a chance to climb out of his rut. He remembers what happened to a reporter who covered a similar incident of a man trapped in a mine: "He crawled in for the story and crawled out with a Pulitzer Prize." Douglas begins playing up the local incident, capitalizing on someone else's misfortune. "How's that for an angle: 'King Tut in New Mexico: White man half-buried by angry Indian spirits.' " The journalist identifies with the trapped man. "There's three of us buried here," he says to the cave victim's hard-boiled, money-grubbing wife (Jan Sterling). "I'm going back in style," he promises. But as the accident becomes a shabby, manufactured *cause célèbre*, his chances for a new start slip away. Fatally stabbed by the black widow, he winds up horrified by his own cheapness. "I'm a $1000-a-day newspaperman; you can have me for nothing," he announces just before he dies.

Billy Wilder, at his most cynical, depicts the crowds who come to gape at someone else's catastrophe, as well as the hustlers who try to make a fast buck by turning the cave site into a jerrybuilt amusement park, with the leering twisted features of Hogarth caricatures. In *Ace in the Hole*, *noir* victimization is writ large, to epic proportions, as it becomes clear that all the characters are as trapped as the man in the cave.

In *No Way Out* and *The Dividing Line*, as in *Ace in the Hole*, the victim theme has a social conscience. The black doctor in *No Way Out* is attacked by a rabid racist and the Mexican boy in *The Dividing Line* is accused of being a rapist and a cop killer, but the films' beleaguered heroes recover from white hostility. Major studio *noir* is not prepared to depict a black man or a Mexican as a hopeless victim, a born loser, or a social menace. In *No Way Out*, the doctor's wife says, "We've been a long time getting here. We're tired, but we're here. We've got a right to be happy." And the film, in which Sidney Poitier is a very dignified doctor, supports her claim. Against all the odds, the nice black family triumphs over the nasty white bigots.

Like race, the fight game provided *film noir* with some of its most pious victims. In such pictures as *Body and Soul*, *Champion*, and *The Set-Up*, the ring is the symbol of a tough world, a metaphor for the hero's struggles in a dog-eat-dog environment. In *Champion*, the boxer is contaminated by his success and by what he had to do in order to make it; in *The Set-Up*, the fighter is the pawn of his managers. The protagonist's moral crisis inevitably centers on a climactic fixed fight in which the victim-hero is paid to lose. At the end of *Champion*, the boxer (Kirk Douglas) fights like a mad man, symbolically battling all the people who tried to obstruct his rise. Against terrific odds, he KOs his opponent—and then dies of brain damage. His disapproving brother bitterly pronounces his epitaph: "He was a champ." The boxer in *The Set-Up* (Robert Ryan) is so clearly on his last legs that his managers count on his defeat simply as a matter of course and don't even bother to tell him that he has to lose. Bounding back from his losing streak with unexpected force, however, he wins the fight. His reward is to be trapped in the empty arena as thugs track him down. With its innocent victim squared off against his inhuman oppressors, and the faces of the crowd

twisted in perverse delight at the sight of blood, *The Set-Up* is as rigged as the fight racket itself.

Noir dramas set in prison suffer from the same symbolic insistence as the fight pictures: prison, like the boxing ring, is too literal, too facile a setting for dramatizing stories of *noir* victims whose lives seem to be closing in on them. In Jules Dassin's schematic *Brute Force*, Burt Lancaster and his cronies plan an escape but are betrayed by a fellow convict. At the climax, Lancaster and a sadistic guard (Hume Cronyn) kill each other in a fight as the prison doctor, standing behind a barred window, intones the film's theme: "There is no escape." Through dialogue, action, and image, the film enforces the point that the prisoners are doomed men, caught both within and outside the prison walls. The outside world, overrun with two-timing dames and avenging con men, is as fierce and as enclosed as the prison society, a point made with equal force in Joseph Losey's equally schematic English thriller *The Criminal* (U.S.: *The Concrete Jungle*) (1960).

Noir stories with a social point to make have less tension than the non-preachy thrillers, just as the *noir* victim who represents only himself is more engaging than such sufferers as prisoners and prize fighters, who represent the entrapment of Modern Man. Victims who live in a real world that turns against them are more persuasive fictional characters than the boxer or the member of a minority group who suffers in a closed-off and obviously symbolic setting. In more open-ended victim stories, crime pops up just around the corner. A single misstep can precipitate disaster. Any movement or action in which the character departs from routine is potentially dangerous, fraught with peril. In these dramas, middle-class routine is pierced by an overheard conversation, a chance encounter, a wrong turn on the way to work. And in that fateful moment the course of a life is unalterably changed.

In *Scarlet Street*, Edward G. Robinson, deciding to go home by a different route, runs straight into trouble: Joan Bennett and Dan Duryea. In *My Name is Julia Ross*, Nina Foch plays an American alone and unemployed in London, who goes for a job interview as companion to a rich lady. Before she has time to catch her breath, she has been cast by her wealthy new employer in the role of Julia Ross, the woman's mad, dead daughter-in-law, killed by the matron's son in a moment of rage. Presented as suicidal and crazy to the villagers in the remote hamlet where the dowager and her weak-willed son live, the new "Julia Ross" will provide a corpse with an alibi. The film is a clever variation on the *noir* theme of unstable identity: who you are can be altered, or eradicated, by the simplest act—by something so mundane as a job interview. A despondent, aspiring screenwriter (William Holden) turns by chance into a driveway off Sunset Boulevard— and into the fatal net of faded film star Norma Desmond (Gloria Swanson). In *The Ministry of Fear*, a man just released from prison for having killed his terminally ill wife goes to a fair, simply because he happens to be passing by. On a whim, he has his fortune told, and in record time is embroiled in the activities of a network of spies.

Noir posits an unstable world in which terror lurks in wait just beneath a deceptively placid reality. In *The Window*, a little boy, going out on the fire escape for some air on a sweltering New York night, sees a murder through a window. In *Rear Window*, a photo-journalist (James Stewart) confined to a wheelchair looks at his neighbors through a telescope. He too discovers—or thinks he discovers—a murder. Violent crime can crop up in *noir* anywhere and at any moment. Murder is often sudden—and, for the voyeurs in *The Window* and *Rear Window*, exhilarating because they are not directly involved. But for Joan Crawford in *Sudden Fear*, or Barbara Stanwyck in *Sorry, Wrong Number*, who discover that their husbands want to do them in, or for Joan Bennett in *The Reckless Moment*, who has to conceal her daughter's accidental murder of her unsavory boyfriend, the sudden intrusion plunges them into a nightmare.

In *noir*, no one is safe from himself or from others—and those "others" include spouses, siblings, neighbors, best friends. Crime occurs even in the most sedate and unexpected settings. Who could have thought Joan Bennett's lovely Balboa house would be the scene of murder? Or

Crawford's swank San Francisco apartment could become a place of "sudden fear?" Or Stanwyck's Sutton Place townhouse turn into a death trap? In these stories, crime escapes from its usual setting—the underworld of the gangster films—to infest a sunny, seemingly innocent and pacific, daytime reality. And the gap between setting and action in these accounts of sudden violence is meant to surprise the audience as much as it does the hapless characters.

The middle-class protagonists in such films as *The Reckless Moment*, *The Woman in the Window*, *Scarlet Street*, *Sudden Fear*, and *Sorry, Wrong Number* are more or less innocent bystanders invaded by crime. They may be unconsciously provocative, but they are not willing, calculating criminals, like a number of the genre's middle-class citizens who are tempted and then victimized by fantasies of quick money and illicit sex.

"I left the same house at the same time for eleven years," announces the banker (Joseph Cotten) at the beginning of *The Steel Trap*. And then, one morning, this ultra-respectable bourgeois, this pillar of his community, decides to steal money from the bank where he has been a trusted employee for so long. "Of course, I wasn't serious about this wild scheme," he tells us, in the voice-over narration, "but I had an uncontrollable urge to probe its possibilities . . . there were moments when I was shocked by the enormity of my own thoughts." Once the idea occurs to him, he is unable to extricate himself from its grip: "Did you ever have one of those nightmares in which you try to run from danger and can't move?" As he plans and then executes the larceny, he begins to invent excuses: "The difference between the honest and the dishonest is a debatable line . . . We're suckers if we don't try to cram as much happiness as possible in our brief time, no matter how; everybody breaks the law." And yet, finally, his stubborn middle-class conscience stops him in his tracks: "I walked and walked and realized with each step what it meant to be a thief, a man without honor or self-respect, a man without a wife, a daughter, a home." He returns the money on a Monday morning, before the bank opens, his guilt safely concealed beneath his public facade; only

The boxer is one of *film noir's* pious victims: Robert Ryan,
in the ring, in Robert Wise's self-consciously symbolic
drama, *The Set-Up*; Jamie Smith, in *Killer's Kiss*.

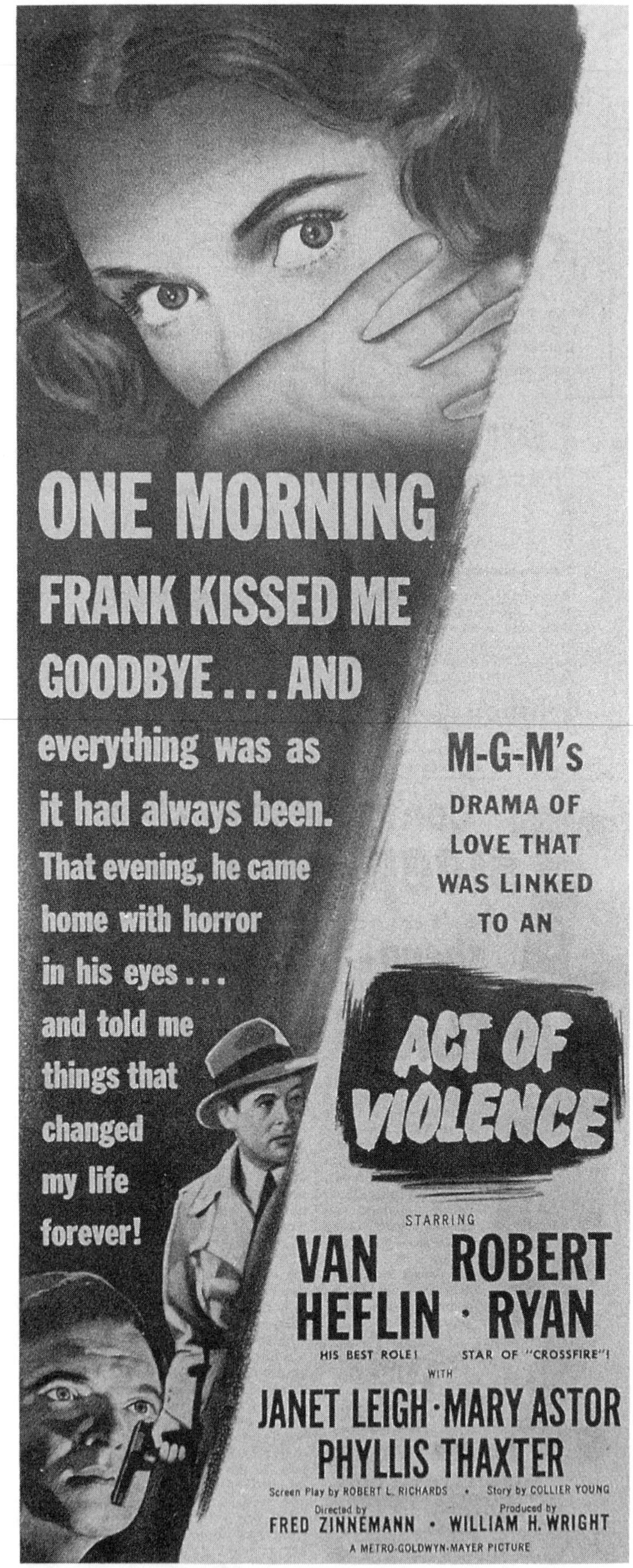

ONE MORNING FRANK KISSED ME GOODBYE... AND everything was as it had always been. That evening, he came home with horror in his eyes... and told me things that changed my life forever!

M-G-M's DRAMA OF LOVE THAT WAS LINKED TO AN

ACT OF VIOLENCE

STARRING

VAN HEFLIN · ROBERT RYAN

HIS BEST ROLE!   STAR OF "CROSSFIRE"!

WITH

JANET LEIGH · MARY ASTOR PHYLLIS THAXTER

Screen Play by ROBERT L. RICHARDS · Story by COLLIER YOUNG
Directed by FRED ZINNEMANN · Produced by WILLIAM H. WRIGHT
A METRO-GOLDWYN-MAYER PICTURE

The ad for *Act of Violence* stresses the recurrent *noir* theme of sudden, annihilating misfortune.

he and his wife know what he has tried to do.

Uncovering the criminal potential of an ultra-bourgeois, *The Steel Trap* is designed to strike a sympathetic chord in the average spectator. The audience actively wants the man to get away with it. The film exploits universal fantasies of being bad, of defying the law, of getting rich quick no matter how; and its subversive undercurrent is not entirely eradicated by the return-to-normal ending.

"I feel like a wheel within a wheel within a wheel," says Dick Powell, an insurance man, to his wife (Jane Wyatt), at the beginning of *Pitfall*. "You and fifty million others," she answers, rather tartly. "You're John Forbes, average American, backbone of the country." "I don't want to be," he says. "What would happen if, just once, I didn't walk through the door at Olympic Insurance?" *Pitfall* is the story of what does happen when idle daydream turns to grim reality, on the day he does *not* follow the straight and narrow. On a routine case of embezzlement, Powell yields to the lure of money and a woman (Lizabeth Scott). He ends up a prisoner in his own home, as the embezzler comes to gun him down. In self-protection, he kills his assailant. He is exonerated but stained by his experience. "You kill a man and that's not a pleasant thing to live with for the rest of your life," the district attorney tells him. A psychiatrist suggests that the risk he took has all the signs of temporary insanity. And his wife asks: "If a man has always been a good husband except for twenty-four hours, how long should he be expected to pay for it? . . . I don't suppose it will ever be the same, but we'll try."

Like the banker in *The Steel Trap*, Forbes resents his averageness: "I was voted the boy most likely to succeed; you were the prettiest girl in class. Something should happen to people like us." Something does, yet the departure from middle-class convention is presented in films like *Pitfall* as perilous. A regular middle-class life may be dull, but the options are treacherous; to leave middle-class containment is to risk danger to life and limb. Such films as *Pitfall* and *The Steel Trap* support the status quo out of fear rather than from strong or healthy moral convictions, and their mealy-mouthed morality may be a symptomatic response to the political witch-hunt that was invading the motion picture industry at the time. The search for communists may have enforced the idea that it is safer to stay home, minding your own business, than to stray into unknown territory. These *noir* thrillers that end up espousing a numbing bourgeois conformity are in part a response to the sense of threat and intimidation instigated by the Congressional investigations, which asked the appalling and intransigent question: "Are you now or have you ever been. . . ?"

In *Side Street*, a baby-faced postman (Farley Granger), another of *noir*'s nice-guy victims, lower in the economic scale than the Cotten and Powell characters, also is tempted by the prospect of easy money. By chance, money is sitting in an empty office where he makes a mail delivery. What could be the risk in taking it? He steals what he thinks is $200—an impulsive act which propels him into the middle of a crime syndicate. The $200 turns out to be $30,000, and the postman becomes a man on the run, cowering in rundown hotels as he tracks down the criminals to whom the money belongs and who don't want to step forward to claim it.

"You know how it is early in the morning on the water, and then you come ashore, and in no time at all you're up to your ears in trouble, and you don't know how it began," says John Garfield, delivering the *noir* victim's theme song, at the opening of *The Breaking Point* (based loosely on Hemingway's *To Have and Have Not*). Because he needs money, he agrees to a shady deal, smuggling some Chinese refugees on his boat. The leader pulls a gun on him and the hero shoots and kills him. Later he gets involved with criminals, and ends up killing them all. Not being able to support his family has led him to "the breaking point," getting involved with crooked characters and using violence to defend himself.

Besides money, the other temptation for the good man gone wrong, the potential *noir* victim, is, of course, sex. Often the two are linked, as in *Double Indemnity*. One look at Joan Bennett, in *The Woman in the Window* and *Scarlet Street*, and Edward G. Robinson is a goner. Barbara Stanwyck throws D.A. Wendell Corey off

The bourgeois hero slips into crime: Joseph Cotten, in *The Steel Trap*.

the track in *The File on Thelma Jordan*. He loses his job and his family, and the ending implies that he will find a new way of salvation, like a penitent hero in a religious drama by T.S. Eliot. Women of a certain kind spell certain disaster for the vulnerable middle-class men, the Mr. Nice Guys, in *noir*. Affable Wendell Corey, smiling Fred MacMurray, debonair Ray Milland, meek Edward G. Robinson, an untried Burt Lancaster or William Holden don't stand a chance against the man-eating, victim-hungry dames of the *noir* underworld.

Sex in *noir* is usually poisoned, presented characteristically not in a romantic context but a psychotic one. Characters are enslaved, victimized, by it. But unlike *noir*'s "wrong men," who are essentially innocent bystanders, the sexually enflamed characters are often potentially dangerous, capable of acts of violence against themselves as well as others. Sexual interest fans psychosis, leading to extreme

jealousy, possessiveness, and often crime. "Love" in *noir* is typically a disease, an affliction. In *Conflict*, Sydney Greenstreet as a psychologist delivers a speech to Humphrey Bogart that could well stand as the *noir* psychotic's theme song: "Love rather than money is the root of all evil," he says. "Sometimes a thought can be like a malignant disease and start to eat away at the will power." Consider what "love" does to a group of *noir* misfits, how it deforms and distorts the personality of characters originally healthy, or at least seemingly so, and how it oozes in bizarre forms out of characters already beyond the pale. It becomes the focus of psychotic behavior, the catalyst for crime. Smitten, Lana Turner and John Garfield become murderers in *The Postman Always Rings Twice*; their powerful sexual response to each other leads them into a maze of criminal action, as they first plot how to kill the woman's husband, and then turn against each other. Humphrey Bogart's infatuation with his wife's sister (in *Conflict*) makes

In *noir*, sex invariably leads to crime, as the posters for *Dead Reckoning* and *Born to Kill*, and the scene from *Phantom Lady*, reveal.

him want to kill his wife. When the insurance man first sees Phyllis Dietrichson, in *Double Indemnity*, he feels "hooked." "I could smell that honeysuckle again, only it was even stronger, now that it was night . . . The machinery had started to move," he states flatly, as he speaks into a tape recorder, leaving a record of his crime, "and nothing could stop it."

In *The Killers* and *Criss Cross*, Burt Lancaster's obsession with unfaithful women leads to his own death. His two lovesick characters use their infatuation as a luxurious form of self-punishment in which romantic longing and a death wish are closely connected.

Sexual obsession in such films as *Laura*, *Human Desire*, and *Leave Her to Heaven* provokes criminal acts. The psychotic lovers, husbands, and wives in these films seek absolute control over the objects of their passion. Like Porphyria's Lover, they would rather see their loved ones dead than alive with someone else. "You are the best part of myself," Waldo Lydecker (Clifton Webb) says to Laura (Gene Tierney),

whom he feels he has created, and whom he cannot bear to see grow away from him. "Do you think I could leave you to a second-rate detective who thinks you are a dame?" He thought he had killed Laura, but he had shot another woman, who simply had the misfortune to be staying in Laura's apartment at the time. His sick fantasy is that he will be able to hold onto her in death: "Love is stronger than life—it reaches beyond the shadow of death."

"I love you so I can't bear to share you with anybody," says Gene Tierney, as the maniacally possessive wife in *Leave Her to Heaven*. She is insanely jealous of her husband's former girlfriend, of his invalid brother to whom he is devoted, of the novel he is writing with a concentration she resents and which she feels excludes her. In her mad efforts to hold onto him, she watches cold-bloodedly as her husband's crippled brother drowns in a lake; she makes herself fall down stairs so she will have a miscarriage (she imagines that the child will come between her and her husband); she even arranges her own death to implicate her sister, whom she imagines is luring her husband away from her. On her deathbed, she tells her husband, "I'll never let you go, Richard."

"You're not chained to your husband," a reasonable Glenn Ford says to Gloria Grahame, *noir*'s ultimate masochist, in *Human Desire*. She is married to a brute (played by Broderick Crawford) who asks her, in effect, to prostitute herself for him, in order to get his job back, and who kills his boss in a jealous rage. They make the ideal sado-masochistic couple: the wife craves punishment; the husband needs to be betrayed. She feels that her only escape route from marriage is to ask Ford to kill her husband. But he stands outside her sick world: "It's all wrong, Vicky," he says. "From the beginning. I feel dirty." "You killed before," she argues, "in the war." Her twisted conclusion is that "It's only people like Carl [her husband] who can kill for something they love." In the end, when her husband strangles her, she gets what she has really wanted all along.

Significantly, the twisted romantic and sexual relationships in *noir* which do *not* lead to crime are unconvincing. In *Gilda*, Glenn Ford

and Rita Hayworth enact one of the most psychotic romances of the decade—and they both live to go off together at the end. Johnny and Gilda, who were once lovers, meet again by chance in Buenos Aires. Johnny works for a powerful businessman who has just married Gilda. "I hate her so I couldn't get her out of my mind for a minute," Johnny explains in a voice-over narration that opens the film. (The "lovers" in *Gilda* talk like a parody of *noir* neuroticism.) "She was in the air I breathed and the food I ate." "I hate you so much that I would even destroy myself to take you down with me," Gilda announces. "I hate you so much I think I'm going to die from it." "Statistics show that there are more women in the world than anything else—except insects," Johnny says.

Strangely, the romance between this fierce misogynist and this castrating *femme fatale* ends happily. After the Baron, who is something of a father figure for them both, is killed by one of his employees just as he is about to kill Johnny and Gilda, the lovers are chastened, magically reunited—and they decide to return to America. The end is believable only if we ignore the rest of the film. That their ferocious love-hate relationship, their deeply embittered distrust of each other, their games of mutual baiting and mental torture, could be so easily resolved is a denial of everything the film has told us about them.

In *Sweet Smell of Success*, Burt Lancaster is a powerful gossip columnist suffering from an incestuous attachment to his sister. "Susie's all I've got," he tells a nervous press agent (Tony Curtis), "and I want my relationship with her to remain on par." He wants the press agent to do some dirty work for him—to discredit the man Susie is engaged to, before morning, when she is to announce her marriage plans. The gossip columnist wants to own his sister the way he owns the town. When he walks onto the balcony of his penthouse apartment, which overlooks Times Square, he is clearly the monarch of all that he surveys, as, in the preceding shot, he has looked in on his sister, asleep in her room, with a fiercely proprietary air. The character recalls the sexually maladjusted gangsters of an earlier movie cycle—like them, he is a supremely powerful man who is sexually damaged. He makes a living by revealing or uncovering other people's

dirty secrets, and he has tried, in a totally warped way, to keep his sister insulated from the corruption in which he lives. He feels that in protecting his sister he is also keeping a part of himself pure. "I'd rather be dead than living with you," she says at the end, just before she walks off, on her own at last. "I don't hate you. I pity you."

In *The Woman on the Beach*, a blind painter (Charles Bickford), his young wife (Joan Bennett), and a coastguardsman (Robert Ryan), enact a neurotic romantic triangle in an isolated, fog-bound oceanside setting. "You've got to set Peggy free," the coastguardsman warns the artist. "You treat her like a slave." "You murdering little sneak," the artist lashes out at his wife. "I can smell your hate. It's no different from your love." But he discovers a way of releasing himself and his wife from their desperate relationship; he burns down his house and the pictures that have obsessed him, thereby exorcising the past.

The "happy" endings in *Gilda*, *Sweet Smell of Success*, and *The Woman on the Beach* are no more persuasive than any other upbeat conclusions in *noir*. Climactic confrontations supposedly loosen the powerful psychotic bonds that have linked the quarreling romantic partners, but in effect contradict what we have been told about them. The relationships in these films are fatally infested, the characters are so deeply disturbed, so mired in self-destructive behavior, that any last-minute psychic exorcism is frankly incredible.

Many *noir* psychotics hold onto romantic obsessions in ways that destroy themselves rather than inflict harm on others. Perhaps not surprisingly, the most memorable of these nervous wrecks are women: Joan Crawford in *Possessed*, Marilyn Monroe in *Don't Bother to Knock*, Deanna Durbin in *Christmas Holiday*. Iconographically, all three actresses make fascinating victims: Durbin, because she is here radically different from her usual homespun image; Crawford, because she is an obviously hard, mean woman playing a pathetically vulnerable one; and Monroe, because her own fragility is here presented, for the first and really the only time in her career, as psychotic.

In *Christmas Holiday*, Deanna Durbin atones

for her failure to save the man she loves by becoming a whore and a torch singer, whose theme song, fittingly enough, is "Always." She maintains her obsession even after the discovery that her husband is a murderer; she cannot change her feelings even after it becomes increasingly clear that she has married a lily-livered mama's boy who is also insane. Waging a deadly battle with the dragon lady mother for possession of her husband, she is trapped in a brutal game of psychological warfare. After her husband breaks out of prison and comes to the club where she sings to attack her, she is "cured" of her enflamed and masochistic loyalty. At the end of the film, she stands alone, seemingly transfigured, staring up at the sky, her compulsions safely behind her. But, as so often in films of the forties, as Barbara Deming notes in her brilliant study, *Running Away from Myself*, the attempted happy resolution goes against the grain of the entire film. Durbin's character has been shown as so pathologically obsessed that it is impossible to believe that her husband's hysterical cruelty toward her after his jailbreak would result in a change of heart. Sustained by her self-imposed role as a guilt-stricken martyr, she is really quite as mad as her husband and his mother.

Christmas Holiday treats its loaded material—there are hints of incest and sadomasochism, along with the heroine's use of prostitution as a form of self-punishment—in a glancing way typical of many kinky *films noirs*. What gives the film some added impact is that its tough, masochistic heroine and its pathological mama's boy are played by the normally sweet-natured Deanna Durbin and Gene Kelly. The clash between the stars' personae and the twisted characters adds to the gnarled psychology that permeates the drama: it is as if, in addition to all their other problems, the characters are also schizophrenic. Durbin is remarkably persuasive as a lowlife *noir* psychotic, departing from her syrupy mode yet retaining echoes of it. Gene Kelly is less successful in a part equally rich. He does not suggest a true and intimidating darkness beneath an agreeable facade. His performance looks like nice Gene Kelly trying to be mean. He is really too lightweight—too much a prisoner of his own image—to fill the role of a self-destructive, emotionally stunted con artist.

In *Don't Bother to Knock*, Marilyn Monroe is a babysitter whose lover was killed in a plane crash. She has never recovered from the trauma of his sudden death. "Everybody tries to come between Philip and me," she whispers, eerily. She tries to kill the child she is babysitting for, accusing the girl of coming between her and Philip and of preventing her from getting married. "Philip is dead. Do you know it?" asks Richard Widmark, as a man she meets in the hotel where she is working. Traumatized, self-abnegating to a pathological degree, unreachable, the woman lives in a closed fantasy world: "I'll be any way you want me to be. From the beginning, I knew you were the very best. Don't leave. I was in a hotel room once, the night before he flew away, for the last time."

As this lost child-woman, hopelessly alienated, dumb, sensitive, inarticulate, Marilyn Monroe is brilliantly cast, revealing dark aspects of her own tortured personality more nakedly than at any other time in her career. As she is taken away to an asylum at the end, her last words are a fragment: "People who love each other . . ."

Monroe playing a victim of thwarted love is very different from Joan Crawford in the same kind of part. Monroe's collapse to madness seems absolute, terrifying in its finality, whereas Joan Crawford as a victim of romantic delusion retains her usual obduracy and strength. She plays an obsessed woman with a fierceness that Monroe would never have been able to summon. In *Possessed*, Crawford as a woman scorned is more tyrant than victim. The toughness that the actress projects, regardless of her role, prevents audience sympathy. Her character is a fiend whose only reality is possession of a man who doesn't want her. Van Heflin's David treats her shabbily, claiming that the war has made him restless, unable to settle down. To be near him, she marries his employer (Raymond Massey), then is thwarted when David falls in love with the man's daughter. She says she will resort to anything in order to keep David, but she is guilty of crimes only in her own imagination. Through it all, as she becomes progressively unhinged, her rich husband remains unnaturally patient, even claiming at the end that he will wait for her probable recovery.

Monroe's babysitter, colored by the actress's own weakness, clearly could not help herself. But Crawford's perverse obsession with a man who continually spurns her suggests willful behavior; her madness is a conscious way of inflicting punishment on others because she cannot have what she wants. There is a kind of doubleness about the character's mania, as if insanity were something that can be called up and placed on display.

The *noir* psychopath, inevitably, is bedeviled, pursued by ghosts from his past; and he is often fatally self-divided. Sometimes the schizoid motif is presented in a literal way, as in *A Stolen Life* or *The Dark Mirror* or *Dead Ringer*, stories about good and bad twin sisters. Sometimes it is dramatized as conflicting aspects of the same personality, as in *So Dark the Night*, *The Lost Weekend*, and *Psycho*. And sometimes it is offered as an exchange between two different but in some ways parallel personalities, as in *Shadow of a Doubt* and *Strangers on a Train*.

The movies about good and bad twins are the least suggestive of these variations on schizophrenia. In *The Dark Mirror*, Terry, the evil sister, kills her fiancé because she senses he loves her good sister Ruth (both are played by Olivia de Havilland) even though he doesn't know Ruth exists; he simply feels a warmth when he is with Ruth and a strange kind of absence when he is with Terry, and he goes to a psychiatrist to ask about the possibility of a split personality in the woman he loves. As the net closes around her, Terry becomes more possessive of Ruth: "You and I are never going to be separated, as long as we live. You and I are going to be together. Always." In collusion with a police officer, Ruth, who all along has been reluctant to believe in Terry's badness, stages her own "suicide" in order to trap her sister. When Terry is caught, she breaks a mirror. "The mirror is everything in reverse," a doctor explains to Ruth.

The film suggests but does not develop the possibility that Terry is Ruth's other self, the "dark mirror" that reflects the negative potential lurking beneath Ruth's sunny mask. But the insistent separation of the characters into icons of good and evil makes the film a superficial melodrama rather than a probing psychological study. Good and evil do not engage in an internal clash but are presented as the essence of two separate characters, as in a medieval morality drama. "One sister could and one couldn't commit murder, and that's all there is to it," the film's resident psychiatrist explains.

The division between virtue and vice in such films as *The Lost Weekend* and *So Dark the Night* is equally simplistic, though here the doubleness exists within a single protagonist. "There are two Don Burnhams," explains the hero of *The Lost Weekend*: "Don the drunk and Don the writer—I've tried to break away from that guy a lot of times, but it's no good—that other Don always wants us to have a drink." Alcoholism is presented as the moral equivalent of the wicked sister in *The Dark Mirror*, eating away at the good Don, keeping him off the track. During his lost weekend, Don succumbs to his demon—alcohol is the devil that must be exorcised before its victim can return to society as a whole person. "Don Burnham died this weekend—of shame, the DTs, moral anemia. He wanted to kill himself." "Get rid of it by writing it down," suggests his girlfriend Helen, who has been fighting his addiction as if it were a rival. Overcoming the writing block which contributed to his collapse, Don vows to record the events of his weekend. In the novel by Charles Jackson on which the film is based, the problem tearing away at the hero is fear of his homosexuality. (In 1940s Hollywood, alcoholism seemed a fair exchange, as a moral and social stigma, for homosexuality.) In both versions of the story, the character's struggle with powerful inner forces takes on the dimensions of a religious conflict. The film's rosy and quite incredible resolution suggests that Don becomes whole after having descended to rock bottom. Utter damnation leads to improbable salvation, according to the drama's artificial scheme. The character's breakdown, presented in a vivid *noir*

The *noir* sexual psychopath: Marilyn Monroe *(opposite)* in the performance of her career, as a babysitter suffering from a romantic fixation, in *Don't Bother to Knock*.

Simplistic schizophrenia: Bette Davis times two, in *Dead Ringer*.

style, with the city weighing down on him during his long, isolated weekend, is far more convincing than his last-minute rehabilitation.

Hitchcock offers the most subtle and unsettling treatments of the divided personality. In his work, the split self is not presented in the obvious and simplistic twins motif, nor as a drama of inner struggle between good and evil, but as an exchange between disparate yet startlingly complementary personalities. In *Shadow of a Doubt*, a teenage girl and her adored uncle, both named Charlie, share a strange kind of psychological bond. "I have a feeling there is something deep inside you that nobody knows about," she tells him. "We're sort of like twins. I have to know." The uncle is a murderer, a killer of rich widows; his niece is an innocent small town girl. What could they possibly have in common? Yet the film implies both visual and psychological connections between them. The first time we see Charlie (Teresa Wright), she is lying on a bed in a listless way that imitates her

uncle's position in the preceding shot. Both are suffering from anomie; she is bored and thinks that a visit from her uncle will revive her and her family. She decides to send him a telegram. But in one of the many reciprocal gestures that occur in the film and that suggest an almost mystical rapport between the two Charlies, he has already sent *her* one, announcing his arrival. It is as if the niece, in summoning her uncle, is also, unconsciously, calling up qualities in herself. When he arrives, she gets the tune of the Merry Widow waltz in her head (her uncle is the Merry Widow murderer). "I think tunes jump from head to head," she says. On the surface, Uncle Charlie is a charming man; it is easy to see why Charlie adores him, and why merry widows dance when he calls. The casting of Joseph Cotten, so earnest and likable, is shrewd, as it underlines the film's theme that evil comes masked in bewitching guises.

The struggle between the characters is compelling because it lacks neat correspondences. The two Charlies are unevenly matched, an unlikely pair, rather than conflicting halves of the same personality. Her uncle educates her to the presence of evil in the world and to possibilities in herself that she had not suspected. When she finally confronts him with being the Merry Widow murderer, he makes a frightening speech to her: "You're just an ordinary little girl living in an ordinary little town. You're a sleepwalker, you're blind. How do you know what the world is really like? Do you know the world is a foul sty? Do you know if you ripped the fronts off houses you'd find swine? The world's a hell: Wake up, Charlie, use your wits, learn something. . ." He concludes menacingly, "The same blood flows through our veins."

Charlie keeps her uncle's secret, allowing him to have a hero's burial, in order to protect her mother, a genuine innocent who would be demolished by the truth about the charming brother she has worshiped. Charlie doesn't "become" her uncle, yet she internalizes the dark knowledge that he has passed on to her, his apocalyptic view of the world as a sty, his profoundly cynical belief of the universal darkness within. She is no longer a naive small town girl. In *Shadow of a Doubt*, as in many of Hitchcock's

A hard-boiled, psychopathic Faust: Tyrone Power as a power-mad spiritualist, in *Nightmare Alley*.

other films, good and evil are intertwined. Because, in this film, the divided self is not magically restored and the knowledge communicated from uncle to niece remains an ongoing threat and possibility, the drama attains a psychological realism rare in American popular cinema. The final statement of the film, as so often in Hitchcock, is that even the most virtuous characters harbor a darkness within.

Many *noir* psychopaths wage a fierce inner battle between their rational selves and their demonic other selves. Often, the dark self stems from sexual obsessions, but in a range of *films noirs* the characters' psychoses are beyond sexual perversity; and these twisted characters, whose madness is only partially explained, are among the most terrifying of *noir* protagonists. Though the films may hint at reasons for the characters' erratic behavior, their evident capacity for violence exceeds whatever motivations are implied. In *Crossfire*, a soldier's anti-Semitism "causes" him to commit murder. In *Sunset Boulevard*,

Norma Desmond's lost fame and fading beauty turn her into a psychopathic recluse. In *Nightmare Alley*, the hero's lust for power contributes to his becoming an amoral spiritualist. Power also fatally corrupts the gang boss in *The Big Combo* and the sheriff in *Touch of Evil*. No one is safe from such characters.

Orson Welles as an officer of the law suffering from a God complex plants evidence against people he wants to prove guilty; it doesn't matter to him whether they *are* guilty. Tyrone Power's career as a mindreader in *Nightmare Alley* is a pop version of the Faust legend: he is a down-and-out opportunist who fakes mental powers in order to fleece millionaires. Trying to control others, he is himself controlled by a nagging sense of guilt that gradually overwhelms him. Descending lower and lower in self-esteem, he ends up a geek in a circus, his mad quest for control having removed him from any connections to the normal world. Richard Conte's motto as the ganglord in *The Big Combo* is "first

One of *noir's* most memorable tyrants: Orson Welles,
Touch of Evil.

is first, and second is nowhere." Because his code allows him no loyalty to anyone, he bombs the two weird henchmen who have remained dumbly faithful to him.

Robert Young in *Crossfire*, as the detective who investigates an apparently motiveless killing in a barroom brawl, explains, "[The murderer's] hate is like a gun. The motive had to be someone who could hate Samuels without knowing him; it had to be inside the killer." It is—he is a crazed anti-Semite. The film, through *raisonneur* Robert Young, tries to present the character's blind prejudice within the frame of pious social drama: "My grandfather was killed just because he was an Irish Catholic," Young says. "Hating is always the same, always senseless. It can end up killing people who wear striped neckties." Yet Robert Ryan's powerful performance resists the kind of neat, limiting social classification that the film wants to attach to his sickness. He plays with an intensity that transcends the film's own boundaries as a liberal social document. Anti-Semitism alone does not fully account for the character's insane behav-

ior—like the sheriff in *Touch of Evil*, the corrupt mentalist in *Nightmare Alley*, the has-been actress in *Sunset Boulevard*, the gangster in *The Big Combo*, the Ryan character's derangement is complex and finally mysterious; it eludes analysis. These characters are more dangerous, more anti-social, than the reasons the films tentatively offer to "explain" their pathological state; the spectacular and unclassifiable nature of their mania gives the films their strong impact—we feel we are in the presence of characters whose evil is profound and beyond understanding.

The protagonists of *On Dangerous Ground* and *In a Lonely Place* have sudden rages only partially accounted for in the scripts. In *On Dangerous Ground*, the city, teeming with crime, seems to be closing in on a policeman (Robert Ryan) who has spent too many years trafficking with underworld types. The "dangerous ground" applies not only to the urban milieu in which he works but to his own emotional condition. He is living on the edge. After he violently attacks a criminal suspect, his boss orders him to go for a rest in the country. The lonely place in *In a Lonely Place* is the isolation enforced on a Hollywood screenwriter (Humphrey Bogart) by his anti-social behavior. His irrational explosions make him the likely suspect in a murder case and also alienate a neighbor (Gloria Grahame) who has grown romantically attached to him. As Ryan and Bogart play these festering characters, they seem completely removed from society, ostracized by the force of their anger. That their eruptions have no simple cause makes them truly alienated, unreclaimable. The ending of *In a Lonely Place*, with the writer neither becalmed nor realigned with the world, is therefore more plausible than that for *On Dangerous Ground*, which suggests that the cop has been redeemed by a kind-hearted blind woman—a sentimental conceit at odds with the feverish *noir* world in which the protagonist is imbedded.

Their perversity largely unexplained, their murderous instincts ultimately eluding definition, some *noir* psychopaths seem to be evil for evil's sake, and are placed on exhibit, as it were, as weird case histories. The killer in *The Spiral Staircase* outlines his philosophy: "There is no room for imperfection in this world . . . What a pity my father didn't live to see me strong — to dispose of the weak of the world whom he detested. He would have admired me for what I am going to do." The film offers too neat a Freudian explanation in presenting its psychopath as a weakling who has been poisoned by his brutish father's cult of masculinity; the only way he can prove himself to his dead father is to kill the maimed and the infirm, to project outward, onto others, his overwhelming sense of his own incompleteness and vulnerability. His sickness is deeper than the film's facile definition of it.

In *Niagara*, Joseph Cotten plays a man who "went wrong" in the war. In the haunting first scene, he is "called" by the falls in the early morning, to commune with their titanic natural force. He is linked to them throughout the film, as if they symbolize the forces churning within him. After he kills his adulterous wife (Marilyn Monroe), he chooses his own destruction by going over the edge of the falls. A character to whom something awful—something irreversible—has happened, he is sick beyond cure and

perhaps beyond explanation, like the psychopath in *The Spiral Staircase*.

Gun Crazy is the case history of a man whose gun fixation dates from his childhood. He is not a bad kid, flashbacks inform us, since he does not use guns to kill living things. As a grown-up, he is played appropriately by a weak actor (John Dall)—the character's fascination with guns, obviously, is a compensation for his own lack of manliness. His obsession begins to turn violent when, at a circus, he encounters a woman who makes her living as a sharpshooter. They meet in a contest, as they shoot matches placed on each other's heads—sexual imagery as blatant as the film's other psychological symbols. The woman (Peggy Cummins), a bewitching psychopath, is an enigma; the film keeps its distance from her, in a way that it does not with the more reasonable male protagonist, whom it attempts at least partially to explain. We have no clue as to how the woman got to be as maniacal as she is. Fearless, taunting, utterly without moral scruples, she goads the passive hero into a cycle of robberies and shootings, her expertise with guns a sign of her essential and unstoppable violence. At the end, as they are on the run, the man shoots her as she is about to kill his childhood friends who have come to reclaim him.

Great pop psychology, *Gun Crazy* makes passing stabs at a variety of meaty subjects: the place of violence in American life; the link between violence and sex; the emasculating obsession with masculinity. It examines the dependence on violence of a passive, fatally wounded man and an amorally seductive woman. Guns replace sex for both characters, and it is shrewd casting that the two actors do not project a strong sensuality.

"The power to kill can be just as satisfying as the power to create. You know I'd never do anything unless I did it perfectly," says John Dall, in a dramatic change of pace, as an aggressive psychopath in Hitchcock's *Rope*. His character manipulates a weak-willed friend (Farley Granger) into committing with him "an immaculate murder. We've killed for the sake of danger and the sake of killing." "How did you feel, during it?" he asks his friend. The question has a sexual undertone: in the killer's mind the

This deceptively plain-looking couple (Peggy Cummins and John Dall) is *Gun Crazy*.

act of murder becomes a metaphor for the sexual act. "I felt tremendous, exhilarated," Dall proclaims. After the murder he hosts a dinner party, taking a wicked delight in using as a table the chest where the murder victim lies. "This party is like the signature of the artist," he boasts to his friend.

Although *Rope* does not label the two young men as homosexuals, it is clear that they are perfectly paired partners in a gay sado-masochistic relationship. In an entirely unliberated way, the film implies a connection between the characters' sexuality and their crime, as if being homosexual has placed them beyond the laws of society. Brandon (the Dall character) is a stereotype of a sneering, fastidious homosexual—a spiritual heir of Oscar Wilde, seduced by elegance and the notion of decadence. He affects a disdainful posture: "Good and evil were invented for the ordinary man." His contempt for humanity is never explained; aside from the fact that he was a bully at school and that his friend

has always been afraid of him, and aside from whatever damage his sexual preference has worked on him, he remains a blank, grinning mask. James Stewart, as a professor who finds him out, says, "This thing must all along have been deep inside you. You've made me ashamed of my concept of superior and inferior. By what right did you decide that that boy in there was inferior and therefore could be killed? Did you think you were God?"

Presented with Hitchcock's characteristic detachment, his bland irony in the face of psychological horror, *Rope* is especially chilling because its blasphemous anti-hero resists categorization. At the end of *Psycho*, Norman Bates is diagnosed as a schizophrenic who has "internalized his mother." He has worked out in a literal way the clash between a strong-willed, guilt-inducing mother and a pliant, secretly rebellious child. The explanation of his psychosis is certainly pat, and may be a particularly droll instance of Hitchcockian irony. With the

"We've killed for the sake of danger and the sake of killing": Farley Granger and John Dall, as psychotic homosexuals, in *Rope* (with James Stewart, who has found them out).

"mother part" of his personality having taken over, Norman is locked up, to be of no further harm to anyone. *Rope* is more disturbing because the criminal cannot be contained by a tight Freudian profile; his evil seems more a matter of intellectual will than a result of psychic damage. *Noir*'s aberrational, deeply anti-social characters—the homosexuals in *Rope*, the gun-crazed couple on the run, the weakling son in *The Spiral Staircase*, the anti-Semite in *Crossfire*—resist whatever fragments of personal history the films supply as reasons for their madness. *Noir* constructs a world in which en-flamed anti-Semites, crazed gunmen, power-mad lawmen, gangsters, and con artists can materialize *without apparent cause*, to menace and terrify those who abide by the rules of the normal world. In *noir*, the bland and the insane live cheek-by-jowl: sometimes, they exist within the same person, waging a battle for supremacy; more often, madness erupts with terrifying suddenness into an environment that is seemingly ordered and safe. In either case, the genre is preoccupied with the vulnerability of seemingly well-adjusted characters to the forces of darkness both within and without.

8
Noir's Legacy

Noir's true heyday was brief: from Billy Wilder's *Double Indemnity* in 1944 to Wilder's *Sunset Boulevard* in 1950. By the end of the decade, *noir's* distinctive signature—its visual style, character types and narrative patterns—seemed repetitive. In the early fifties *noir* began, in various ways, to be eroded from within as it slipped into an unmistakably B category. The genre had always been low budget, but in the forties it had attracted the interest of major stars and directors. In the fifties it began to look threadbare. But the development and decline of a genre is a complicated process, of course, and good *films noirs* continued to be produced throughout the decade, and later.

Touch of Evil (1958) is now commonly regarded as the genre's epitaph, but *Odds Against Tomorrow* (1959), Robert Wise's strikingly designed thriller about a bank robbery, and *Psycho* (1960), which recounts an average woman's plunge into crime, contain many traditional *noir* motifs. *Psycho's* memorable opening, in which the camera moves from the bleaching daylight of Phoenix at mid-afternoon to the dark interior of a hotel room, announces a descent from day to night, from order to disorder, from rationality to error and chaos, that recalls many of the

Visual entrapment, in *Windows*, Gordon Willis' 1980 city thriller.

best and most typical *noir* dramas. From the dark self that lies in wait beneath the sunny facade of its normal heroine, to its psycho villain split between his own personality and that of his mother, to the birds he has stuffed in a gruesome parody of resurrection, to the appearance of the heroine's sister, halfway through the film, who in looks and manner so closely resembles her as to constitute another kind of "resurrection," to the name of the city (Phoenix) in which the story begins (which recalls the mythical bird that rises from its own ashes), the film is preoccupied, both visually and thematically, with the quintessential *noir* theme of doubleness.

Despite its gothic embellishments, *Psycho* is a vindication of the continuing strength of *noir* motifs, since at the time the film was made, *noir* was no longer a dominant influence. The genre in many ways was a product of its time, a response of film-makers, perhaps even on an unconscious level, to the stresses of the immediate postwar period, as well as a retrospective acknowledgment of wartime traumas. *Noir* unleashed a series of dark allegories of the national state of mind during the forties.

The genres that thrived during the fifties were westerns, science fiction thrillers, and musicals. Westerns and science fiction movies provided metaphors for a different set of national traumas than the ones that were filtered into *noir*. The strongest genre pieces of the fifties offer symbolic readings of two disasters, the HUAC (House Un-American Activities Committee) witch-hunt for communists, and the fear generated by atomic energy. (Although both catastrophes had their roots in the forties, their impact was not registered in popular culture until the fifties.) Such archetypal films of the period as *High Noon* and *The Invasion of the Body Snatchers* reflected current fears about what happens to non-conformists. The number of mutants that terrorized American cities in the fantasy movies of the time—*The Beast from 20,000 Fathoms* and all his fellows—translated anxiety of nuclear holocaust into popular storytelling molds; and the recurrent theme of personality takeover surely at some level spoke to the political hysteria fostered by Senator Joe McCarthy.

Noir thrives on confusion and a breakdown of values, and, in prospect, the utter political absurdity of the search for communists in the late forties and early fifties contained ripe possibilities for *noir* stories of paranoia, and of nightmarish disruptions of everyday routine. But the fact remains that no significant *films noirs* were concerned, either directly or metaphorically, with the contemporary political scene. The genre worked most effectively in recording private rather than large-scale social traumas; its most congenial framework was domestic: murderously angry husbands and wives, embattled parents, siblings and lovers. One of the eroding factors in the fifties thrillers surfaced in such films as *The Big Combo* and *The Phenix City Story* where crime no longer springs from the aberrant individual but is instead a corporate enterprise, run like a business. This view of crime as a widespread, almost communal undertaking, counters the traditional *noir* interest in the isolated criminal whose actions are controlled not by an impersonal conglomerate but by a complex interweaving of character and fate.

The genre is most at home in the postwar forties, at a time when the nation re-entered private life. In the fifties, *noir* lost its sustained high achievement as it began to tamper with generic elements that had become traditional. Some of these variations extended the life of the genre, while others hastened its virtual eclipse by the end of the decade.

The Prowler (1951) and *The Narrow Margin* (1952) are both fine thrillers that nonetheless inverted *noir* molds in ways that signalled the end of a movie cycle. *The Prowler* is a variation on *Double Indemnity*. This time it is the man, a thoroughly corrupt cop who invades the house of a well-to-do couple, who is the criminal instigator. The film's female protagonist noticeably departs from *noir* convention: instead of the vamp that audiences might expect, given the triangular romance the movie sets up, the character is passive, forlorn, loyal to the husband who is mostly absent pursuing his career, and hesitant about entering into an affair with the persistent policeman. Yet the intruder obviously answers some need in her. She originally called the police to her house to report the presence of a prowler; we are not told the prowler actually

Variations on *noir* formulas: in *The Prowler*, the woman (Evelyn Keyes) is innocent, the man (Van Heflin) is the criminal: (*below*) in *The Narrow Margin*, Marie Windsor's *femme fatale* costume is only a masquerade because she is really a policewoman testing detective Charles MacGraw's trustworthiness.

existed, but in effect the policeman who answers her distress calls becomes a prowler, slowly taking over her life, which in some ways is really what she wanted. Instead of Barbara Stanwyck, draped in a towel, nostrils flaring, spitting out her seductive words through clenched teeth, the movie offers Evelyn Keyes, tremulous, faded, sad-eyed. In *The Prowler*, it is the man who is seductive, fatally tempted by the promise of the woman's sensuality, and by the indications of wealth in her Southern California Spanish-style house, a dead ringer for the shadowed Dietrichson house in *Double Indemnity*.

The Narrow Margin also plays with *noir's* traditional iconographic depiction of women. The movie begins with deceptive ordinariness: a detective and his partner come to Chicago to escort a mobster's widow (Marie Windsor),

raven-haired and tough, to a trial in Los Angeles at which she is going to testify. She is carrying a list of names, and as she and her two escorts walk down the rickety stairway of the tenement in which she lives, the detective's assistant is shot. On the train, the detective befriends a pleasant blonde woman, who is traveling with her child and a nanny. Slyly the film inverts *noir* stereotypes, as the "widow" turns out to be a police officer (a decoy who has been planted to see if the detective could be bought by the mob), and the Grace Kelly-like blond turns out to be the mobster's widow. Ideally cast as a tough moll, Marie Windsor performs the role broadly. Her dialogue sounds like a parody of the hard-boiled school; and the exaggeration is a tip-off that *noir* conventions are being burlesqued. The detective is fooled by appearances, since he never for a moment figures the Windsor dame as a police officer, or the pleasant blonde as a gangster's widow. Like *The Prowler, The Narrow Margin* depends for its full impact on audience familiarity with earlier *noir* stories—both films are echoes of a fading genre.

Part of the process of change and transformation, leading to the eventual disappearance of *noir* as a popular genre, included two distinct and oddly divergent tendencies, one in the direction of simplification of *noir* motifs, the other a baroque elaboration of traditional elements. Early in the decade, several thrillers had a severely limited focus in story and setting and thereby differed from the labyrinthine plotting that marked the genre in the forties. In *Jeopardy*, Barbara Stanwyck spends most of the film trying to find a way to save her husband from drowning when his foot is trapped in the timbers of a rotting pier. In *Beware My Lovely*, Ida Lupino is held hostage in her house by a madman (Robert Ryan) throughout the film. In *Dangerous Crossing*, Jeanne Crain's new husband disappears almost as soon as their honeymoon aboard a luxury liner begins, and the rest of the drama hinges on whether or not the distraught woman really has a husband at all. These three films have bare storylines which rely in a simplified and almost abstract way on *noir* themes of psychological and physical entrapment. The suspense comes from the concentrated structure: from the start, a heroine is plunged headlong into a catastrophe, and the films focus exclusively on her plight. The three films are exciting thrillers which nonetheless lack the dimension of earlier *films noirs*.

The contrasting late *noir* tendency is exaggeration tinged with satire. Such films as *Kiss Me Deadly, The Big Combo, Screaming Mimi, Touch of Evil*, all represent *noir's* decadence. With Welles, the overdone treatment grows as much out of his own temperament as from his overwrought attempts to visualize a tired story. The bravura rendering of *noir* motifs in *Touch of Evil*, at any rate, is a display to be enjoyed for its own sake, quite apart from usual considerations of story and character development. It is easy to see why the film has been tagged as *noir's* epitaph, since it subjects motifs to what is probably their most theatrical elaboration. Robert Warshow wrote that *Shane* looked like the final western ever made because it pushed generic elements to the breaking point, treating them with calculated virtuosity. Overheated to a turbulent boil, *Touch of Evil* has something of the same place of dubious honor with respect to *noir*. The border city in the film is a festering cesspool, populated with a bunch of sweaty Mexicans lurking menacingly in the rotting, colonnaded streets. Crawling with human vermin, this city is the perfect setting for the corrupt sheriff to flourish in as well as an obvious trap for the distinguished Mexican-American lawyer (Charlton Heston) and his Anglo-Saxon wife (Janet Leigh). The film opens with a bomb exploding in the back of a car. It ends with a chase through oil derricks on the outskirts of town. The chase is a bravura set-piece, with wild camera angles and an elaborate soundtrack mixing dialogue, music, and voices on a radio. A cheap little thriller about a power-mad sheriff is transformed, by Welles' operatic style, into a galvanizing vision of evil.

In the sixties and seventies the genre was clearly a self-consciously resurrected form. Thrillers made "in the *noir* style" became a nostalgic exercise, touched with that note of condescension which often results when one generation reconstructs artifacts of an earlier era's popular culture. For the film-makers of the sixties and seventies, *"film noir"* seems to mean Bogart and Raymond Chandler. Such films as *Marlowe* (1969), *The Long Goodbye* (1974), *Farewell, My Lovely* (1975), and *The Big Sleep* (1978) are salutes to a bygone movie and literary tradition which fail, in different ways, to make Chandler's world either tangible or flavorful.

Based on *The Little Sister*, Chandler's novel about Hollywood, *Marlowe* looks like an ordinary television crime drama, with television actor James Garner providing a stolid interpretation of Chandler's legendary sleuth. Chandler's contrived plotting and snappy dialogue are at odds with the film's neutrally rendered contemporary setting and its bland use of color. The only well-chosen location is Marlowe's dim office located in the magnificent Bradbury Building in downtown Los Angeles, a recurrent background in high *film noir*. And the only character who transcends the inappropriately sunny background and the flat sixties lighting is Rita Moreno, playing a psychotically jealous stripper who turns out to be the villain. Moreno lends a soiled quality to the dancer; she has a toughness and seductiveness that have an authentic *noir* tang.

Michael Winner's *The Big Sleep* also has entirely the wrong look. The story has been transferred to England, with most of the outdoor scenes set in a country landscape, all lush green foliage and rolling hills. Where is the fog, so crucial a part of the Howard Hawks version? And where is the decorum, essential to the texture of Hawks' work as well as of Chandler's original? The violence and the sexual perversity that are part of the story are here blatantly handled. As General Sternwood's bad daughter (the role played by Martha Vickers in the 1946 version), harsh-voiced Candy Clark is crude, coming on like Southern white trash. She is hard and stupid, a freaked-out seventies kook; and she reduces Chandler's mysterious catalyst to someone who is plainly weird. Understandably enough, Winner did not want to duplicate the tone of the famous Hawks film; but his own counter choices—sunny skies, English countryside, kinky characters—deny the flavor of the material. The film's only appealing element is Robert Mitchum, himself an authentic *noir* icon,

as Philip Marlowe. His voice-over narration evokes the forties with only the faintest hint of parody or condescension, with at any rate no more of these qualities than can be found in the original *noir* dramas. Mitchum plays Marlowe in something of a stupor. He seems especially languid and sleepy-eyed, even for him, and he makes no pretense of doing anything more than simply lending his presence to the film. Yet that presence is really good enough—stolid, he-manly, beyond corruption; with a lazy, oozing, pot-bellied sexuality. But the actor looks like an anachronism in Winner's updating.

Dick Richards' *Farewell, My Lovely* provides a more congenial frame for Mitchum's Marlowe. Richards sets the film in the forties though the milieu is palpably a studied recreation rather than the real thing. To suggest the texture of old photographs the images are coated with a yellow gauze—the blurred quality is intended to distance characters and events. The film is beautiful to look at, but the photo album color and the exaggerated period details only point up the film-makers' lack of confidence in the material: everything seems to be enclosed in quotation marks. *Farewell, My Lovely* is a film *about* a bygone Hollywood style and, as such, shares many of the attitudes toward old movies in the films of Mel Brooks and Peter Bogdanovich. Bogdanovich resurrects superannuated modes in an affectionate, celebratory spirit; Brooks' satiric thrusts at outmoded movie conventions are harsher yet contain an implicit fondness for their corniness and sentimentality. A product of the cinematic self-consciousness of seventies film-makers, *Farewell, My Lovely* is more a nostalgic evocation of an old movie style than a full-fledged *film noir*.

Robert Altman is certainly not one merely to recreate or mimic a defunct genre, and his version of *The Long Goodbye* offers aggressive changes on the Chandler original. Subjecting the original story to cynical revisions, Altman has made a movie very much of and for the seventies. Chandler's *The Long Goodbye* is a story of a male friendship; Marlowe, obeying that gentlemanly code of honor that is so strong an aspect of his appeal, maintains his loyalty to a friend in trouble, even at considerable risk to his

Dick Richards' 1975 version of *Farewell, My Lovely* (with Robert Mitchum) is a self-conscious homage to *film noir*.

own well-being. His trust turns out to be justified, as his friend—despite incriminating appearances—is in fact innocent. As often in Chandler, a woman is responsible, and in *The Long Goodbye* she turns out to be a positive murdering fiend. Altman's film utterly violates Chandler's as well as Marlowe's code: the friend in this version is guilty; the woman merely an adulteress; and an enraged Marlowe, feeling a keen sense of betrayal, tracks down his friend in Mexico and shoots him, in an act of cold-blooded murder that Chandler's Marlowe would never commit. What is Altman saying? That Marlowe's code is no longer applicable to the cynical seventies? That trust and loyalty are irrelevant and misplaced feelings, and certainly have no part in the life of a private eye? Elliot Gould's sloppy, boyish Marlowe is deliberately a far cry from the sartorial neatness of Bogart and Dick Powell. Behaving altogether with a cuteness that would have given Bogart the shudders, Gould plays Marlowe as a mumbler

who lives in a pig sty and holds absent-minded conversations with his cat. He is on the wrong track most of the time, as the old Marlowes also were, but he also seems to be a natural fall guy in a way that the forties hard-boiled anti-heroes were not. He is ill-treated by the police, like all the Marlowes, but he does not hold his own with them as his predecessors did. This Marlowe gets his revenge at the end, in a radical and quite unexpected gesture, when he kills his betraying friend and then walks away, seemingly purged, to the ironic strains of "Hooray for Hollywood." The film ends with intentional dissonance: the music sends up the whole story, dismissing it as a Hollywood fabrication with a we-know-better-than-to-believe-this smugness, while the sudden killing is meant to jolt us, since Gould's character has seemed incapable of such a brutal and decisive action.

This revisionist *noir* is outfitted with Altman's usual tricks: muffled, overlapping dialogue; elaborate deep focus compositions (lots of reflections in glass in a chic Malibu beach house where much of the story takes place). Altman's leisurely pacing has an openness and an improvisational quality that sets up a deliberate contrast with the forties films; his is a very different kind of "cool" than the hard-boiled variety. *The Long Goodbye* is a stylish piece of work which shows little faith in the ability of Chandler to hold a contemporary audience. As opposed to the self-conscious recreation of *Farewell, My Lovely*, the film attempts to break the *noir* formula; but rather than suggesting provocative possibilities for the genre, Altman's work looks like a self-enclosed exercise.

Arthur Penn, like Altman a conscientious revisionist, tries in *Night Moves* to do to the private eye mold what he did to the western in *Little Big Man* and *The Left-Handed Gun* and to the gangster story in *Bonnie and Clyde*—that is, to give it a distinctly modern flavor. Like Chandler's plots, *Night Moves* blends two parallel stories: the private eye spies on his wife, who is having an affair, at the same time that he is pursuing a professional assignment, trying to locate the missing daughter of a wealthy client. The inner story (the hunt for the missing girl) is a reprise of forties conventions, and practically indecipherable in its twisted plotting; but the outer story gives the private eye more of a private life than was ever extended to the Spades and Marlowes of old. Interestingly, the film uses his profession as a metaphor for his own incompleteness; surveillance, which is a way of life for the character, is a sign of his remoteness. Harry Moseby (Gene Hackman) sees the world as a network of clues, and can live only by tracing and spying. He conducts a search for his father, and when he finally locates him, sitting on a park bench, he "spies" on him and then leaves. Moody, vulnerable, unknowable and yet intrigued by the unknowability of others, passionately involved in discovering the truth, in finding the puzzle's missing piece, Harry (as brilliantly played by Hackman, who performed much the same kind of part in *The Conversation*) is a significant extension of the tight-lipped private eye impersonated by Bogart.

Private eye detective dramas appeared at sporadic intervals in the sixties and seventies, to varying but never spectacular effect: Paul Newman in *Harper*, Jack Nicholson in *Chinatown*; the vastly overrated *The Late Show* with Art Carney as an aging, bloated private eye and dead-faced Lily Tomlin as a seventies kook who wants to locate a missing cat; parodies like *Gumshoe, The Black Bird*, and *The Cheap Detective*. Other thrillers with *noir* echoes—Don Siegel's remake of *The Killers*, the byzantine *Point Blank*, Siegel's Clint Eastwood movies, *Bunny Lake is Missing, Dead Ringer*—have been on the whole more successful than the Chandler-based series, though none has had the impact of the original forties pictures.

Many *noir* conventions have nonetheless had a continuing influence on American filmmaking: the use of the city; Expressionistic heightening and distortion to create suspense and to convey personality transformation; the notions of the criminal as a complex, divided character and of the criminal possibilities—the potential for violence—within the most seemingly ordinary people. Almost all thrillers since the fifties have some elements of *noir*, in mood or atmosphere, in acting style, settings, lighting. And the *noir* look infiltrated other genres as well: *Pursued* is obvious *film noir* even though a west-

Elliott Gould, as a bedraggled, uncool Philip Marlowe, in Robert Altman's revisionist version of *The Long Goodbye*.

ern, and a costume melodrama like *Reign of Terror* has distinct *noir* overtones. Although full-blown *films noirs* are indeed rare, thrillers with *noir* echoes, and dramas of various kinds that demonstrate the strength and endurance of the genre's conventions, continue to appear.

Noir conventions were adopted by French film-makers in the fifties and sixties. Godard's *Breathless* is certainly a salute to the American crime cycle of the forties, with Jean-Paul Belmondo playing a distinctly Gallic version of the *noir* loner. And the thrillers of Jean-Pierre Melville are heavily indebted to *noir* in both visual design and narrative pattern. Melville's cold, oddly still crime movies have a self-consciously abstract quality that no major studio American thriller would dare risk.

The work of two current film-makers—Paul Schrader and Walter Hill—is especially evocative of the *noir* strain. Schrader's familiarity with *noir* as critic and moviegoer has certainly influenced his own work, particularly in *Taxi Driver* (for which he wrote the script) and *Hard Core* (which he wrote as well as directed). In both films the city is a potent dramatic presence. New York in *Taxi Driver* is as infested a cityscape as any in the darkest *noir* of the forties. It seems not only to reflect the loner hero's terrifying disconnectedness and ferocity, but almost to function as a catalyst for it as well. A place of all-night movies and of sex for sale, the crumbling, dank city is an inferno in which steam drifts up from holes in the street and blinking neon lights perform their own demented dance of death; the city is a symbol of the anti-hero's tortured state of mind. The night scenes, with Travis' taxi snaking through the mean streets, have a preternaturally eerie quality. Schrader and the director, Martin Scorsese, make no pretense of presenting New York realistically; only those viewers with the most paranoid sense of what city life is really like could accept the film's version of the city as true-to-life. The film's dark city is a city of the imagination—of the Ex-

pressionist imagination, with an artistic lineage that can be traced back through the forties to German cinema and painting of the twenties.

Its story is not as compelling as that of *Taxi Driver*, but *Hard Core* also renders the city—this time, Los Angeles—as a wicked, corrupting environment, a collection of porn shops and brothels. Schrader, who comes from a strict Midwestern Calvinist family, has a puritan's riveted fascination with sin. Clearly, in the director's mind, "the city" is virtually a synonym for sexual wickedness.

Walter Hill (*The Driver, The Warriors*) is, like Schrader, a neo-Expressionist for whom the city is a rich symbolic backdrop. In *The Driver*, Hill uses *noir* conventions in an abstract way that strongly recalls Melville's cool style. His characters have no names, no inner lives; they are masks. The Driver, who is tops in his field (he drives getaway cars in hold-ups), is a *noir* loner, hiding out in dumpy downtown hotels. His eyes hidden behind dark glasses, he is a cold, dangerous character, capable of swift violence. His most human contact is in his battle of wits with a compulsive cop who is determined to nail him. In the forties, the Driver would have been killed; but in this modern allegory, he wanders off into the night as his arch-enemy, the Cop, has a fit because once again the Driver has eluded him.

The city is a cold presence in the film, as remote, as abstract, as menacing as the nameless characters. Hill begins and ends his story with spectacular chase sequences through the empty streets of downtown Los Angeles at night, with its mixture of sleek high-rise apartment buildings, its modernistic hotels, and its peeling bars and low-life rooming houses. A movie-smart director, Hill adds to the echoes of classic *films noirs* by setting much of the action in Union Station, one of the most-used backgrounds in films of the forties. *The Driver* is a true homage to the genre, a highly stylized and unappreciated contemporary *film noir*.

Film noir, then, has made a steady contribution to the look of American movies. Visual elements first formulated and developed in *noir* continue to appear in a variety of crime stories and melodramas. In its heyday, *film noir* had the best track

The city as a sexual inferno, in two latter-day *films noirs*: *Taxi Driver* (with Robert De Niro); *Hard Core* (with George C. Scott).

Cars as a place of isolation (Robert De Niro and Martin Scorsese, in *Taxi Driver*) and as a weapon (in *The Driver*) in two contemporary thrillers.

record of any Hollywood genre. It was hard to go entirely wrong with *noir* stories, which provided ready-made visual opportunities. Even the thinnest and most purely formulaic examples of the genre had some style and atmosphere. *Noir* had popular appeal—the stories were usually tense and engrossing—and it allowed for, indeed virtually demanded, some psychological complexity. Dramas of people in crisis, *noir* illuminated the night world of the other self that bedevils us all. Visually and thematically it was a genre of genuine richness, one that flourished at a particular moment in American history, but one that has had a lasting impact on film style. *Noir* is being rediscovered on college campuses and in revival theaters, as American *cinéastes* are finally catching up with the discovery of French critics over twenty-five years ago, that *film noir* constitutes a body of striking work that represents the American film industry in its most neurotic, subversive, and visually provocative phase. *Noir* exposes the underside of the American Dream in a mode that mixes German Expressionism with a native hard-boiled realism. In the verve and colloquial tanginess of its dialogue, in its range of provocative themes, in its gallery of taut performances, its studied compositions in light and shadow, its creation of sustained suspense, and its dramatic use of the city, the *noir* canon is an exemplar of Hollywood craftsmanship at its finest. In the flickering images of a movie screen, *film noir* seizes and penetrates a universal heart of darkness.

Noir in France: Alain Delon as a masked, hard-boiled hero, in Jean-Pierre Melville's *Le Samourai* (1972).

Selected Bibliography

Agee, James. *Agee on Film*. Boston: Beacon Press, 1964.

Allen, Dick, and David Chacko. *Detective Fiction: Crime and Compromise*. New York: Harcourt Brace Jovanovich, 1974.

Alloway, Lawrence. *Violent America: The Movies, 1946-1964*. New York: The Museum of Modern Art, 1971.

Appel, Alfred. *Nabokov's Dark Cinema*. New York: Oxford University Press, 1974.

Ball, John, editor. *The Mystery Story*. New York: Penguin Books, 1978.

Baxter, John. *Hollywood in the Thirties*. New York: A.S. Barnes; London: The Tantivy Press, 1968.

Bergman, Andrew. *We're in the Money: Depression America and Its Films*. New York: New York University Press, 1971.

Borde, Raymond, and Etienne Chaumeton. *Panorama du film noir américain*. Paris: Les Editions de Minuit, 1955.

Braudy, Leo. *The World in a Frame: What We See in Films*. New York: Doubleday Anchor Press, 1976.

Bridgman, Richard. *The Colloquial Style in America*. New York: Oxford University Press, 1966.

Burnett, W.R. *Little Caesar*. New York: The Dial Press, 1958.

Cain, James M. *Double Indemnity*. New York: Vintage Books, 1978.

_____. *Mildred Pierce*. New York: Vintage Books, 1978.

_____. *The Postman Always Rings Twice*. New York: Vintage Books, 1978.

_____. *Serenade*. New York: Vintage Books, 1978.

Camus, Albert. *The Rebel*. New York: Vintage Books 1956.

_____. *The Stranger*. New York: Vintage Books, 1954.

Cawelti, John G. *Adventure, Mystery, and Romance: Formula Stories as Art and Popular Culture*. Chicago and London: The University of Chicago Press, 1976.

Chandler, Raymond. *The Big Sleep*. New York: Vintage Books, 1976.

_____. *The Blue Dahlia*. Carbondale: Southern Illinois University Press, 1976.

_____. *Farewell, My Lovely*. New York: Vintage Books, 1976.

_____. *The Long Goodbye*. New York: Ballantine Books, 1971.

Cheney, Sheldon. *Expressionism in Art*. New York: Liveright, 1958.

Deming, Barbara. *Running Away from Myself*. New York: Grossman, 1969.

Durgnat, Raymond. "The Family Tree of *Film Noir*," in *Cinema* (UK), 1970.

_____. *The Strange Case of Alfred Hitchcock or, the Plain Man's Hitchcock*. Cambridge, Massachusetts: The MIT Press, 1974.

Durham, Philip. *Down These Mean Streets a Man Must Go: Raymond Chandler's Knight*. Chapel Hill: University of North Carolina Press, 1963.

Eisinger, Chester E. *Fiction of the Forties*. Chicago and London: University of Chicago Press, 1963.

Eisner, Lotte H. *Fritz Lang*. New York: Oxford University Press, 1977.

_____. *The Haunted Screen*. Berkeley and Los Angeles: University of California Press, 1965.

Everson, William K. *The Detective in Film*. Secaucus, New Jersey: Citadel Press, 1972.

Farber, Manny. *Negative Space*. New York: Praeger, 1971.

Ferguson, Otis. *The Film Criticism of Otis Ferguson*. Philadelphia: Temple University Press, 1971.

Frohock, W.M. *The Novel of Violence in America 1920-1950*. Dallas: Southern Methodist University, 1973.

Gabree, John. *Gangsters from Little Caesar to The Godfather*. New York: Pyramid, 1973.

Greene, Graham. *The Ministry of Fear*. New York: Penguin Books, 1978.

Gross, Miriam, editor. *The World of Raymond Chandler*. New York: A&W Publishers, 1977.

Gurko, Leo. *The Angry Decade*. New York: Dodd, Mead, 1947.

_____. *Heroes, Highbrows and The Popular Mind*. Indianapolis: Bobbs-Merrill, 1953.

Hammett, Dashiell. *The Big Knockover*. New York: Vintage Books, 1972.

_____. *The Continental Op*. New York: Vintage Books, 1975.

_____. *The Glass Key*. New York: Vintage Books, 1972.

_____. *The Maltese Falcon*. New York: Vintage Books, 1972.

Haycraft, Howard. *Murder for Pleasure: The Life and Times of the Detective Story*. New York: Biblo and Tannen, 1968.

Hemingway, Ernest. *To Have and Have Not*. New York: Charles Scribner's Sons, 1970.

_____. "The Killers," in *Men Without Women*. New York: Charles Scribner's Sons, 1932.

Higham, Charles, and Joel Greenberg. *Hollywood in the Forties*. New York: A.S. Barnes; London: The Tantivy Press, 1968.

Hirsch, Foster. *Edward G. Robinson*. New York: Pyramid, 1975.

_____. *Joseph Losey*. Boston: G.K. Hall, 1980.

Hughes, Dorothy M. *In a Lonely Place*. New York: Bantam Books, 1979.

_____. *Ride the Pink Horse*. New York: Bantam Books, 1979.

Jacobs, Diane. *Hollywood Renaissance*. Cranbury, New Jersey: A.S. Barnes; London: The Tantivy Press, 1977.

Kaminsky, Stuart. *American Film Genres*. Dayton, Ohio: Pflaum-Standard, 1974.

Kaplan, E. Ann, editor. *Women in Film Noir*. London: BFI, 1978.

Karimi, Amir Massoud. *Toward a Definition of the American Film Noir (1941-1949)*. New York: Arno Press, 1976.

Karpf, Stephen Louis. *The Gangster Film: Emergence, Variation and Decay of a Genre 1930-1940*. New York: Arno Press, 1973.

Kracauer, Siegfried. *From Caligari to Hitler: A Psychological History of the German Film*. Princeton: Princeton University Press, 1947.

Landrum, Larry N., and Pat Browne, and Ray B. Browne, editors. *Dimensions of Detective Fiction*. Popular Press, 1976.

MacShane, Frank. *The Life of Raymond Chandler*. New York: Penguin Books, 1978.

McArthur, Colin. *Underworld USA*. New York: The Viking Press, 1972.

McCarthy, Todd, and Charles Flynn. *Kings of the Bs: Working Within the Hollywood System*. New York: E.P. Dutton, 1975.

Madden, David. *James M. Cain*. New York: Twayne Publishers, 1970.

_____. ed. *Tough Guy Writers of the Thirties*. Carbondale: Southern Illinois University Press, 1968.

Nevins, Jr., Francis M. *The Mystery Writer's Art*. Bowling Green, Ohio: Bowling Green University Popular Press, 1970.

O'Hara, John. *Appointment in Samarra*. New York: Random House, 1934.

Phillips, Cabell. *The 1940s: Decade of Triumph and Trouble*. New York: Macmillan, 1975.

Rosow, Eugene. *Born to Lose: The Gangster Film in America*. New York: Oxford University Press, 1978.

Ruehlmann, William. *Saint with a Gun: The Unlawful American Private Eye*. New York: New York University Press, 1974.

Ruhm, Herbert, editor. *The Hard-Boiled Detective: Stories from Black Mask Magazine 1920-1951*. New York: Vintage Books, 1977.

Sarris, Andrew. *The American Cinema: Directors and Directions 1929-1968*. New York: E.P. Dutton, 1968.

Schrader, Paul. "Notes on *Film Noir*," in *Film Comment* (Spring 1972).

Shadoian, Jack. *Dreams and Dead Ends: The American Gangster/Crime Film*. Cambridge, Massachusetts: The MIT Press, 1977.

Silver, Alain, and Elizabeth Ward, eds. *Film Noir, An Encyclopedic Reference to the American Style*. Woodstock: The Overlook Press, 1979.

Solomon, Stanley. *Beyond Formula: American Film Genre*. New York: Harcourt Brace Jovanovich, 1976.

Tyler, Parker. *Magic and Myth of the Movies*. New York: Simon & Schuster, 1970.

Warshow, Robert. "The Gangster as Tragic Hero," in *The Immediate Experience*. New York: Atheneum, 1970.

Wolfe, Peter. *Graham Greene: The Entertainer*. Carbondale: Southern Illinois University Press, 1972.

Wood, Robin. *Hitchcock's Films*. New York: A.S. Barnes; London: The Tantivy Press, 1977.

Woolrich, Cornell (as William Irish). "Angel Face," in *Crime On Her Mind*, ed. by Michele E. Slung. New York: Pantheon, 1975.

_____. *Angels of Darkness*. New York: The Mysterious Press, 1978.

_____. *The Black Angel*. New York: P.F. Collier & Son, 1943.

_____. *Nightwebs*. New York: Avon, 1974.

_____. "Rear Window," in *Stories into Film*, edited by William Kittridge and Steven M. Krauzer. New York: Harper & Row, 1979.

Willett, John. *Expressionism*. New York: McGraw-Hill, 1970.

Wilson, Edmund. "The Boys in the Back Room," "Why Do People Read Detective Stories?" in *Classics and Commercials: A Literary Chronicle of the Forties*. New York: Vintage Books, 1962.

Selected Filmography

ANGEL FACE. RKO. 1952. Screenplay: Frank Nugent and Oscar Millard; from an unpublished story by Chester Erskine. Director: Otto Preminger. Director of Photography: Harry Stradling. Music Score and Conductor: Dimitri Tiomkin. Art Directors: Albert S. D'Agostino, Carroll Clark. Editor: Frederic Knudtson. Cast: Robert Mitchum, Jean Simmons, Mona Freeman, Herbert Marshall.

THE ASPHALT JUNGLE. MGM. 1950. Screenplay: Ben Maddow and John Huston; from the novel by W.R. Burnett. Director: John Huston. Director of Photography: Harold Rosson. Music: Miklos Rozsa. Art Directors: Cedric Gibbons, Randall Duell. Editor: George Boemler. Cast: Sterling Hayden, Louis Calhern, Jean Hagen, Sam Jaffe, Marilyn Monroe.

BEWARE, MY LOVELY. Filmmakers-RKO. 1952. Screenplay: Mel Dinelli; from his play and short story *The Man*. Director: Harry Horner. Director of Photography: George E. Diskant. Music: Leith Stevens. Art Directors: Albert S. D'Agostino, Alfred Herman. Editor: Paul Weatherwax. Cast: Ida Lupino, Robert Ryan.

BEYOND A REASONABLE DOUBT. RKO. 1956. Screenplay: Douglas Morrow. Director: Fritz Lang. Director of Photography: William Snyder. Music: Herschel Burke Gilbert. Art Director: Carroll Clark. Editor: Gene Fowler Jr. Cast: Dana Andrews, Joan Fontaine, Sidney Blackmer, Philip Bourneuf, Shepperd Strudwick, Barbara Nichols.

BEYOND THE FOREST. Warner Brothers. 1949. Screenplay: Lenore Coffee; from the novel by Stuart Engstrand. Director: King Vidor. Director of Photography: Robert Burks. Music: Max Steiner. Art Director: Robert Haas. Editor: Rudi Fehr. Cast: Bette Davis, Joseph Cotten, David Brian, Ruth Roman, Dona Drake.

THE BIG CARNIVAL (ACE IN THE HOLE). Paramount. 1951. Screenplay: Billy Wilder, Lesser Samuels, and Walter Newman. Director: Billy Wilder. Director of Photography: Charles B. Lang. Music: Hugo Friedhofer. Art Directors: Hal Periera, Earl Hedrick. Editor: Arthur Schmidt. Cast: Kirk Douglas, Jan Sterling, Porter Hall, Frank Cady, Ray Teal.

THE BIG CLOCK. Paramount. 1948. Screenplay: Jonathan Latimer, adapted by Harold Goldman; from the novel by Kenneth Fearing. Director: John Farrow. Director of Photography: John F. Seitz. Music: Victor Young. Art Directors: Hans Dreier, Roland Anderson, Albert Nozaki. Editor: Gene Ruggiero. Cast: Ray Milland, Charles Laughton, Maureen O'Sullivan, Elsa Lanchester.

THE BIG COMBO. Security-Theodora-Allied Artists. 1955. Screenplay: Philip Yordan. Director: Joseph H. Lewis. Director of Photography: John Alton. Music: David Raskin. Production Designer: Rudi Feld. Editor: Robert Eisen. Cast: Cornell Wilde, Jean Wallace, Richard Conte, Brian Donlevy.

THE BIG HEAT. Columbia. 1953. Screenplay: Sydney Boehm; from the novel by William P. McGivern. Director: Fritz Lang. Director of Photography: Charles Lang. Music: Daniele Amfitheatrof. Art Director: Robert Peterson. Editor: Charles Nelson. Cast: Glenn Ford, Gloria Grahame, Jocelyn Brando, Alexander Scourby, Lee Marvin, Jeanette Nolan.

THE BIG SLEEP. Warner Brothers. 1946. Screenplay: William Faulkner, Leigh Brackett, and Jules Furthman; from the novel by Raymond Chandler. Director: Howard Hawks. Director of Photography: Sid Hickox. Music: Max Steiner. Art Director: Carl Jules Weyl. Editor: Christian Nyby. Cast: Humphrey Bogart, Lauren Bacall, Martha Vickers, Dorothy Malone.

BLACK ANGEL. Universal. 1946. Screenplay: Roy Chanslor; from the novel by Cornell Woolrich. Director: Roy William Neill. Director of Photography: Paul Ivano. Music: Frank Skinner. Art Directors: Jack Otterson, Martin Obzina. Editor: Saul A. Goodkind. Cast: Dan Duryea, June Vincent, Peter Lorre, Broderick Crawford, Constance Dowling, Wallace Ford.

THE BLUE DAHLIA. Paramount. 1946. Screenplay: Raymond Chandler. Director: George Marshall. Director of Photography: Lionel Lindon. Music: Victor Young. Art Directors: Hans Dreier, Walter Tyler. Editor: Arthur Schmidt. Cast: Alan Ladd, Veronica Lake, William Bendix, Howard da Silva, Tom Powers.

BODY AND SOUL. Enterprise-United Artist. 1947. Screenplay: Abraham Polonsky. Director: Robert Rossen. Director of Photography: James Wong Howe. Music: Hugo Friedhofer. Art Director: Nathan Juran. Editor: Francis Lyon, Robert Parrish. Cast: John Garfield, Lilli Palmer, Anne Revere, William Conrad, Canada Lee.

THE BREAKING POINT. Warner Brothers. 1950. Screenplay: Ranald MacDougall; from the novel *To Have and Have Not* by Ernest Hemingway. Director: Michael Curtiz. Director of Photography: Ted McCord. Music: Ray Heindorf. Art Director: Edward Carrere. Editor: Alan Crosland Jr. Cast: John Garfield, Phyllis Thaxter, Patricia Neal, Juano Hernandez, Wallace Ford.

BRUTE FORCE. Universal-International. 1947. Screenplay: Richard Brooks; from an unpublished story by Robert Patterson. Director: Jules Dassin. Director of Photography: William Daniels. Music: Miklos Rozsa. Art Directors: Bernard Herzbrun, John F. DeCuir. Editor: Edward Curtiss. Cast: Burt Lancaster, Hume Cronyn, Charles Bickford, Yvonne De Carlo, Ann Blyth, Ella Raines, Sam Levene, Howard Duff, Art Smith.

CALL NORTHSIDE 777. 20th Century-Fox. 1948. Screenplay: Jerome Cady and Jay Dratler, adapted by Leonard Hoffman and Quentin Reynolds; from *Chicago Times* articles by James P. McGuire. Director: Henry Hathaway. Director of Photography: Joe MacDonald. Music Director: Alfred Newman. Art Directors: Lyle Wheeler, Mark-Lee Kirk. Editor: J. Watson Webb Jr. Cast: James Stewart, Richard Conte, Lee J. Cobb, Helen Walker, Betty Garde, Howard Smith, Moroni Olsen, E.G. Marshall.

CAPE FEAR. Universal-International. 1962. Screenplay: James R. Webb; from the novel *The Executioners* by John D. MacDonald. Director: J. Lee Thompson. Director of Photography: Samuel Leavitt. Music: Bernard Herrmann. Art Directors: Alexander Golitzen, Robert Boyle. Editor: George Tomasini. Cast: Gregory Peck, Robert Mitchum, Polly Bergen.

CHINATOWN. Paramount. 1974. Screenplay: Robert Towne. Director: Roman Polanski. Director of Photography: John A. Alonzo. Music: Jerry Goldsmith. Production Designer: Richard Sylbert. Art Director: W. Stewart Campbell. Editor: Sam O'Steen. Cast: Jack Nicholson, Faye Dunaway, John Huston, John Hillerman, Diane Ladd.

CHRISTMAS HOLIDAY. Universal. 1944. Screenplay: Herman J. Mankiewicz; from the novel by W. Somerset Maugham. Director: Robert Siodmak. Director of Photography: Woody Bredell. Music: Hans J. Salter. Art Directors: John B. Goodman, Robert Clatworthy. Editor: Ted Kent. Cast: Deanna Durbin, Gene Kelly, Gladys George, Gale Sondergaard.

CLASH BY NIGHT. Wald-Krasna-RKO. 1952. Screenplay: Alfred Hayes; from the play by Clifford Odets. Director: Fritz Lang. Director of Photography: Nicholas Musuraca. Music: Roy Webb. Art Directors: Albert S. D'Agostino, Carroll Clark. Editor: George J. Amy. Cast: Barbara Stanwyck, Paul Douglas, Robert Ryan, Marilyn Monroe.

CONFLICT. Warner Brothers. 1945. Screenplay: Arthur T. Horman and Dwight Taylor; from an original story by Robert Siodmak and Alfred Neumann. Director: Curtis Bernhardt. Director of Photography: Merritt Gerstad. Music Score: Frederick Hollander. Art Director: Ted Smith. Editor: David Weisbart. Cast: Humphrey Bogart, Alexis Smith, Sydney Greenstreet, Rose Hobart.

CORNERED. RKO. 1945. Screenplay: John Paxton; from an unpublished story by John Wexley. Director: Edward Dmytryk. Director of Photography: Harry J. Wild. Music: Roy Webb. Art Directors: Albert S. D'Agostino, Carroll Clark. Editor: Joseph Noriega. Cast: Dick Powell, Walter Slezak, Micheline Cheirel, Morris Carnovsky, Steven Geray.

CRISS CROSS. Universal-International. 1949. Screenplay: Daniel Fuchs; from the novel by Don Tracy. Director: Robert Siodmak. Director of Photography: Franz Planer. Music Score: Miklos Rozsa. Art Directors: Boris Leven, Bernard Herzbrun. Editor: Ted J. Kent. Cast: Burt Lancaster, Yvonne De Carlo, Dan Duryea, Stephen McNally, Richard Long.

CROSSFIRE. RKO. 1947. Screenplay: John Paxton; from the novel *The Brick Foxhole* by Richard Brooks. Director: Edward Dmytryk. Director of Photography: J. Roy Hunt. Music: Roy Webb. Art Directors: Albert S. D'Agostino, Alfred Herman. Editor: Harry Gerstad. Cast: Robert Young, Robert Mitchum, Robert Ryan, Gloria Grahame, Paul Kelly, Sam Levene, Lex Barker.

CRY OF THE CITY. 20th Century-Fox. 1948. Screenplay: Richard Murphy; from the novel *The Chair for Martin Rome* by Henry Edward Helseth. Director: Robert Siodmak. Director of Photography: Lloyd Ahern. Music Score: Alfred Newman. Art Directors: Lyle Wheeler, Albert Hogsett. Editor: Harmon Jones. Cast: Victor Mature, Richard Conte, Fred Clark, Shelley Winters, Betty Garde, Berry Kroeger, Debra Paget, Hope Emerson.

D.O.A. Popkin-United Artists. 1950. Screenplay: Russell Rouse and Clarence Green. Director: Rudolph Maté. Director of Photography: Ernest Laszlo. Music Score: Dimitri Tiomkin. Art Director: Duncan Cramer. Editor: Arthur H. Nadel. Cast: Edmond O'Brien, Pamela Britton, Luther Adler, Beverly Campbell, Neville Brand.

THE DARK CORNER. 20th Century-Fox. 1946. Screenplay: Jay Dratler and Bernard Schoenfeld; from the short story by Leo Rosten. Director: Henry Hathaway. Director of Photography: Joe MacDonald. Music: Cyril Mockridge. Art Directors: James Basevi, Leland Fuller. Editor: J. Watson Webb. Cast: Mark Stevens, Lucille Ball, Clifton Webb, William Bendix, Cathy Downs, Constance Collier.

THE DARK MIRROR. Universal-International. 1946. Screenplay: Nunnally Johnson. Director: Robert Siodmak. Director of Photography: Milton Krasner. Music Score: Dimitri Tiomkin. Production Designer: Duncan Cramer. Editor: Ernest Nims. Cast: Olivia De Havilland, Lew Ayres, Thomas Mitchell, Dick Long.

DARK PASSAGE. Warner Brothers. 1947. Screenplay: Delmer Daves; from the novel by David Goodis. Director: Delmar Daves. Director of Photography: Sid Hickox. Music Score: Franz Waxman. Art Director: Charles H. Clarke. Editor: David Weisbart. Cast: Humphrey Bogart, Lauren Bacall, Bruce Bennett, Agnes Moorehead.

DEADLINE AT DAWN. RKO. 1946. Screenplay: Clifford Odets; from the novel by William Irish (Cornell Woolrich). Director: Harold Clurman. Director of Photography: Nicholas Musuraca. Music: Hanns Eisler. Art Directors: Albert D'Agostino, Jack Okey. Editor: Roland Gross. Cast: Susan Hayward, Paul Lukas, Bill Williams, Joseph Calleia, Osa Massen, Lola Lane, Steven Geray.

DIRTY HARRY. Warner Brothers. 1971. Screenplay: Harry Julian Fink, Rita M. Fink, and Dean Riesner. Director: Don Siegel. Director of Photography: Bruce Surtees. Music: Lalo Schifrin. Art Director: Dale Hennesy. Editor: Carl Pingitore. Cast: Clint Eastwood, Reni Santoni, Harry Guardino, Andy Robinson, John Larch, Josef Sommer.

DOUBLE INDEMNITY. Paramount. 1944. Screenplay: Raymond Chandler and Billy Wilder; from the novel by James M. Cain. Director: Billy Wilder. Director of Photography: John F. Seitz. Music Score: Miklos Rozsa. Supervising Art Director: Hans Dreier. Editor: Doane Harrison. Cast: Fred MacMurray, Barbara Stanwyck, Edward G. Robinson.

EDGE OF DOOM. Goldwyn-RKO. 1950. Screenplay: Philip Yordan and Ben Hecht; from the novel by Leo Brady. Director: Mark Robson, with additional scenes by Charles Vidor. Director of Photography: Harry Stradling. Music Score: Hugo Friedhofer. Art Director: Richard Day. Editor: Daniel Mandell. Cast: Dana Andrews, Farley Granger, Joan Evans, Robert Keith, Paul Stewart, Mala Powers, Adele Jergens.

THE ENFORCER. Warner Brothers. 1951. Screenplay: Martin Rackin. Director: Bretaigne Windust and (uncredited) Raoul Walsh. Director of Photography: Robert Burks. Music Score: David Buttolph. Art Director: Charles H. Clarke. Editor: Fred Allen. Cast: Humphrey Bogart, Zero Mostel, Ted de Corsia, Everett Sloane, King Donovan, Susan Cabot.

FALLEN ANGEL. 20th Century-Fox. 1946. Screenplay: Harry Kleiner; from the novel by Marty Holland. Director: Otto Preminger. Director of Photography: Joseph LaShelle. Music: David Raksin. Art Directors: Lyle Wheeler, Leland Fuller. Editor: Harry Reynolds. Cast: Alice Faye, Dana Andrews, Linda Darnell, Charles Bickford, Anne Revere.

FAREWELL, MY LOVELY. ITC-Kastner/Avco Embassy. 1975. Screenplay: David Zelag Goodman; from the novel by Raymond Chandler. Director: Dick Richards. Director of Photography: John A. Alonzo. Music: David Shire. Art Director: Angelo Graham. Editors: Walter Thompson, Joel Cox. Cast: Robert Mitchum, Charlotte Rampling, John Ireland, Sylvia Miles, Anthony Zerbe.

THE FILE OF THELMA JORDAN. Paramount. 1950. Screenplay: Ketti Frings. Director: Robert Siodmak. Director of Photography: George Barnes. Music: Victor Young. Art Director: Hans Dreier, Earl Hedrick. Editor: Warren Low. Cast: Barbara Stanwyck, Wendell Corey, Paul Kelly, Joan Tetzel, Minor Watson.

GILDA. Columbia. 1946. Screenplay: Marion Parsonnet, adapted by Jo Eisinger; from an original story by E.A. Ellington. Director: Charles Vidor. Director of Photography: Rudolph Maté. Music Director: Morris Stoloff. Art Directors: Stephen Goosson, Van Nest Polglase. Editor: Charles Nelson. Cast: Rita Hayworth, Glenn Ford, George Macready, Joseph Calleia, Steven Geray, Gerald Mohr.

THE GLASS KEY. Paramount. 1942. Screenplay: Jonathan Latimer; from the novel by Dashiell Hammett. Director: Stuart Heisler. Director of Photography: Theodor Sparkuhl. Music: Victor Young. Art Directors: Hans Dreier, Haldane Douglas. Editor: Archie Marshek. Cast: Brian Donlevy, Veronica Lake, Alan Ladd, Bonita Granville, Richard Denning, William Bendix.

GUN CRAZY. King Brothers–United Artists. 1950. Screenplay: MacKinlay Kantor and Millard Kaufman: from the *Saturday Evening Post* story *Gun Crazy* by MacKinlay Kantor. Director: Joseph H. Lewis. Director of Photography: Russell Harlan. Music: Victor Young. Production Designer: Gordon Wiles. Editor: Harry Gerstad. Cast: Peggy Cummins, John Dall, Berry Kroeger, Morris Carnovsky, Rusty Tamblyn.

HIGH SIERRA. Warner Brothers. 1941. Screenplay: John Huston and W.R. Burnett; from the novel by W.R. Burnett. Director: Raoul Walsh. Director of Photography: Tony Gaudio. Music: Adolph Deutsch. Art Director: Ted Smith. Editor: Jack Killifer. Cast: Humphrey Bogart, Ida Lupino, Arthur Kennedy, Joan Leslie, Henry Hull.

HOUSE ON 92ND STREET. 20th Century-Fox. 1945. Screenplay: Barré Lyndon, Charles G. Booth, and John Monks Jr.; from an unpublished story by Charles G. Booth. Director: Henry Hathaway. Director of Photography: Norbert Brodine. Music: David Buttolph. Art Directors: Lyle Wheeler, Lewis Creber. Editor: Harmon Jones. Cast: William Eythe, Lloyd Nolan, Signe Hasso, Gene Lockhart, Leo G. Carroll.

HUMAN DESIRE. Columbia. 1954. Screenplay: Alfred Hayes; from the novel *La Bete Humaine* by Emile Zola. Director: Fritz Lang. Director of Photography: Burnett Guffey. Music Score: Daniele Amfitheatrof. Art Director: Robert Peterson. Editor: William A. Lyon. Cast: Glenn Ford, Gloria Grahame, Broderick Crawford, Edgar Buchanan.

IN A LONELY PLACE. Columbia. 1950. Screenplay: Andrew Solt; from the novel by Dorothy B. Hughes. Director: Nicholas Ray. Director of Photography: Burnett Guffey. Musical Score: George Antheil. Art Director: Robert Peterson. Editor: Viola Lawrence. Cast: Humphrey Bogart, Gloria Grahame, Frank Lovejoy, Carl Benton Reid, Art Smith, Jeff Donnell.

JEOPARDY. MGM. 1952. Screenplay: Mel Dinelli and Maurice Zim. Director: John Sturges. Director of Photography: Victor Milner. Music: Dimitri Tiomkin. Art Directors: Cedric Gibbons, William Ferrari. Editor: Newell P. Kimlin. Cast: Barbara Stanwyck, Barry Sullivan, Ralph Meeker.

KANSAS CITY CONFIDENTIAL. United Artists. 1952. Screenplay: George Bruce and Harry Essex. Director: Phil Karlson. Director of Photography: George E. Diskant. Music: Paul Sawtell. Art Director: Edward L. Ilou. Editor: Buddy Small. Cast: John Payne, Coleen Gray, Preston Foster, Dona Drake, Jack Elam, Neville Brand, Lee Van Cleef.

KEY LARGO. Warner Brothers. 1948. Screenplay: Richard Brooks and John Huston; from the play by Maxwell Anderson. Director: John Huston. Director of Photography: Karl Freund. Music: Max Steiner. Art Director: Leo K. Kuter. Editor: Rudi Fehr. Cast: Humphrey Bogart, Edward G. Robinson, Lauren Bacall, Lionel Barrymore, Claire Trevor, Thomas Gomez. 101 minutes.

THE KILLERS. Universal. 1946. Screenplay: Anthony Veiller and John Huston (uncredited); from the short story by Ernest Hemingway. Director: Robert Siodmak. Director of Photography: Woody Bredell. Music: Miklos Rozsa. Art Directors: Jack Otterson, Martin Obzina. Editor: Arthur Hilton. Cast: Burt Lancaster, Edmond O'Brien, Ava Gardner, Albert Dekker, Sam Levene, Virginia Christine, Queenie Smith.

KILLER'S KISS. United Artists. 1955. Screenplay: Stanley Kubrick. Director: Stanley Kubrick. Director of Photography: Stanley Kubrick. Music: Gerald Fried. Editor: Stanley Kubrick. Cast: Frank Silvera, Jamie Smith, Irene Kane.

THE KILLING. Kubrick-Harris-United Artists. 1956. Screenplay: Stanley Kubrick; from the novel *The Clean Break* by Lionel White. Director: Stanley Kubrick. Director of Photography: Lucien Ballard. Art Director: Ruth Sobotka Kubrick. Music: Gerald Fried. Editor: Betty Steinberg. Cast: Sterling Hayden, Coleen Gray, Vince Edwards, Jay C. Flippen, Marie Windsor, Ted De Corsia, Elisha Cook Jr., Timothy Carey.

KISS ME DEADLY. Parklane-United Artists. 1955. Screenplay: A.I. Bezzerides; from the novel by Mickey Spillane. Director: Robert Aldrich. Director of Photography: Ernest Laszlo. Art Director: William Glasgow. Music: Frank De Vol. Editor: Michael Luciano. Cast: Ralph Meeker, Albert Dekker, Paul Stewart, Maxine Cooper, Gaby Rodgers, Wesley Addy, Cloris Leachman.

KISS OF DEATH. 20th Century-Fox. 1947. Screenplay: Ben Hecht and Charles Lederer; from a story by Eleazar Lipsky. Director: Henry Hathaway. Director of Photography: Norbert Brodine. Music: David Buttolph. Art Directors: Lyle Wheeler, Leland Fuller. Editor: J. Watson Webb Jr. Cast: Victor Mature, Brian Donlevy, Coleen Gray, Richard Widmark, Karl Malden.

KISS TOMORROW GOODBYE. Warner Brothers. 1950. Screenplay: Harry Brown; from the novel by Horace McCoy. Director: Gordon Douglas. Director of Photography: J. Peverell Marley. Music: Carmen Dragon. Production Design: Wiard Ihnen. Editors: Truman K. Wood, Walter Hannemann. Cast: James Cagney, Barbara Payton, Helena Carter, Ward Bond, Luther Adler, Barton MacLane, Steve Brodie, Rhys Williams, John Litel.

THE LADY FROM SHANGHAI. Columbia. 1948. Screenplay: Orson Welles; from the novel *Before I Die* by Sherwood King. Director: Orson Welles. Director of Photography: Charles Lawton Jr. Music Score: Heinz Roemheld. Art Directors: Stephen Gosson, Sturges Carné. Editor: Viola Lawrence. Cast: Rita Hayworth, Orson Welles, Everett Sloane, Glenn Anders, Erskine Sanford.

LADY IN THE LAKE. MGM. 1947. Screenplay: Steve Fisher; from the novel by Raymond Chandler. Director: Robert Montgomery. Director of Photography: Paul C. Vogel. Music Score: David Snell. Art Directors: Cedric Gibbons, Preston Ames. Editor: Gene Ruggiero. Cast: Robert Montgomery, Lloyd Nolan, Audrey Totter, Tom Tully, Leon Ames, Jayne Meadows.

LAURA. 20th Century-Fox. 1944. Screenplay: Jay Dratler, Samuel Hoffenstein, and Betty Reinhardt; from the novel by Vera Caspary. Director: Otto Preminger. Director of Photography: Joseph LaShelle. Music Score: David Raksin. Art Directors: Lyle Wheeler, Leland Fuller. Editor: Louis Loeffler. Cast: Gene Tierney, Dana Andrews, Clifton Webb, Vincent Price, Judith Anderson.

LEAVE HER TO HEAVEN. 20th Century-Fox. 1945. Screenplay: Jo Swerling; from the novel by Ben Ames Williams. Director: John M. Stahl. Director of Photography: Leon Shamroy. Music Score: Alfred Newman. Art Directors: Lyle Wheeler, Maurice Ransford. Editor: James B. Clark. Cast: Gene Tierney, Cornel Wilde, Jeanne Crain, Vincent Price, Gene Lockhart.

THE LINEUP. Columbia. 1958. Screenplay: Stirling Silliphant; from characters created by Lawrence L. Klee in the CBS Television series *The Lineup*. Director: Don Siegel. Director of Photography: Hal Mohr. Music: Mischa Bakaleinikoff. Art Director: Ross Bellah. Editor: Al Clark. Cast: Eli Wallach, Robert Keith, Warner Anderson, Richard Jaeckel.

THE LONG GOODBYE. United Artists. 1973. Screenplay: Leigh Brackett; from the novel by Raymond Chandler. Director: Robert Altman. Director of Photography: Vilmos Zsigmond. Music Score: John Williams. Editor: Lou Lombardo. Cast: Elliott Gould, Nina van Pallandt, Sterling Hayden, Mark Rydell, Henry Gibson, Jim Bouton.

M. Columbia. 1951. Screenplay: Norman Reilly Raine and Leo Katcher, with additional dialogue by Waldo Salt; based on the 1931 screenplay by Thea von Harbou. Director: Joseph Losey. Director of Photography: Ernest Laszlo. Music Score: Michel Michelet. Art Director: Martin Obzina. Editor: Edward Mann. Cast: David Wayne, Howard de Silva, Martin Gabel, Luther Adler, Glenn Anders, Dorothy Comingore.

THE MALTESE FALCON. Warner Brothers. 1941. Screenplay: John Huston; from the novel by Dashiell Hammett. Director: John Huston. Director of Photography: Arthur Edeson. Music: Adolph Deutsch. Art Director: Robert Haas. Editor: Thomas Richards. Cast: Humphrey Bogart, Mary Astor, Gladys George, Peter Lorre, Barton MacLane, Sydney Greenstreet, Ward Bond, Jerome Cowan, Elisha Cook Jr.

MARLOWE. MGM. 1969. Screenplay: Stirling Silliphant; from the novel *The Little Sister* by Raymond Chandler. Director: Paul Bogart. Director of Photography: William H. Daniels. Music: Peter Matz. Art Directors: George W. Davis, Addison Hehr. Editor: Gene Ruggiero. Cast: James Garner, Gayle Hunnicutt, Carroll O'Connor, Rita Moreno, Sharon Farrell.

MILDRED PIERCE. Warner Brothers. 1945. Screenplay: Ranald MacDougall; from the novel by James M. Cain. Director: Michael Curtiz. Director of Photography: Ernest Haller. Music: Max Steiner. Art Director: Anton Grot. Editor: David Weisbart. Cast: Joan Crawford, Jack Carson, Zachary Scott, Eve Arden, Ann Blyth.

MINISTRY OF FEAR. Paramount. 1945. Screenplay: Seton I. Miller; from the novel by Graham Greene. Director: Fritz Lang. Director of Photography: Henry Sharp. Music Score: Victor Young. Art Directors: Hal Pereira, Hans Dreier. Editor: Archie Marshek. Cast: Ray Milland, Marjorie Reynolds, Carl Esmond, Hillary Brooke, Percy Waram, Dan Duryea.

MURDER, MY SWEET. RKO. 1944. Screenplay: John Paxton; from the novel *Farewell, My Lovely* by Raymond Chandler. Director: Edward Dmytryk. Director of Photography: Harry J. Wild. Music: Roy Webb. Art Directors: Albert S. D'Agostino, Carroll Clark. Editor: Joseph Noreiga. Cast: Dick Powell, Claire Trevor, Anne Shirley, Otto Kruger, Mike Mazurki, Miles Mander.

MY NAME IS JULIA ROSS. Columbia. 1945. Screenplay: Muriel Roy Bolton; from the novel *The Woman In Red* by Anthony Gilbert. Director: Joseph H. Lewis. Director of Photography: Burnett Guffey. Music: Mischa Bakaleinikoff. Art Director: Jerome Pycha Jr. Editor: James Sweeney. Cast: Nina Foch, Dame May Whitty, George Macready, Roland Varno, Queenie Leonard.

THE NAKED CITY. Universal-International. 1948. Screenplay: Albert Maltz and Malvin Wald; from an unpublished story by Malvin Wald. Director: Jules Dassin. Director of Photography: William Daniels. Music: Miklos Rozsa, Frank Skinner. Art Director: John F. DeCuir. Editor: Paul Weatherwax. Cast: Barry Fitzgerald, Howard Duff, Dorothy Hart, Don Taylor, Ted de Corsia, House Jameson, Tom Pedi, Enid Markey.

THE NAKED KISS. Allied Artists. 1964. Screenplay: Samuel Fuller. Director: Samuel Fuller. Director of Photography: Stanley Cortez. Music: Paul Dunlap. Art Director: Eugene Lourié. Editor: Jerome Thoms. Cast: Constance Towers, Anthony Eisley, Michael Dante, Virginia Grey, Patsy Kelly, Betty Bronson.

THE NARROW MARGIN. RKO. 1952. Screenplay: Earl Felton. Director: Richard Fleischer. Director of Photography: George E. Diskant. Art Directors: Albert S. D'Agostino, Jack Okey. Editor: Robert Swink. Cast: Charles McGraw, Marie Windsor, Jacqueline White, Gordon Gebert, Queenie Leonard.

NIAGARA. 20th Century-Fox. 1953. Screenplay: Charles Brackett, Walter Reisch, and Richard Breen. Director: Henry Hathaway. Director of Photography: Joe MacDonald. Music: Sol Kaplan. Art Directors: Lyle Wheeler, Maurice Ransford. Editor: Barbara McLean. Cast: Marilyn Monroe, Joseph Cotten, Jean Peters, Casey Adams, Don Wilson, Lurene Tuttle, Russell Collins.

NIGHT AND THE CITY. 20th Century-Fox. 1950. Screenplay: Jo Eisinger; from the novel by Gerald Kersh. Director: Jules Dassin. Director of Photography: Max Greene. Music: Franz Waxman. Art Director: C.P. Norman. Editors: Nick De Maggio, Sidney Stone. Cast: Richard Widmark, Gene Tierney, Googie Withers, Hugh Marlowe, Francis L. Sullivan, Herbert Lom, Mike Mazurki.

THE NIGHT HAS A THOUSAND EYES. Paramount. 1948. Screenplay: Barré Lyndon and Jonathan Latimer; from the novel by Cornell Woolrich. Director: John Farrow. Director of Photography: John F. Seitz. Music: Victor Young. Art Directors: Hans Dreier, Franz Bachelin. Editor: Eda Warren. Cast: Edward G. Robinson, Gail Russell, John Lund, Virginia Bruce, William Demarest, Richard Webb.

NIGHT MOVES. Warner Brothers. 1975. Screenplay: Alan Sharp. Director: Arthur Penn. Director of Photography: Bruce Surtees. Music: Michael Small. Art Director: George Jenkins. Editor: Dede Allen. Cast: Gene Hackman, Susan Clark, Edward Binns, Harris Yulin.

NIGHTMARE. United Artists. 1955. Screenplay: Maxwell Shane; from the short story by William Irish (Cornell Woolrich). Director: Maxwell Shane. Director of Photography: Joe Biroc. Music: Herschel Burke Gilbert. Art Director: Frank Sylos. Editor: George Gittens. Cast: Edward G. Robinson, Kevin McCarthy, Connie Russell, Virginia Christine, Rhys Williams.

NIGHTMARE ALLEY. 20th Century-Fox. 1947. Screenplay: Jules Furthman; from the novel by William Lindsay Gresham. Director: Edmund Goulding. Director of Photography: Lee Garmes. Music Score: Cyril Mockridge. Art Directors: Lyle Wheeler, J. Russell Spencer. Editor: Barbara McLean. Cast: Tyrone Power, Joan Blondell, Coleen Gray, Helen Walker.

ODDS AGAINST TOMORROW. Harbel-United Artists. 1959. Screenplay: John O. Killens and Nelson Gidding; from the novel by William P. McGivern. Director: Robert Wise. Director of Photography: Joseph Brun. Music: John Lewis. Art Director: Leo Kerz. Editor: Dede Allen. Cast: Harry Belafonte, Robert Ryan, Gloria Grahame, Shelly Winters, Ed Begley, Carmen DeLavallade.

ON DANGEROUS GROUND. RKO. 1951. Screenplay: A.I. Bezzerides; from the novel *Mad With Much Heart* by Gerald Butler. Director: Nicholas Ray. Director of Photography: George E. Diskant. Music Score: Bernard Herrmann. Art Directors: Albert S. D'Agostino, Ralph Berger. Editor: Roland Gross. Cast: Ida Lupino, Robert Ryan, Ward Bond, Charles Kemper, Ed Begley.

OUT OF THE PAST. RKO. 1947. Screenplay: Geoffrey Homes (Daniel Mainwaring); from his novel *Build My Gallows High*. Director: Jacques Tourneur. Director of Photography: Nicholas Musuraca. Music Score: Roy Webb. Art Directors: Albert S. D'Agostino, Jack Okey. Editor: Samuel E. Beetley. Cast: Robert Mitchum, Jane Greer, Kirk Douglas, Rhonda Fleming.

PANIC IN THE STREETS. 20th Century-Fox. 1950. Screenplay: Richard Murphy, adapted by Daniel Fuchs. Director: Elia Kazan. Director of Photography: Joe MacDonald. Music: Alfred Newman. Art Directors: Lyle Wheeler, Maurice Ransford. Editor: Harmon Jones. Cast: Richard Widmark, Paul Douglas, Barbara Bel Geddes, Walter (Jack) Palance, Zero Mostel, Alexis Minotis.

PHANTOM LADY. Universal. 1944. Screenplay: Bernard C. Schoenfeld; from the novel by William Irish (Cornel Woolrich). Director: Robert Siodmak. Director of Photography: Woody Bredell. Music: Hans J. Salter. Art Directors: John B. Goodman, Robert Clatworthy. Editor: Arthur Hilton. Cast: Franchot Tone, Ella Raines, Alan Curtis, Aurora, Thomas Gomez, Fay Helm, Elisha Cook Jr.

PICKUP ON SOUTH STREET. 20th Century-Fox. 1953. Screenplay: Samuel Fuller. Director: Samuel Fuller. Director of Photography: Joe MacDonald. Music: Leigh Harline. Art Directors: Lyle Wheeler, George Patrick. Editor: Nick De Maggio. Cast: Richard Widmark, Jean Peters, Thelma Ritter, Murvyn Vye, Richard Kiley.

PITFALL. United Artists. 1948. Screenplay: Karl Kamb; from the novel by Jay Dratler. Director: André de Toth. Director of Photography: Harry Wild. Music: Louis Forbes. Art Director: Arthur Lonergan. Editor: Walter Thompson. Cast: Dick Powell, Lizabeth Scott, Jane Wyatt, Raymond Burr, John Litel, Byron Barr, Ann Doran.

POINT BLANK. MGM. 1967. Screenplay: Alexander Jacobs, David Newhouse, and Rafe Newhouse; from the novel *The Hunter* by Richard Stark (Donald Westlake). Director: John Boorman. Director of Photography: Philip H. Lathrop. Music: Johnny Mandel. Art Directors: George W. Davis, Albert Brenner. Editor: Henry Berman. Cast: Lee Marvin, Angie Dickinson, Keenan Wynn, Carroll O'Connor, Michael Strong, John Vernon.

POSSESSED. Warner Brothers. 1947. Screenplay: Sylvia Richards and Ranald MacDougall; from the *Cosmopolitan* magazine novelette *One Man's Secret* by Rita Weiman. Director: Curtis Bernhardt. Director of Photography: Joseph Valentine. Music Score: Franz Waxman. Art Director: Anton Grot. Editor: Rudi Fehr. Cast: Joan Crawford, Van Heflin, Raymond Massey, Geraldine Brooks.

THE POSTMAN ALWAYS RINGS TWICE. MGM. 1946. Screenplay: Harry Ruskin and Niven Busch; from the novel by James M. Cain. Director: Tay Garnett. Director of Photography: Sidney Wagner. Music Score: George Bassman. Art Directors: Cedric Gibbons, Randall Duell. Editor: George White. Cast: Lana Turner, John Garfield, Cecil Kellaway, Hume Cronyn, Leon Ames, Audrey Totter.

THE PROWLER. United Artists. 1951. Screenplay: Hugo Butler. Director: Joseph Losey. Director of Photography: Arthur Miller. Music Score: Lyn Murray. Art Director: Boris Leven. Editor: Paul Weatherwax. Cast: Van Heflin, Evelyn Keyes, John Maxwell, Katharine Warren.

RAW DEAL. Eagle-Lion. 1948. Screenplay: Leopold Atlas and John C. Higgins. Director: Anthony Mann. Director of Photography: John Alton. Music Score: Paul Sawtell. Art Director: Edward L. Ilou. Editor: Alfred De Gaetano. Cast: Dennis O'Keefe, Claire Trevor, Marsha Hunt, John Ireland, Raymond Burr.

THE RECKLESS MOMENT. Columbia. 1949. Screenplay: Henry Garson and Robert W. Soderberg, adapted by Mel Dinelli and Robert E. Kent; from the short story *The Blank Wall* by Elisabeth Saxnay Holding. Director: Max Ophuls. Director of Photography: Burnett Guffey. Music Score: Hans Salter. Art Director: Cary Odell. Editor: Gene Havlick. Cast: James Mason, Joan Bennett, Geraldine Brooks, Shepperd Strudwick.

SCARLET STREET. Universal. 1945. Screenplay: Dudley Nichols; from the novel and play *La Chienne* by Georges de la Fouchardíere in collaboration with Mouezy-Eon. Director: Fritz Lang. Director of Photography: Milton Krasner. Music Score: Hans J. Salter. Art Director: Alexander Golitzen. Editor: Arthur Hilton. Cast: Edward G. Robinson, Joan Bennett, Dan Duryea, Jess Barker, Margaret Lindsay, Rosalind Ivan.

THE SET-UP. RKO. 1949. Screenplay: Art Cohn; from the poem by Joseph Moncure March. Director: Robert Wise. Director of Photography: Milton Krasner. Music Director: Constantin Bakaleinikoff. Art Directors: Albert S. D'Agostino, Jack Okey. Editor: Roland Gross. Cast: Robert Ryan, Audrey Totter, George Tobias, Alan Baxter, Wallace Ford, Percy Helton.

SHADOW OF A DOUBT. Universal. 1943. Screenplay: Thornton Wilder, Sally Benson, and Alma Reville; from a story by Gordon McDonell. Director: Alfred Hitchcock. Director of Photography: Joseph Valentine. Music Score: Dimitri Tiomkin. Art Directors: John B. Goodman, Robert Boyle. Editor: Milton Carruth. Cast: Teresa Wright, Joseph Cotten, Macdonald Carey, Henry Travers, Patricia Collinge.

SIDE STREET. MGM. 1950. Screenplay: Sydney Boehm. Director: Anthony Mann. Director of Photography: Joseph Ruttenberg. Music Score: Lennie Hayton. Art Directors: Cedric Gibbons, Daniel B. Cathcart. Editor: Conrad A. Nervig. Cast: Farley Granger, Cathy O'Donnell, James Craig, Paul Kelly.

SO DARK THE NIGHT. Columbia. 1946. Screenplay: Martin Berkeley and Dwight Babcock. Director: Joseph H. Lewis. Director of Photography: Burnett Guffey. Music: Morris W. Stoloff, Hugo Friedhofer. Art Director: Carl Anderson. Editor: Jerome Thoms. Cast: Steven Geray, Micheline Cheirel, Eugene Borden, Ann Codee.

SORRY, WRONG NUMBER. Paramount. 1948. Screenplay: Lucille Fletcher; from her radio play. Director: Anatole Litvak. Director of Photography: Sol Polito. Music Score: Gene Merritt, Walter Oberst. Art Directors: Hans Dreier, Earl Hedrick. Editor: Warren Low. Cast: Barbara Stanwyck, Burt Lancaster, Ann Richards, Wendell Corey, Ed Begley, William Conrad.

THE STRANGER. International-RKO. 1946. Screenplay: Anthony Veiller; from a story by Victor Trivas. Director: Orson Welles. Director of Photography: Russell Metty. Music Score: Bronislau Kaper. Art Director: Perry Ferguson. Editor: Ernest Nims. Cast: Edward G. Robinson, Loretta Young, Orson Welles.

STRANGERS ON A TRAIN. Warner Brothers. 1951. Screenplay: Raymond Chandler and Czenzi Ormonde, adapted by Whitfield Cook; from the novel by Patricia Highsmith. Director: Alfred Hitchcock. Director of Photography: Robert Burks. Music: Dimitri Tiomkin. Art Director: Ted Haworth. Editor: William H. Ziegler. Cast: Farley Granger, Ruth Roman, Robert Walker, Leo G. Carroll, Patricia Hitchcock, Marion Lorne.

THE STREET WITH NO NAME. 20th Century-Fox. 1948. Screenplay: Harry Kleiner. Director: William Keighley. Director of Photography: Joe MacDonald. Music: Lionel Newman. Art Directors: Lyle Wheeler, Chester Gore. Editor: William Reynolds. Cast: Mark Stevens, Richard Widmark, Lloyd Nolan, Barbara Lawrence.

SUDDEN FEAR. Kaufman-RKO. 1952. Screenplay: Lenore Coffee and Robert Smith; from the novel by Edna Sherry. Director: David Miller. Director of Photography: Charles Lang Jr. Music: Elmer Bernstein. Art Director: Boris Leven. Editor: Leon Barsha. Cast: Joan Crawford, Jack Palance, Gloria Grahame, Bruce Bennett.

SUNSET BOULEVARD. Paramount. 1950. Screenplay: Charles Brackett, Billy Wilder, and D.M. Marshman Jr. Director: Billy Wilder. Director of Photography: John F. Seitz. Music Score: Franz Waxman. Art Director: Hans Dreier, John Meehan. Editor: Arthur Schmidt. Cast: William Holden, Gloria Swanson, Erich von Stroheim, Nancy Olson, Fred Clark, Cecil B. DeMille, Hedda Hopper, Buster Keaton, Anna Q. Nilsson, H. B. Warner.

SWEET SMELL OF SUCCESS. United Artists. 1957. Screenplay: Clifford Odets, adapted by Ernest Lehman; from the short story *Tell Me About It Tomorrow* by Ernest Lehman. Director: Alexander MacKendrick. Director of Photography: James Wong Howe. Music: Elmer Bernstein. Art Director: Edward Carrere. Editor: Alan Crosland Jr. Cast: Burt Lancaster, Tony Curtis, Susan Harrison, Martin Milner, Sam Levene, Barbara Nichols, Queenie Smith, Autumn Russell.

TAXI DRIVER. Columbia. 1976. Screenplay: Paul Schrader. Director: Martin Scorsese. Director of Photography: Michael Chapman. Music: Bernard Herrmann. Art Director: Charles Rosen. Editors: Tom Rolf, Melvin Shapiro. Cast: Robert DeNiro, Jodie Foster, Albert Brooks, Peter Boyle, Cybill Shepherd, Leonard Harris, Harvey Keitel.

THEY LIVE BY NIGHT. RKO. 1948. Screenplay: Charles Schnee, adapted by Nicholas Ray; from the novel *Thieves Like Us* by Edward Anderson. Director: Nicholas Ray. Director of Photography: George E. Diskant. Music: Leigh Harline. Art Directors: Albert S. D'Agostino, Al Herman. Editor: Sherman Todd. Cast: Cathy O'Donnell, Farley Granger, Howard Da Silva, Jay C. Flippen, Helen Craig.

THIS GUN FOR HIRE. Paramount. 1942. Screenplay: Albert Maltz and W.R. Burnett; from the novel by Graham Greene. Director: Frank Tuttle. Director of Photography: John Seitz. Music: Frank Loesser and Jacques Press. Editor: Archie Marshek. Cast: Alan Ladd, Veronica Lake, Robert Preston, Laird Cregar.

TOUCH OF EVIL. Universal-International. 1958. Screenplay: Orson Welles; from the novel *Badge of Evil* by Whit Masterson. Director: Orson Welles. Director of Photography: Russell Metty. Music: Henry Mancini. Art Directors: Alexander Golitzen, Robert Clatworthy. Editors: Virgil M. Vogel, Aaron Stell. Cast: Charlton Heston, Janet Leigh, Orson Welles, Joseph Calleia, Akim Tamiroff, Marlene Dietrich, Ray Collins, Dennis Weaver, Mercedes McCambridge, Zsa Zsa Gabor, Keenan Wynn, Joseph Cotten.

UNDERWORLD U.S.A. Globe-Columbia. 1961. Screenplay: Samuel Fuller; from the *Saturday Evening Post* articles by Joseph F. Dinneen. Director: Samuel Fuller. Director of Photography: Hal Mohr. Music: Harry Sukman. Art Director: Robert Peterson. Editor: Jerome Thoms. Cast: Cliff Robertson, Dolores Dorn, Beatrice Kay, Arlene Francis, Robert Emhardt, Larry Gates, Richard Rust.

WHERE THE SIDEWALK ENDS. 20th Century-Fox. 1950. Screenplay: Ben Hecht, adapted by Victor Trivas, Frank P. Rosenberg, and Robert E. Kent; from the novel *Night Cry* by William L. Stuart. Director: Otto Preminger. Director of Photography: Joseph LaShelle. Music: Cyril Mockridge. Art Directors: Lyle Wheeler, J. Russell Spencer. Editor: Louis Loeffler. Cast: Dana Andrews, Gene Tierney, Gary Merrill, Bert Freed.

WHILE THE CITY SLEEPS. RKO. 1956. Screenplay: Casey Robinson; from the novel *The Bloody Spur* by Charles Einstein. Director: Fritz Lang. Director of Photography: Ernest Laszlo. Music: Herschel Burke Gilbert. Art Director: Carroll Clark. Editor: Gene Fowler Jr. Cast: Dana Andrews, Rhonda Fleming, George Sanders, Howard Duff, Thomas Mitchell, Vincent Price, Sally Forrest, John Barrymore Jr., Ida Lupino, Mae Marsh.

WHITE HEAT. Warner Brothers. 1949. Screenplay: Ivan Goff and Ben Roberts. Director: Raoul Walsh. Director of Photography: Sid Hickox. Music Score: Max Steiner. Art Director: Edward Carrere. Editor: Owen Marks. Cast: James Cagney, Virginia Mayo, Edmond O'Brien, Margaret Wycherly, Steve Cochran.

THE WINDOW. RKO. 1949. Screenplay: Mel Dinelli; from the novelette *The Boy Cried Murder* by Cornell Woolrich. Director: Ted Tetzlaff. Director of Photography: William Steiner. Music Score: Roy Webb. Art Directors: Walter E. Keller, Sam Corso. Editor: Frederic Knudtson. Cast: Barbara Hale, Bobby Driscoll, Arthur Kennedy, Paul Stewart, Ruth Roman.

THE WOMAN IN THE WINDOW. International-RKO. 1945. Screenplay: Nunnally Johnson; from the novel *Once Off Guard* by J.H. Wallis. Director: Fritz Lang. Director of Photography: Milton Krasner. Music: Arthur Lange. Art Director: Duncan Cramer. Editors: Marjorie Johnson, Gene Fowler Jr. Cast: Edward G. Robinson, Joan Bennett, Raymond Massey, Edmond Breon, Dan Duryea, Dorothy Peterson.

THE WRONG MAN. Warner Brothers. 1956. Screenplay: Maxwell Anderson and Angus MacPhail; from *The True Story of Christopher Emmanuel Balestrero* by Maxwell Anderson. Director: Alfred Hitchcock. Director of Photography: Robert Burks. Music: Bernard Herrmann. Art Directors: Paul Sylbert, William L. Kuehl. Editor: George Tomasini. Cast: Henry Fonda, Vera Miles, Anthony Quayle, Esther Minciotti.

Index

Numerals in italics indicate illustrations.

Other titles of interest

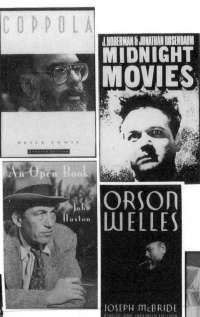
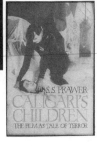